BLACKSTONE'S GUIDE TO

The Employment Equality Regulations 2003

BLACKSTONE'S GUIDE TO

The Employment Equality Regulations 2003

Nicholas De Marco

Barrister, Blackstone Chambers

OXFORD
UNIVERSITY PRESS

OXFORD

UNIVERSITY PRESS

Great Clarendon Street, Oxford OX2 6DP

Oxford University Press is a department of the University of Oxford.
It furthers the University's objective of excellence in research, scholarship,
and education by publishing worldwide in

Oxford New York

Auckland Bangkok Buenos Aires Cape Town Chennai
Dar es Salaam Delhi Hong Kong Istanbul Karachi Kolkata
Kuala Lumpur Madrid Melbourne Mexico City Mumbai Nairobi
São Paulo Shanghai Singapore Taipei Tokyo Toronto

with an associated company in Berlin

Oxford is a registered trade mark of Oxford University Press
in the UK and in certain other countries

Published in the United States
by Oxford University Press Inc., New York

© Nicholas De Marco 2004

The moral rights of the author have been asserted
Database right Oxford University Press (maker)

Crown copyright material is reproduced under Class Licence Number C01P0000148
with the permission of HMSO and the Queen's Printer for Scotland

First published 2004

British Library Cataloguing in Publication Data

Data available

Library of Congress Cataloging in Publication Data

Data available

ISBN 0–19–927265–4 (pbk)

1 3 5 7 9 10 8 6 4 2

Typeset in Times
by Cambrian Typesetters, Frimley, Surrey
Printed in Great Britain
on acid-free paper by
Ashford Colour Press Ltd,
Gosport, Hampshire

Contents–Summary

Contents

Contents

Foreword by Lord Lester of Herne Hill QC[1]

Nicholas De Marco has written a timely, well-constructed, and practical guide to the new equality legislation forbidding discrimination and harassment based on religious belief and sexual orientation. The complex legislation is lucidly explained within the historical context of the long struggle to provide effective redress for the victims of these forms of unfair and unjustifiable discrimination. The guide also locates the legislation within the wider context of European human rights, European Union, and UK anti-discrimination legislation tackling other forms of discrimination.

Some perplexing puzzles are examined in the guide. Does someone who believes the bizarre teachings of a new-age religious cult have a 'similar philosophical belief' (to use the legislative phrase) to someone who believes in the Assumption of the Virgin Mary or that God spoke to Moses from a burning bush? More seriously, is the gaping exception apparently permitting a religious body to exclude a gay or lesbian cleaner from employment compatible with the EU Framework Directive, and can it be interpreted narrowly to make it compatible? What kind of justification is permissible to defeat claims of indirect discrimination based on religion or sexual orientation?

The guide is constructed in a user-friendly way to make this complex legal regime accessible not only to discrimination lawyers but also to personnel managers, trade union officers, and advice centres. It highlights areas where there is an apparent mismatch between the Framework Directive and the implementing Regulations, making comparisons with other parts of the anti-discrimination legislative code. It deserves to be read and used by everyone affected by this important new legislation: judges, members of employment tribunals, employers, trade unions, NGOs, and members of groups vulnerable to discrimination.

I hope that sooner rather than later the law-makers will reform the opaque, incomplete, and incoherent state of this area of law. Meanwhile, works of this kind provide invaluable guides to the perplexed, the disadvantaged, and those in a position to provide genuine equality of treatment without discrimination.

Anthony Lester

---

[1] Lord Lester of Herne Hill QC is a practising barrister at Blackstone Chambers and a Liberal Democrat peer. He introduced a Civil Partnership Bill and an Equality Bill in the House of Lords. As Special Adviser to the Home Secretary (Roy Jenkins) between 1974 and 1976, he developed policy on what became the Sex Discrimination Act 1975 and the Race Relations Act 1976.

Preface

It has been a great pleasure to write this book. The Regulations pose exciting and dynamic new challenges for lawyers specializing in employment and discrimination law. More important, they should help change the lives of many who have suffered discrimination and harassment on grounds of their religion or belief, or their sexual orientation, and who have never before had a legal remedy. They could also play a significant part in the development of domestic discrimination law, and a general culture of equality.

Most of this book was written in early November 2003, a few weeks before the Regulations came into force. As there was no case law to help interpret the Regulations, it was necessary to combine statutory interpretation with a certain amount of speculation. This has been both challenging and rewarding. Only time will tell how the courts and tribunals will interpret the Regulations, and this book does not pretend to be any more than an effort to explain what the Regulations mean and how they might apply. Any mistakes are mine.

I am most grateful to everybody at my publisher, OUP, for supporting and investing in this project, and for all their helpful suggestions. Thanks must also go to everyone at Blackstone Chambers for their advice and support, and for allowing me the time to work on this project. I am also grateful to ACAS for agreeing to let us publish their useful guidance on the Regulations in full which appear in the appendices of this book. Special thanks are due to Anthony Lester, who has made an unrivalled contribution to domestic discrimination law both as a lawyer and law-maker, for his kind agreement to write a foreword to this book. Finally, thanks to Shomsul Islam for his patience and support during the long days and nights taken to write this book.

This book contains the law up to and including 27 November 2003.

Where a hypothetical complainant is referred to throughout this book as 'he', this should be read to include both genders.

Nicholas De Marco
Blackstone Chambers
Temple
London EC4Y 9BW
27 November 2003

Table of Cases

EUROPEAN LEGISLATION

CONVENTIONS

Table of Abbreviations

DDA	Disability Discrimination Act 1995
EE (Religion or Belief) Regulations	Employment Equality (Religion or Belief) Regulations 2003
EE (Sexual Orientation) Regulations	Employment Equality (Sexual Orientation) Regulations 2003
Framework Directive	Council Directive 2000/78/EC of 27 November 2000 establishing a framework for equal treatment in employment and occupation respectively
GOR	genuine occupational requirement
HRA	Human Rights Act 1998
RRA	Race Relations Act 1976
SDA	Sex Discrimination Act 1975

1

INTRODUCTION TO THE REGULATIONS

1.1 HISTORY AND OVERVIEW OF THE REGULATIONS

The EE (Religion or Belief) Regulations and the EE (Sexual Orientation) Regulations came into force in Great Britain on 1 and 2 December 2003. Together, they represent the most important development in discrimination law for years. For the first time, discrimination, on grounds of religion or belief and sexual orientation, is unlawful. Previously, employers could discriminate against their employees because of their religion or their sexual orientation. The courts and tribunals were powerless to intervene, unless the employer broke other legislation.

Over the years there has been increasing dissatisfaction with this state of affairs. How could it be right that a Jewish or Sikh employee had protection from discrimination, because under the RRA (Race Relations Act 1976) Jews and Sikhs were categorized as ethnic or racial groups, but a Muslim had no protection when he was subjected to discrimination because he was part of a religious and not a racial group? Why could a woman complain to an employment tribunal because she was subjected to name-calling and bullying because she was a woman, but when she was subjected to the same level of harassment because she was a lesbian she could not bring a complaint?

In the end the change in the law came from Europe. The Framework Directive, agreed by the Council of the European Union in 2000, sought to establish a 'general framework for equal treatment in employment and occupation' across the European Union member states. Discrimination on grounds of religion or belief, disability, age, or sexual orientation in employment was prohibited. A separate Directive on race was also agreed in June of the same year. Under domestic discrimination law, discrimination on grounds of race, sex, and disability was already unlawful—some amendments were necessary to bring the legislation into conformity. Britain was given until October 2006 to draft and put in place complicated legislation prohibiting discrimination on grounds of age. Legislation making discrimination on grounds of religion or belief and sexual orientation unlawful had to be in force by December 2003.

The Government decided to transpose the Framework Directive (in so far as it related to religion or belief/sexual orientation discrimination) into national law as secondary legislation—relying on its powers to do so under the European Communities Act 1972. Hence there was little parliamentary debate or media interest in the passage of these important Regulations through Parliament in June 2003.

The reason for considering both these Regulations together in one book is that they are remarkably similar. They are both based on the Framework Directive. They both prohibit discrimination previously lawful in Britain. They both came into force at the same time. They both share a common definition of discrimination and victimization, and a novel definition of harassment and positive action. They both apply to the same sectors of society, overwhelmingly employees, but also some college and university students. Indeed the language of the Regulations is, in most part, identical.

This book follows the structure of both Regulations together, only dealing with them separately when necessary. Chapter 2 discusses the discrimination prohibited in Part I of the Regulations. It examines the definition of 'religion or belief' and 'sexual orientation', the definition of discrimination, victimization and harassment. Chapter 3 concerns the scope of the Regulations—to whom they apply (Part II of the Regulations). Chapter 4 explains how the Regulations extend liability to 'other unlawful acts', such as an employer's liability for the harassment of his employees (Part III of the Regulations). Chapter 5 considers the genuine occupational requirement by which certain jobs can be exempt from the Regulations. Chapter 6 concerns the general exceptions to the Regulations listed in Part IV of both of them, including provisions for employers to take 'positive action'. Chapter 7 looks at enforcement—it considers the jurisdiction of the courts and tribunals, the burden of proof, and the procedures used for binging complaints under the Regulations (Part V of the Regulations). Chapters 8 and 9 examine specific issues that might arise in relation to religion or belief and sexual orientation discrimination respectively. These chapters should be particularly useful for employers concerned to see whether their organization complies with the Regulations, to employees and their representatives interested to know what type of behaviour may constitute discrimination, and to lawyers seeking illustrations of discrimination and harassment on grounds of religion or belief and sexual orientation. The book has six appendices, which include both Regulations in full, the Framework Directive on which they are based, and the ACAS guidance on the Regulations.

It is hoped that this book will be a valuable tool for employment and discrimination lawyers who are likely to advise on or act in cases concerning these Regulations. It should also be of interest for academics and students interested in the important development of discrimination law these Regulations represent. However, this book is also aimed at employers and personnel managers, trade union and employee representatives, and community activists concerned about religion or belief and sexual orientation discrimination. Primarily, it is a practical guide to the Regulations for anyone seeking to understand how they operate or to rely on them.

As the Regulations prohibit discrimination that was previously lawful, there is no case law to assist in their interpretation. But it is not necessary to start from scratch. Most of the concepts used in the Regulations are based on those found in the Race Relations Act 1976 (RRA) and SDA (Sex Discrimination Act 1975), and the law arising from race and sex discrimination can, and often is in this book, used to assist in explaining how the Regulations operate. It would be a mistake, however, for lawyers familiar with discrimination law to assume these Regulations add nothing new. They do. The statutory definition of harassment is one of the most important examples of this, but there are others, as there are important and novel issues that arise, such as how one defines 'religion or belief' or how the concept of a genuine occupational requirement applies to sexual orientation. Navigating these untrodden paths requires particular attention.

1.2 DISCRIMINATION ON GROUNDS OF RELIGION OR BELIEF BEFORE THE REGULATIONS

It was not unlawful for an employer to discriminate against one of his employees on grounds of religion or belief before the Employment Equality (Religion or Belief) Regulations 2003 (EE (Religion or Belief) Regulations) came into force. The right not to be discriminated against on grounds of religion had a partial and fragmented existence. For instance, since the Human Rights Act 1998 (HRA) came into force, everyone has a right to freedom of thought, conscience, and religion under Article 9 of the Convention. Taken with Article 14 (prohibition on discrimination) it is unlawful for a public authority to discriminate against a citizen on grounds of his religion or belief. Article 9 and Article 10 (freedom of expression) of the Convention are amongst the most important rights in a democratic society, and courts and tribunals must guard these rights with vigilance. 'Very weighty reasons' will be required to be advanced by a State to justify discrimination on grounds of religion (see, eg, *Hoffmann v Austria* (1994) 17 EHRR 293, E Ct HR, paragraph 36: 'a distinction based essentially on a difference in religion alone is not acceptable'). However, as explained in greater detail below (section 1.3), the HRA, and with it Convention jurisprudence, has limited effect in complaints brought against private employers in the employment tribunals.

In Northern Ireland there is legislation that not only protects freedom of religion and belief, but goes much further. Section 75 of the Northern Ireland Act 1998, for instance, makes it unlawful for a public authority to discriminate against a person on grounds of religious belief and 'political opinion'. The Act provides constitutional protection against discrimination on grounds of religion. The Fair Employment and Treatment (Northern Ireland) Order 1998 allows action designed to secure fair participation in employment by members of the Protestant or Roman Catholic community, including direct discrimination in pursuit of affirmative action in certain circumstances. But this legislation, which is part of the Northern Ireland 'peace process', is intended to meet a particular set of circumstances unique to the province. It has no effect on employment rights in Great Britain, and provides little assistance as to how the Regulations operate.

The closest domestic discrimination law came to a prohibition on religion or belief discrimination was in relation to race discrimination. A series of cases established that what could be described as religious discrimination could be treated as racial discrimination under the RRA in certain circumstances. However, it was first necessary to establish the group discriminated against was a 'racial group' for the purposes of the RRA. Being members of a religion was not enough.

In *Seide v Gillette Industries Ltd* [1980] IRLR 427, EAT, for instance, the Employment Appeal Tribunal was able to find Jews were protected by the RRA where the discrimination against a Jewish man was not because of his Jewish faith but because he was a member of the Jewish race or of Jewish ethnic origin. The House of Lords went further in *Mandla v Dowell Lee* [1983] 2 AC 548, HL, finding Sikhs constituted a 'racial group' for the purposes of the RRA by virtue of certain important shared characteristics. The case involved the operation of a 'no turban rule', something that would certainly amount to discrimination on grounds of religion or belief. The House of Lords found that the rule constituted indirect racial discrimination because a smaller proportion of Sikhs than non-Sikhs could comply with it.

On the other hand, in *Crown Suppliers (PSA) Ltd v Dawkins* [1993] ICR 517, CA, the Court of Appeal held that Rastafarians could not constitute a racial group for the purposes of the RRA. The complainant was refused employment because he indicated he was unwilling to cut his dreadlocks. This was not unlawful discrimination under the RRA as there was nothing to distinguish Rastafarians from other West Indians on racial grounds. The case would have to be decided differently if brought under the EE (Religion or Belief) Regulations since it is Rastafarianism—a religion or belief—that distinguishes Rastafarians from others.

In *J H Walker Ltd v Hussain* [1996] IRLR 11, EAT, the Employment Appeal Tribunal upheld the decision of the industrial tribunal that there could be no direct racial discrimination against Muslims as 'the true nature of Islam is not within' the RRA. The RRA Act does not mention religion and it was not possible to treat Muslims as an ethnic grouping (although it was possible to find there had been indirect racial discrimination against the applicants in the circumstances).

Thus, a case of what could be described as 'religious discrimination' could only succeed under the old rule if it 'fit' into the requirements necessary to bring a case of race discrimination: the religious group would have to be capable of constituting a racial group. The old law meant that if an employer advertised a job with a notice,

'Jews and Sikhs need not apply' he would commit an act of unlawful direct discrimination; if his notice read 'Muslims and Hindus need not apply' he would not.

This anomalous situation was unacceptable, but it is only with the EE (Religion or Belief) Regulations that it is beginning to be eroded. Even now, however, fundamental inconsistencies continue. The Regulations only apply to employment (and to further and higher education). A Muslim or Hindu subjected to discrimination in relation to the supply of goods and services, for instance, would have no protection, because the Regulations do not extend to those spheres, whereas a Jew or Sikh would, as the RRA does. In this sense the step forward in discrimination law that the Regulations represent makes a single and comprehensive equality law a more obvious final destination.

1.3 DISCRIMINATION ON GROUNDS OF SEXUAL ORIENTATION BEFORE THE REGULATIONS

The situation in relation to discrimination on grounds of sexual orientation before the Regulations was remarkably similar as that in relation to discrimination on grounds of religion or belief. The biggest difference was that, rather than trying to 'fit' into concepts of race discrimination, complainants of sexual orientation discrimination often tried to 'fit' their complaints into the structure of sex discrimination legislation.

In many ways, however, the development towards sexual orientation equality has been a far more rapid one. Less than 40 years ago homosexuality was completely unlawful in Britain. Anyone found practising homosexuality, even if in private between consenting adults, could be locked up in prison. Only in recent years have certain laws that directly discriminated against gay men been repealed. The age of consent legislation provided that people of one sexual orientation could lawfully have consensual sex at one age, whereas people of another sexual orientation would be treated as having unlawful sex—statutory rape—if they had consensual sex at the same age. The Armed Forces banned any person from service if they were lesbian or gay, and they could investigate, punish, and dismiss lesbian and gay officers they discovered by covert operations with impunity—merely because of sexual orientation. Sexual orientation discrimination has been ingrained within the law, national institutions, and society. Only very recently has the idea of sexual orientation equality been given legal roots.

One of the areas of sharpest controversy surrounding sexual orientation discrimination ironically relates to the subject matter of the other Regulations considered in this book: religion. Many organized religions regard sexual orientation discrimination as a fundamental and immutable tenet of their faith. It is perhaps no surprise, then, that the most contentious provision of these Regulations, Regulation 7(3) is the one that attempts to accommodate the potential explosive conflict between deeply

5

held religious views and homosexuality—it does so, however, by creating a special exception for 'organized religion', allowing employers in this area considerable freedom from the prohibition on discrimination contained in the body of the Regulations.

The HRA, and before that the case law of the European Convention on Human Rights, has had the most significant impact on the development of the law on sexual orientation discrimination. Discrimination on grounds of sexual orientation is contrary to Article 8 (right to private and family life) and Article 14 (prohibition of discrimination) of the Convention. 'Particularly weighty reasons' are required to justify discrimination on grounds of sexual orientation, just as with sex discrimination (see, eg, *L and V v Austria* (2003) 36 EHRR 55, E Ct HR at paragraph 45). The impact of this on domestic law has been particularly important. In a series of cases, the European Court and Commission on Human Rights has found domestic legislation that discriminates against homosexuals to be unlawful; see, eg: *Dudgeon v United Kingdom* (1981) 4 EHRR 149, E Ct HR (a Northern Ireland statute making consenting homosexual sex between adults a criminal offence was in breach of Article 8); *Sutherland v UK* (1997) 24 EHRR CD 22, E Comm HR (different age of consent laws for heterosexuals and homosexuals was unlawful discrimination, contrary to Articles 8 and 14); and *Smith and Grady v United Kingdom* (2000) 29 EHRR 493, E Ct HR (dismissal of gay and lesbian servicemen and women from armed forces on grounds of sexual orientation was contrary to Article 8).

Since the HRA came into force, the Convention has had an important influence on the development of domestic sexual orientation discrimination law. The high point was reached in the Court of Appeal decision of *Mendoza v Ghaidan* [2002] EWCA Civ 1533, [2003] 2 WLR 478, CA. The Court held at paragraph [32], 'Sexual orientation is now clearly recognized as an impermissible ground of discrimination, on the same level as the examples, which is all that they are, specifically set out in the text of article 14', and went on to read words into housing legislation to protect homosexuals from discrimination.

In many ways, the protection against discrimination on grounds of sexual orientation found in the Convention goes further than that found in the Regulations—both in quality and scope. But the HRA and Convention protection is fundamentally limited to acts by public authorities. Although it can be applied in other circumstances in certain situations, and complainants in employment tribunal cases should always consider whether it is possible to rely on it, the HRA will be of limited assistance in most employment tribunal complaints against private employers. The extent to which the HRA can be applied in actions between employees and private employers remains unclear.

This has been examined by the Employment Appeal Tribunal in a case concerning sexual orientation discrimination before the introduction of the Regulations. In *X v Y* [2003] IRLR 561, EAT, it was indicated that there *may* be circumstances in which it would be right for an employment tribunal to question whether the statutory right not to be unfairly dismissed should be interpreted, so far as it is possible to do so, in a way which is compatible with Convention rights (by the interpretative provision in s 3 of the HRA, and the Act's application to the employment tribunal by s 6), but the EAT did not think it right to do so in that case. It remains open, therefore, for a party to argue that the employment tribunal should interpret the Regulations compatibly with Convention rights—but whether or not this is a valid approach has yet to be finally resolved.

The advantages of the Regulations, on the other hand, is that they have effect against all employers.

Attempts to 'fit' sexual orientation discrimination complaints into sex discrimination legislation have generally failed over the years. In one of the most significant decisions, the European Court of Justice found that an employer's benefit (a travel concession) available only to an employee's 'common law opposite sex spouse', and not a same-sex partner, was not unlawful, since it was not discrimination on grounds of sex, and sexual orientation discrimination was not unlawful under European law (see, Case C-249/96, *Grant v South-West Trains Ltd* [1998] ICR 449, ECJ). A number of domestic cases have adopted the same approach to sexual orientation cases brought as sex discrimination cases. The 'final nail in the coffin' was the decision of the House of Lords in *Macdonald v Ministry of Defence & Pearce v Governing Body of Mayfield Secondary School* [2003] UKHL 34, [2003] ICR 937. School pupils had subjected a lesbian teacher to a terrible campaign of harassment. The harassment mainly took the form of verbal abuse, and she was repeatedly called names such as 'lesbian', 'dyke', 'lesbian shit', 'lemon', 'lezzie', or 'lez'. After finally having to resign her job on grounds of ill health caused by the harassment she brought a complaint of sexual harassment. The House of Lords found that the harassment she had suffered could not be unlawful under the SDA as the reason for it was her sexual orientation and not her sex.

The *Macdonald* decision demonstrates the real difference the Regulations will make. Employees subjected to homophobic abuse in the future will not have the virtually impossible task of trying to present their cases under the SDA. They now have a free-standing right not be subjected to harassment on grounds of their sexuality. This, in itself, will be of enormous significance to many workers.

1.4 TOWARDS A UNIFIED APPROACH TO DISCRIMINATION

The anomaly discussed in section 1.2, above, applies to sexual orientation discrimination as it does to discrimination on grounds of religion or belief. A lesbian teacher will have protection from sexual orientation harassment by school students under the obligations put on employers by the EE (Sexual Orientation) Regulations. She will also have protection against discrimination by the school under the HRA where it is run by a local authority. A lesbian student will have protection under the Regulations where she is studying in a further or higher education institute. But a lesbian schoolgirl in a private school will have no protection from the same harassment, since school students are not covered by the Regulations, and the HRA does not cover private schools.

These anomalies are largely the result of the fact that discrimination law in Britain has developed in piecemeal fashion. A variety of different Acts of Parliament, Statutory Instruments and European Directives prohibit discrimination on a variety of different grounds, and often on the basis of different principles. There are now 30 different Acts of Parliament, 38 Statutory Instruments, 11 Codes of Practice, and 12 European Directives and Recommendations concerning discrimination. In addition there is the HRA and the case law of both the Strasbourg and domestic courts. Discrimination under some of these provisions, such as the RRA and SDA, have a relatively wide scope, applying to employment, education, and the provision of goods and services for instance. Others, such as the Regulations, are limited to employment and parts of education.

The piecemeal approach itself can lead to discriminatory results. The fact that a Jew or Sikh applicant for housing to a private Housing Association will be protected from discrimination (by the RRA), whereas a Muslim applicant in the same situation will not, is today both illogical and indefensible.

Fundamental terms and concepts in different anti-discrimination law have different meanings. The Regulations' definition of harassment and positive action, for instance, is different from that found in other provisions (though others are moving towards a shared definition because of the influence of EC law). A statutory duty for public authorities to promote equality in respect of one area of discrimination (race) does not apply to others.

Along with inconsistency and potential injustice, the result is that it is extremely confusing for employers and employees alike to understand what measures they must take, or what rights they have, to combat discrimination.

The piecemeal approach is not by design but by accident, and by incremental reform, often forced by Europe. The decision to set up a new, single, statutory equality and human rights commission, replacing the separate statutory commissions dealing with race, sex, and disability discrimination, illustrates the inevitable direction in which equality law must proceed. There are increased calls from politicians, lawyers, equality experts, and representatives of employers and employees to have a single, unified, comprehensive equality law that ties together the various strands of existing anti-discrimination law. Such a law could iron out the existing anomalies and be much easier to understand and apply than the present legislative arrangements. Like the HRA, a single equality law could have constitutional status, in recognition of the importance of the principle of non-discrimination. To the extent that there was a duty on all public bodies to promote equality, the law could also lead to a reduction in employment tribunal and other contentious litigation. For those concerned about religion or belief and sexual orientation discrimination, the advantage of a single equality law would be that it could afford people of different religions or beliefs, and different sexual orientations, equality across the board, and not just within the sphere of employment.

The Regulations considered in this book are of great importance in themselves. The prohibition of discrimination on grounds of religion or belief and sexual orientation will have a major impact on the lives of many, and will provoke new challenges and questions for employers, lawyers, courts, and tribunals. But they will also have an impact on the whole landscape of domestic discrimination law. As concepts from the fields of race, sex, and disability discrimination law and from human rights law have influenced and helped shape these Regulations, so the application of these Regulations will affect other areas. In particular, they make the prospect of a comprehensive single equality law appear as the logical and inevitable next step in the progress of UK discrimination law.

2

THE DISCRIMINATION PROHIBITED

2.1 INTRODUCTION

Part I of both the EE (Religion or Belief) and the EE (Sexual Orientation) Regulations set out the type of conduct prohibited. Part I defines the grounds of discrimination, the different types of discrimination (direct, indirect, and victimization), and harassment. Apart from obvious differences in describing the grounds (ie, religion or belief, or sexual orientation) the content and numbering of the Regulations is the same in both Regulations.

Regulation 1(2) provides that the Regulations do not extend to Northern Ireland, where separate Regulations will be introduced to fit into the special framework of discrimination that exists there (promoting equality between Protestants and Catholics).

The definitions of discrimination, victimization, and harassment in the Regulations are central to their operation. References to discrimination elsewhere in the Regulations are to discrimination falling within Regulation 3 (discrimination on grounds of religion or belief/sexual orientation) or 4 (discrimination by way of victimization), and references to harassment are to harassment on grounds of religion or belief/sexual orientation as defined in Regulation 5 (see Regulation 2(2) of both Regulations). Therefore understanding what constitutes discrimination for the purposes of the Regulations will be one of the most important issues.

2.2 DEFINITION OF 'RELIGION OR BELIEF'

2.2.1 The Definition of 'Religion or Belief' in Regulation 2(1)

Regulation 2 of the EE (Religion or Belief) Regulations defines what is meant by religion or belief. According to Regulation 2(1), religion or belief:

means any religion, religious belief, or similar philosophical belief.

The Government preferred this broad definition of religion or belief to a more precise definition, or one that lists the religions or beliefs covered. This is understandable considering the large number of religions and beliefs that exist, the fact that new ones might develop, and the argument that may arise as to what constitutes a valid religion or belief.

All religions are covered by the Regulations, as is the holding of a particular religious belief. There is no distinction made between 'organized' religions and more disparate groups. It is unnecessary to prove a group is a religion and not a 'cult' since the latter are likely to hold religious beliefs.

The breadth of the Regulations means that a person who is discriminated against because of his belief in what might be considered as the bizarre teachings of a New-Age religious cult should have the same protection as a person who believes in the Assumption of the Virgin Mary, that God spoke to Moses from the burning bush, or that the cow is sacred.

2.2.2 What is a 'Similar Philosophical Belief'?

There has been some controversy over the use of the words 'similar philosophical belief' in the Regulations. What does the word 'similar' suggest? Why must a philosophical belief be similar to a religious one for it to be afforded protection? These questions are particularly important in relation to philosophical beliefs that do not have a place for a Supreme Being, doubt the existence of God, are positively atheistic, or are predicated on the absence of belief in anything. Do atheists and humanists hold a belief similar to religion? Many would be offended to be told they do. How can a person who holds no belief in God (as opposed to positively disputing the existence of God) be described as having a 'philosophical belief' at all, let alone a similar one? Yet it would be perverse if the Regulations protected a person who was discriminated against at work because he was a Buddhist, for instance, but did not offer any protection from discrimination for an atheist who happened to work alongside fanatical Christians.

This question was addressed in the House of Lords debate approving the Regulations. The Government minister responsible for moving the motion approving the Regulations in the Lords, Lord Sainsbury of Turville, said:

Members of Muslim, Christian and other communities have been dismissed, victimised and turned down for work unfairly simply because of their faith. Of those who are not religious, atheists and humanists, for example, who have also experienced discrimination at work because of their beliefs *or absence of them*. These regulations will make this kind of unacceptable treatment unlawful. (Hansard, HL; vol 649, col 786 (17 June 2003), emphasis added)

During the debate that followed, Lord Lester of Herne Hill QC suggested the Minister's statement might be a *'Pepper v Hart'* statement—showing what the Government's intention on this question was—and the Minister was asked if, in his reply, he could make it absolutely clear that discrimination because of a lack of religious belief was covered by the Regulations, so that a humanist, agnostic, atheist, 'or any other godless person or person without faith' is protected. The Minister replied:

It is clearly the intention that where people have strongly held views, which include humanism, or atheism or agnosticism, they would be covered under the phrase 'or similar philosophical belief'. (Hansard, HL; vol 649, col 792 (17 June 2003))

Thus the definition should be given a broad interpretation, consistent with these statements. Non-religious beliefs, such as atheism, and the absence of a religious belief, come within the definition of 'similar philosophical belief'.

This broad approach is also more likely to be compatible with the Framework Directive. The Directive prohibits discrimination on grounds of 'religion or belief'; no further definition is given. The word 'similar' is not used. Furthermore, it is compatible with the approach of the European Court of Human Rights in interpreting the right to a religious belief protected by Article 9 of the Convention. In *Kokkinakis v Greece* (1993) 17 EHRR 397, ECtHR, the Court held at paragraph 31 that Article 9 rights were a 'precious asset for atheists, agnostics, sceptics and the unconcerned'.

2.2.3 Are Political Beliefs Covered by the Regulations?

A more difficult question is whether political beliefs are covered by the words 'similar philosophical belief'. Consultative and explanatory material on the Regulations issued by the Government strongly indicated that the Regulations did not protect political beliefs. The phrase 'similar philosophical belief' could suggest there must be a connection with God or religion, even though not necessarily a belief in religion. Thus atheism would be a similar philosophical belief, as its central tenet relates to the (non-existence of) God. Secularism (belief that religion should be ignored or excluded), agnosticism (belief that the existence of God is unknown and probably unknowable), and humanism (a philosophy that rejects supernaturalism and asserts the essential worth of man) would all fall within this interpretation. Political beliefs that are not based on an attitude towards God or religion may therefore be excluded.

But it is also arguable that the Regulations will cover some political beliefs. A person may hold a political ideology as strongly as any religion or other similar philosophical belief, such as humanism, the ideology may have a similar coherent system of beliefs, or world-view, but it may not have the question of the existence of God as its focus. For instance, a communist may argue that his political belief is a 'similar philosophical belief' in the sense of the Regulations; he has an ideology, or belief system, that could be described as a philosophy. The same may be true for a libertarian. However the expression of a particular political idea, for instance opposition to a European Single Currency, or belief in the repatriation of immigrants, cannot be protected by the Regulations. A single political idea cannot properly be described as a philosophy, which implies a system of beliefs or principles, let alone a 'similar philosophical belief' as a religious belief. So if a person is discriminated against because of his political ideology, for instance, then it is possible he will be able to rely on the Regulations. If, on the other hand, a person is discriminated against because of a particular political opinion he holds he is unlikely to be able to rely on the Regulations. These difficult issues are likely to be resolved by the courts and tribunals in time. For more discussion on this issue, see section 8.3, below.

2.3 DEFINITION OF 'SEXUAL ORIENTATION'

The definition of sexual orientation is found within Regulation 2(1) of the EE (Sexual Orientation) Regulations. This simple definition provides that:

sexual orientation means a sexual orientation towards—
   (a) persons of the same sex;
   (b) persons of the opposite sex; or
   (c) persons of the same sex and of the opposite sex.

So discrimination against a person on the grounds that they are homosexual, heterosexual, or bisexual is covered. Other types of sexual proclivity, such as sadomasochism or paedophilia, are not covered by the definition of sexual orientation. For further discussion on the meaning of sexual orientation, see section 9.2, below.

2.4 PROHIBITED ACTS

Part I of both Regulations go on to set out, in identical terms, the type of conduct that is prohibited by the Regulations. First, Regulation 3 prohibits discrimination on grounds of either religion or belief, or sexual orientation (see section 2.5 below). This includes direct and indirect discrimination. Secondly, discrimination by way of victimization is prohibited by Regulation 4 (see section 2.6 below). Thirdly, harassment on grounds of religion or belief, or sexual orientation is prohibited by Regulation 5 (see section 2.7 below). Naturally, each type of prohibited act has its own definition and has to be considered separately. A person may be the victim of all three or any one of the prohibited types of conduct.

The types of conduct prohibited reflect those prohibited by the RRA/SDA, and so authorities under those acts will be of relevance; however, there are some important differences, such as the separate statutory definition of harassment (in race and sex legislation, harassment has formerly been considered as a type of discrimination). These issues are reviewed below.

As the word 'discrimination' is used in both Regulation 3 (discrimination on grounds of religion or belief/sexual orientation) and Regulation 4 (victimization) of both Regulations, an originating application to an employment tribunal that just complains of 'discrimination' without more is likely to be sufficient to include a complaint for either form of discrimination (see *Quarcoopome v Sock Shop Holdings Ltd* [1995] IRLR 353, EAT, for the similar position under the RRA).

2.5 DISCRIMINATION ON GROUNDS OF RELIGION OR BELIEF/SEXUAL ORIENTATION

Regulation 3 of the Regulations prohibits discrimination on grounds of religion or belief and discrimination on grounds of sexual orientation. As with discrimination law generally, two types of discrimination are outlawed, 'direct' and 'indirect' discrimination. Regulation 3(1)(a) prohibits direct discrimination, defined as where a person (A) treats another (B) less favourably, on grounds of religion or belief/sexual orientation, than he treats or would treat other persons. Regulation 3(1)(b) prohibits indirect discrimination where A applies to B a 'provision, criterion or practice' which he applies to others in the same position as B who are not of the same religion or belief/sexual orientation, and which puts B and persons of the same religion or belief/sexual orientation as B at a disadvantage, and which A cannot show to be a proportionate means of achieving a legitimate aim.

2.5.1 Direct Discrimination

The wording of Regulation 3(1)(a) is essentially the same as that used in s 1 of both the RRA and the SDA (which provide that a person discriminates against another if he treats that other less favourably on grounds of race/sex than he would treat other persons). The DDA (Disability Discrimination Act 1995), on the other hand, does not distinguish between direct and indirect discrimination—all discrimination, other than victimization, is capable of justification under the DDA. The case law under the RRA/SDA will therefore give guidance as to the operation of Regulation 3(1)(a) of both Regulations. Regulation 3(1)(a) transposes the definition of direct discrimination in Article 2(2)(b) of the Framework Directive.

2.5.1.1 *Direct Discrimination Cannot be Justified*
The distinction between direct and indirect discrimination is most significant in that, under both the Regulations and the Framework Directive, direct discrimination cannot be justified. Whilst an employer is entitled to apply a genuine occupational requirement (GOR) to a particular job that would allow what would otherwise be

discrimination (see Chapter 5 below), there are very strict conditions for this. The test of justification, where an employer can show that an act that would otherwise be discriminatory was in fact a proportionate means of achieving a legitimate aim (see section 2.5.2.6 below) only applies to indirect discrimination. Direct discrimination cannot be justified. Therefore unless an employer can show the less favourable treatment on grounds of religion or belief/sexual orientation was in pursuance of a genuine occupational requirement, or one of the limited exceptions discussed in Chapter 6 below, then it will automatically be unlawful.

2.5.1.2 *Less Favourable Treatment*
Regulation 3(1)(a) prohibits less favourable treatment on grounds of religion or belief/sexual orientation. This can be anything from refusing an applicant a job or a promotion, to simply burdening an employee with more arduous tasks than he gives a relevant comparator.

Indeed, words or acts of discouragement can amount to less favourable treatment (see *Simon v Brimham Associates* [1987] IRLR 307, CA, on the same issue under the RRA). For example, if an applicant for a job in a Jewish-owned company was told that it was probably not worth his while applying because he was Muslim and the directors of the company were suspicious of Muslims, then this would be direct discrimination even if the directors would not have discriminated at all.

2.5.1.3 *Grounds of Discrimination*
The less favourable treatment must obviously be on grounds of religion or belief to fall within the EE (Religion of Belief) Regulations, or on grounds of sexual orientation to fall within the EE (Sexual Orientation) Regulations, but the complainant does not need to show the discriminator acted *solely* on those grounds, so long as he can show he *substantially* acted on them. So, where an employer (A) refuses B a job, and gives the job to C, where B and C have similar qualifications, if B can show that the substantial reason A gave C the job was that she was a heterosexual woman, whereas B was a lesbian, then even if another reason was that C could start working for A two weeks before B could, it will still be direct discrimination.

2.5.1.4 *Regulation 3(2) of the EE (Religion or Belief) Regulations*
The Religion or Belief Regulations include a paragraph explaining that the reference in Regulation 3(1)(a) to A treating B less favourably than he would treat other persons, on grounds of religion or belief, 'does not include A's religion or belief' (Regulation 3(2)).

There is some confusion as to the meaning and effect of this provision. A similar provision is not included in the EE (Sexual Orientation) Regulations. It has been suggested that the provision might mean that A does not discriminate against B on grounds of religion or belief when A has the same religion or belief as B. So, if A was a Hindu he would not be discriminating against B on grounds of religion if B was also a Hindu. This reading would not make sense and would be contrary to the whole body of discrimination law. It is quite possible for a female boss to discriminate in favour of male employees. It is just as possible that a Hindu might prefer not to employ other Hindus and therefore discriminate against job applicants on grounds of their religion even though it is the same religion as his.

The better reading of Regulation 3(2) is that it is merely clarifying what is always the case in discrimination law: it is not the motivation of the alleged discriminator that is important, but the grounds for the discrimination. Thus, what is meant by A discriminating against B 'on grounds of religion of belief' is that the *reason* for the discrimination is B's religion or belief (or A's perception of B's religion etc). It does not matter what A's religion or belief is. The reference 'religion or belief' in Regulation 3(1)(a) of the Regulations does not therefore include A's religion or belief. This is both a more logical reading of the Regulations and one that is compatible with the prohibition of discrimination on grounds of religion, regardless of the motivations of the alleged discriminator. Furthermore, there is nothing in the Framework Directive that could justify the former reading of the Regulation, and it would thus be arguably *ultra vires* the Directive to give it that meaning. It will, however, be for the courts and tribunals to determine which of these two interpretations is correct.

2.5.1.5 *Discriminator's Perception Important*

A highly significant point about the Regulations is that, in determining whether or not a person has discriminated against another on grounds of the other's religion or belief/sexual orientation, the person discriminated against does not have to show he was of that religion or belief/sexual orientation. It is enough that the discriminator perceived he was. Paragraph 9 of the Office of the Deputy Prime Minister's Notes on the draft EE (Sexual Orientation) Regulations state:

Direct discrimination 'on grounds of sexual orientation' can also include discrimination based on A's perception of B's sexual orientation, whether the perception is right or wrong. This means that people will be able to bring a claim even if the discrimination was based on (incorrect) assumptions about their sexual orientation. Nor will they be required to disclose their sexual orientation in bringing a claim—it will be sufficient that they have suffered a disadvantage because of the assumptions made about their orientation.

The same guidance is given in relation to the EE (Religion or Belief) Regulations. Thus, where a job applicant is not given a job because it is thought he is Catholic, then even if he is not he has been discriminated against on grounds of religion or belief—ie not on the grounds of *his* religion or belief, but on the grounds of *the perception of his* religion or belief. Likewise, a person refused promotion because his boss thinks he is gay is protected by the legislation whether or not he is in fact gay.

This is important for two reasons. First, it releases a victim of discrimination from the otherwise difficult and potentially embarrassing task of proving he has a particular belief or sexual orientation, and that his employer knew about it. Secondly, it focuses on the discrimination itself, and demonstrates that it is the act of discrimination itself that is condemned, not whether or not the discrimination was based on correct facts. Discrimination on grounds of a person's religion, for instance, can be just as objectionable whether or not the person who suffers from it actually holds that religion.

2.5.1.6 *Discrimination on Grounds of Another's Religion or Belief/Sexual Orientation*

In similar fashion, Regulation 3(1)(a) covers discrimination against a person on grounds of the religion or belief/sexual orientation of another person. So, if a homophobic employer discriminates against an employee because the employee has a gay son, or mixes with gay friends, then this is unlawful even though the employee is himself heterosexual: the discrimination is on *grounds* of sexual orientation. Likewise, where an employee is treated less favourably by his employer because he has refused to ban Muslims from entering the employer's building, this is discrimination against the employee, whatever his individual religion or belief, on grounds of religion or belief.

2.5.1.7 *Motivation for Discrimination*

As with domestic discrimination law generally, it is not necessary to show the discriminator had a discriminatory motivation for his act. Even where a person treats another less favourably for an 'innocent' motive, he may have unlawfully discriminated. Examples of this can be found from the case law of the RRA/SDA. For instance, in *R v Commission for Racial Equality, ex p Westminster CC* [1984] ICR 770, the High Court held that there can be discrimination on racial grounds without there being an intention to discriminate on those grounds: an employer who treats a black employee less favourably on racial grounds for 'worthy motives' is guilty of unlawful discrimination. In that case the employer refused to appoint a black road sweeper to the position of refuse collector. All the refuse collectors were white and their union objected to the black applicant, ostensibly on grounds of his poor attendance record. The employer believed the real reason for the objection was that the applicant was black, but decided not to appoint him anyway for the otherwise 'innocent' motive of preventing industrial action by the union. The employer may not have been motivated by racial prejudice, but he had still discriminated on racial grounds.

It is easy to see how this is important in the context of discrimination on grounds of religion or belief/sexual orientation. Where an employer refuses to employ a gay man as a fire-fighter, for instance, not because he himself intends to discriminate—he may be very sympathetic to homosexuals—but because he thinks it will disrupt the cohesion of his team of employees, this is likely to be direct discrimination. Similarly, if a restaurant owner dismissed a Hasidic Jew from his job as a waiter, not because he himself is prejudiced, but because some of his customers have made anti-Semitic remarks or complained about having to be served by the Hasidic Jew, then although the owner may be solely motivated by the desire not to lose his customers, this is most likely to be direct discrimination.

2.5.1.8 *Comparators*
For a complainant to show he has been treated less favourably than another person in the same circumstances on grounds of his religion or belief/sexual orientation, he must identify a comparator. If, for instance, the complainant is a Sikh complaining that he was not promoted because of his religion, whereas a Christian with the same qualifications as him was promoted, then the Christian with the same qualifications as the Sikh will be his comparator. Identifying a comparator is rarely as straightforward as this, however.

2.5.1.9 *Hypothetical Comparator Allowed*
A person's (A) conduct will be unlawful if he treats another (B) less favourably than he treats or '*would treat*' other persons. So even if there is no direct comparator to B—ie nobody in the same position but of a different religion or belief/sexual orientation—then a hypothetical comparator can be applied. If B can show that A treats him less favourably than he would treat a heterosexual employee because B is gay, for instance, then there is direct discrimination even if A does not actually employ a heterosexual employee. B might be A's only employee, but A might have told B, on discovery that he was gay, that he did not want B to work for him anymore. In this case, A did not treat B less favourably than another employee on grounds of sexual orientation, but he treated him less favourably than he *would* have treated another employee on those grounds, and it is thus direct discrimination contrary to Regulation 3(1)(a).

2.5.1.10 *Comparator's Circumstances must be the Same*
As with race and sex discrimination, the relevant circumstances of the comparator (for instance his job, his experience, or his disciplinary record) must be 'the same, or not materially different' as the person claiming to have been discriminated against. The case law under the RRA/SDA will be useful for examples of how the same relevant circumstances test is applied in different situations. It will be for the court or tribunal to determine whether or not the relevant circumstances are the same. Therefore, where a person is uncertain that they can identify an actual comparator with the same relevant circumstances as them, it may be safer for them to suggest a hypothetical comparator with the same circumstances.

2.5.1.11 *Stereotyping*
Stereotyping is a common problem. Managers may often share widely held stereotypes that suggest people of a certain religion or belief/sexual orientation are more or less sensitive, promiscuous, or hard-working than others. If the employer makes promotion or recruitment decisions, for instance, based on such stereotypes this may be directly discriminatory.

For example, if an employer considers the fact that a person is a committed Christian who runs a Sunday school is more likely to be dedicated and hard working than an atheist who goes running on a Sunday morning, and this is a substantial reason for him deciding to appoint the Christian, this may be directly discriminatory. Conversely, if an employer prefers not to appoint a committed Muslim because he fears he might be a 'kill-joy' and not go drinking with the other workers on a Friday night, this is also likely to be direct discrimination based on stereotyping. In order to avoid stereotyping, employers should consider whether interview questions, for instance, are really necessary to reveal a person's qualifications, or whether they are superfluous for that purpose but may lead to the danger of stereotyping (see Chapters 8 and 9 for more examples of these points).

2.5.2 Indirect Discrimination

2.5.2.1 *The Concept of Indirect Discrimination*
The Framework Directive provides a clear definition of indirect discrimination. Article 2(2)(b) provides:

indirect discrimination shall be taken to occur where an apparently neutral provision, criterion or practice would put persons having a particular religion or belief . . . or a particular sexual orientation at a particular disadvantage compared with other persons unless:

    (i) that provision, criterion or practice is objectively justified by a legitimate aim and the means of achieving that aim are appropriate and necessary.

Article 2(2)(b) is not transposed word for word in the Regulations, and some of the differences are considered below. However, generally, Regulation 3(1)(b) reflects the approach taken in the Directive. The Regulation provides that A discriminates against B when:

A applies to B a provision, criterion or practice which he applies or would apply equally to persons not of the same [religion or belief/sexual orientation] as B, but—

    (i) which puts or would put persons of the same [religion or belief/sexual orientation] as B at a particular disadvantage when compared with other persons,

    (ii) which puts B at that disadvantage, and

    (iii) which A cannot show to be a proportionate means of achieving a legitimate aim.

Indirect discrimination thus occurs when a provision, criterion or practice applied equally to all individuals without differentiation has a disproportionate and unjustified adverse impact on a particular group. One of the earliest developments of the concept was by the US Supreme Court in *Griggs v Duke Power Co* 401 US 424 (1971). Educational disadvantages resulting from segregation meant black people did disproportionately worse than whites at an employer's aptitude test. The test had no business justification and was therefore indirectly discriminatory. The Court held that 'practices that are fair in form, but discriminatory in operation', and not just overt discrimination, were prohibited.

The concept of indirect discrimination is a well-established feature of domestic discrimination law. However, the definition of indirect discrimination in EC law and domestic discrimination law has not been identical. This has led, in turn, to a difference in the definitions applied in the SDA, amended by the Sex Discrimination (Indirect Discrimination and Burden of Proof) Regulations 2001 (SI 2660/2001) to reflect the European approach, and the RRA. However, this has now changed due to the Race Directive and the Race Regulations Act 1976 (Amendment) Regulations 2003 (SI 2003/1626). Since July 2003, a new s 1A of the RRA supplements s 1(1)(b) of the act and brings the RRA into line with s 1(1)(b) and (2) of the SDA. The Regulations covered in this book are based on the EC approach so case law from 2003 onwards under the SDA or RRA should be applicable. Earlier case law should, however, be treated with some caution, although it will generally assist in setting out the principles to be applied when considering indirect discrimination. The definition of indirect discrimination under the amended SDA, RRA, and the Regulations is more favourable to the complainant than it was under the old domestic law.

2.5.2.2 *Provision, Criterion or Practice*

For indirect discrimination to occur, the first thing to show is that A has applied to B 'a provision, criteria or practice' which whilst neutral on the face has a disproportionate and unjustified impact on B and members of the group (religion or belief/sexual orientation) to which B belongs.

The wording here is significantly broader than existed under s 1(1)(b) of the SDA and RRA. Under those provisions, and before the RRA and SDA were amended to bring them into line with EC Directives, indirect discrimination could only occur with respect to the application of a 'requirement or condition'. Many claims for indirect discrimination under the old law foundered because of the stringency of this test. It was often difficult for a complainant to show a requirement or condition was applied to him. Proving a provision, criterion, or practice was applied is much easier, particularly as 'practice' suggests conduct alone will be enough.

A few examples demonstrate the significance of this more liberal wording. In *Perera v Civil Service* (No 2) [1983] 428 ICR (CA) the Court of Appeal considered a complaint by a Sri Lankan barrister who had been refused a post in the Civil Service in England. He had failed to meet several of the selection criteria (eg practical experience in England, ability to communicate in English, etc). He complained that the criteria were indirectly (racially) discriminatory and were 'requirements or conditions'. The Court rejected his claim because they said a requirement or condition means a 'must'—something that has to be complied with. The only requirement or condition in the case was for candidates to be either a qualified solicitor or barrister. He fulfilled that condition. There was no requirement or condition that a candidate for the job have practical experience in England or ability to communicate in English; these were just general factors which the interviewing board took into account—failure on any of them would not be an absolute bar to getting the job. (See, also, *Meer v Tower Hamlets LBC* [1988] IRLR 399, CA). If a similar case arose under the Regulations, then the claim would not fail on the ground that the criteria were not absolute 'musts'; the Regulations cover a 'criterion', so whether or not each or all of them were 'musts' is irrelevant. Of course there may still be a question of causation (ie if the criterion was so peripheral that its application to the complainant made no material difference to his circumstances, the reason he did not get the job was unconnected), but the broader words in the Regulations at least enable a complainant to get over what was previously an often difficult and technical hurdle.

Consider a particular workplace in which the employer (A) and his employees share the practice of going to the pub for a drink every Friday night to discuss work. A new employee, B, may not be required to come, he may simply be invited and pressurized to join in this practice. He may feel unable to do so because his religion or belief prevents him drinking at all, or going out on a Friday night, or perhaps because his sexual orientation makes him feel uncomfortable in a pub of A's choice. If his refusal to participate in this routine practice leads to a disadvantage, such as a failure to receive promotion, then this may be indirect discrimination. The practice of Friday night drinks is not a requirement or condition, but it could be a practice applied to B.

2.5.2.3 *Identifying the Right 'Pool'*

According to the Regulations, the application of the provision, criteria, or practice by A to B must put 'persons of the same [religion or belief/sexual orientation] as B at a particular disadvantage' when compared to other persons of a different religion or belief/sexual orientation. The first issue is therefore to identify the right pool for B's comparison. Consider B is an observant Jewish social worker complaining that he has been indirectly discriminated against, in terms of the opportunities for promotion, because social workers are only offered promotion after they have completed a set number of residential visits on a Saturday, and B cannot attend such visits because they occur on the Sabbath. The pool to which B belongs will be Jewish social workers that observe the Sabbath. The first question, under Regulation 3(2)(b)(i), will be whether the criterion of having to attend residential visits on a Saturday to obtain promotion puts that pool, Jewish social workers that observe the Sabbath, at a disadvantage compared with 'other persons'.

In cases of religious discrimination in particular, it will be important to define the group B belongs to accurately and with regard to the relevant aspects of his religion or belief. Thus in the example given above, it would be mistaken for B to identify the group to which he belongs as Jewish social workers, since the majority of this group are unlikely to observe the Sabbath. If an employee who is a Shi'ite Muslim is complaining that the practice discriminates against Shi'ite Muslims, but not Sunni Muslims, it is important he identifies the group to which he belongs as Shi'ite Muslims, and not Muslims generally.

For example, in *Wetstein v Misprestige Management Services Ltd* (EAT/523/91, 19 March 1993, unreported), the Employment Appeals Tribunal found in a race discrimination case that the number of Jews who observed the Sabbath was only 5–10% and thus not enough to demonstrate indirect discrimination in circumstances where they had to work until 5pm on a Friday even during winter (eg after sunset and therefore the beginning of the Sabbath). It was not possible in that case for the complainant to say he belonged to the group, 'religious Jews who observe the Sabbath' because that group is based on religion or belief and does not come under the definition of 'racial group' for the purposes of the RRA, whereas Jews as a whole are a 'racial group' regardless of religion. Under the EE (Religion or Belief) Regulations, the complainant could show that religious Jews who observe the Sabbath, as a group, would be put at a disadvantage compared to the whole group consisting of non-religious Jews, Jews who don't observe the Sabbath, and non-Jews. The requirement to work on the Sabbath would put persons of the same religious belief as the complainant at a disadvantage.

The words 'particular disadvantage' have their ordinary and common sense meaning. They mean the same as the word 'detriment' under the RRA/SDA. To prove a particular disadvantage it is not necessary to show financial loss (see, eg *Chief Constable of the West Yorkshire Police v Khan* [2001] ICR 1065 (HL)).

Next it is necessary to find the pool of comparators in relation to whom B claims that the group he is a member of has been put at a disadvantage. That group will be persons not of the same religion or belief/sexual orientation as B, but otherwise persons whose relevant circumstances are the same, or not materially different (Regulation 3(3) of the EE (Religion or Belief) Regulations and 3(2) of the EE (Sexual Orientation) Regulations). So, if we consider the above example of the observant Jewish social worker, the comparators must be non-observant Jewish social workers in the same, or at least not in materially different, circumstances. If there are no people that fall into this group, then it is again possible to choose a hypothetical comparator. As discussed above (section 2.5.1.7), it will often be easier for a complainant to demonstrate he was put at a disadvantage compared to a hypothetical comparator, because the danger of identifying an actual comparator is that the court or tribunal will find the complainant is not actually in the same circumstances as the comparator (see, for an example of this under the SDA, *Shamoon v Chief Constable of the Royal Ulster Constabulary* [2003] 2 All ER 26 (HL)).

2.5.2.4 *Statistical and Expert Evidence*

Statistical evidence may be required to demonstrate indirect discrimination. In order to show that the group the complainant belongs to will be put at a disadvantage by a particular practice, compared with others, it is often necessary to show that a disproportionate number of people from the complainant's group can comply with a practice as compared with others.

Consider a practice of asking job applicants to disclose all previous criminal convictions. A gay man might argue that this puts him at a disadvantage because he has a minor conviction for the offence of having sex in a public toilet with another man. Or it may be that the offence for which he was committed has since been repealed as a result of further equality in the law: an 18-year-old man having homosexual sex with a 17-year-old would have been committing a criminal offence only a few years ago, whilst an 18-year-old man having heterosexual sex with a 17-year-old girl would not. If the gay complainant wanted to show the practice of asking for disclosure of previous convictions put the group to which he belonged, homosexuals, at a disadvantage compared with heterosexuals, he might need to produce statistical evidence. If he could show that a greater proportion of homosexuals had convictions for minor offences of a similar nature, compared with heterosexuals in the same relevant circumstances, then he may be able to establish indirect discrimination.

When compiling statistical evidence, it is the proportion of a particular group that is disadvantaged by a practice that is important, not the overall number, or ratio (see, *Perera v Civil Service* [1982] ICR 350, EAT).

However, statistical evidence is by no means always required to prove indirect discrimination. This is perhaps particularly true in the case of the Regulations. It will often not be possible to produce statistical evidence related to the uncharted territory into which these new Regulations go. For instance, in a sexual orientation discrimination case it would be difficult to compile accurate statistics about the proportion of job applicants who were bisexual compared to the proportion of job applicants who were heterosexual, because that information is unknown and difficult to gather. Whether or not a person of a particular religion or sexual orientation would be put at a disadvantage compared to others might often be a question of expert evidence, but not necessarily statistical evidence. Expert theological, sociological, or economic evidence may be more relevant than statistical evidence.

2.5.2.5 *Whether the Complainant Himself is Put at a Disadvantage*
In addition to showing that the group to which the complainant belongs is or would be put at a disadvantage by the practice complained of, it is necessary to show the complainant himself is, in fact, put at that disadvantage (Regulation 3(1)(b)(ii)). Thus, it will not be enough for a Buddhist complainant to show that a particular practice puts Buddhists as a group at a disadvantage when, for whatever reasons (of religion, or maybe because the practice does not apply to him) the individual complainant is not himself put at that disadvantage.

2.5.2.6 *Justification*
The most difficult and controversial issue in cases of indirect discrimination usually relates to justification. Unlike direct discrimination, justification applies to cases of alleged indirect discrimination where the provision, criterion, or practice applied can be shown by the person relying on it to be a proportionate means of achieving a legitimate aim (Regulation 3(1)(b)(iii)).

In short, where it is reasonably necessary for a business to operate a particular practice (eg only opening between Monday to Friday between the hours of 9am and 5pm, and requiring all its employees to work within those hours) then, subject to whether the practice is a proportionate means of achieving that business aim, the employer should be able to justify the practice and it would not be indirectly discriminatory contrary to Regulation 3(1)(b). Unfortunately, however, the definition and operation of justification can be significantly more complicated than that and requires further discussion.

The test for justification in the Regulations reflects the European law approach. This approach is also to be found in the more recent case law under the RRA/SDA and the Equal Pay Act 1970. In the leading ECJ case on the question of justification, Case 170/84 *Bilka-Kaufhaus GmbH v Weber von Hartz* [1986] ECR 1607 (ECJ), the Court considered the indirectly discriminatory effect on women of a policy excluding part-time workers from an occupational pension scheme. Dealing with justification, the Court endorsed the Commission's approach that:

. . . it is not sufficient to show that in adopting a pay practice which in fact discriminates against women workers the employer sought to achieve objectives other than discrimination against women, . . . in order to justify such a pay practice . . . the employer must . . . put forward objective economic grounds relating to the management of the undertaking. It is also necessary to ascertain whether the pay practice in question is necessary and in proportion to the objectives pursued by the employer. (Para 35 of the judgment)

This test thus has three limbs:

(i) whether the otherwise discriminatory measure has a non-discriminatory objective;

(ii) whether the measure is in fact necessary for the employer; and

(iii) whether the measure taken is a proportionate means of achieving the objective.

These three limbs are, in turn, to be found in the test for justification set out in Art 2.2(b)(i) of the Framework Directive:

that provision, criterion or practice is objectively justified by a legitimate aim and the means of achieving that aim are appropriate and necessary.

However, the Regulations fail to transpose the three limbs. Instead, Regulation 3(1)(b)(iii) limits indirect discrimination to cases in which the alleged discriminator 'cannot show to be a proportionate means of achieving a legitimate aim'.

Why did the Government decide to leave out the requirement that the practice or measure be 'necessary'? Paragraph 14 of the Office of the Deputy Prime Minister's Notes on the draft Regulations states that if the Directive's formulation was simply copied out 'there might be a risk that this would be interpreted as a very strict requirement for example, that the legitimate aim pursued was essential to the employer's business'. So the Government was concerned that courts and tribunals might make it too difficult for an employer to justify a measure that would otherwise be indirectly discriminatory. An absolute necessity test is rejected. However, the Notes also say, at paragraph 13, that the Framework Directive uses the words 'proportionate' and 'appropriate and necessary' interchangeably, and they really mean the same thing, not a test of absolute necessity but 'one of proportionality involving balancing between the discriminatory effects of a measure and the importance of the aim pursued'.

The Regulations should therefore be interpreted as implementing the Directive here, and not as attempting to create a different, easier test of justification. The Government's stated intention would appear to be to incorporate the EC law test but in language that did not lead courts and tribunals to mistake that test for an absolute necessity test. It would be inconsistent, and contrary to EC law, to apply one test for justification in cases involving race and sex discrimination, and another, less burdensome one for the employer, in cases of discrimination on grounds of religion or belief/sexual orientation. The case law of the ECJ on justification for indirect discrimination, and the cases under the RRA/SDA and Equal Pay Act that apply it, should thus be followed when interpreting the Regulations.

2.5.2.7 How Justification Works

In seeking to justify a practice that disadvantages people on grounds of religion or belief/sexual orientation, the employer must first identify a legitimate aim. Business efficacy or health and safety are common examples that often arise as legitimate objectives. The employer must prove not only that the aim was legitimate, but also that the practice complained of was in fact applied to pursue that aim. So it will not be good enough for an employer to create a *post-facto* justification for a practice—the practice must have been applied to pursue the legitimate objective.

Secondly, if the employer demonstrates a legitimate aim for the provision, criterion, or practice, he must then show it is proportionate to apply it. This requires an objective balance to be struck between the discriminatory effect of the practice and the importance of the aim pursued. The more serious the discriminatory effect, the more important the aim pursued must be to justify it. On the other hand, where the discriminatory effect of the practice is very minor, the aim sought to be achieved need not be so important.

The employer has to show the practice applied is the least onerous reasonably available to him. If the employer can reasonably achieve his aim by a practice that has less of a discriminatory effect than the one he adopts, he ought to choose the least discriminatory means. A failure to do so may make the practice disproportionate.

It is for the employer to demonstrate the practice pursues a legitimate aim and is proportionate to that aim; he has the burden of proof.

The justification process, and in particular the assessment of proportionality, will be a matter for the court or tribunal to determine, based on the facts before them and, in many cases, on the credibility of the witnesses. So long as the court or tribunal conducts this exercise based on the correct legal principles, an appeal tribunal will be slow to interfere in their assessment (see, eg, *Raval v Department of Health and Social Security* [1985] ICR 685, for a case on this question under the RRA).

2.5.2.8 *Motivation*

As with direct discrimination, it is not necessary to show the alleged discriminator intended to discriminate to succeed in a claim for indirect discrimination. Indeed, the concept of indirect discrimination could not work if it depended on a discriminatory motive, as indirect discrimination occurs when a practice that is neutral (non-discriminatory) is applied, but the practical effect of the application of the practice is to disadvantage a particular group.

2.6 VICTIMIZATION

2.6.1 Introduction

Regulation 4 of both Regulations prohibits discrimination by way of victimization. According to Regulation 4(1) a person (A) discriminates against another (B) if he treats B less favourably than others because B has:

(a) brought proceedings against A or any other person under these Regulations;

(b) given evidence or information in connection with proceedings brought by any person against A or any other person under these Regulations;

(c) otherwise done anything under or by reference to these Regulations in relation to A or any other person; or

(d) alleged that A or any other person has committed an act which (whether or not the allegation so states) would amount to a contravention of these Regulations

or if A knows B intends to do any of the above, or suspects B has done or intends to do any of them.

Again, the wording here is similar (though not exactly the same) to that used in the RRA (s 3(1)(a)), the SDA (s 5(1)(a)), and the DDA (s 55(1)), and the case law under those provisions will be relevant in interpreting Regulation 4.

The acts described in Regulation 4(1) sub-paragraphs (a) to (d) are commonly described as 'protected acts', because an employee is protected if he does any of them.

2.6.2 Establishing Victimization

A complaint of victimization must therefore establish:

(i) that there has been less favourable treatment;

(ii) that the less favourable treatment was in relation to others in the same situation;

(iii) that the reason for the less favourable treatment was that B did a protected act, or A knows B intends to do a protected act, or suspects B has done or intends to do one; and

(iv) that B's conduct, or A's perception of B's conduct, is conduct falling within one of the protected acts; and finally

(v) the allegation, evidence, or information made/given was not false and was not made/given in bad faith.

2.6.2.1 *Less Favourable Treatment*

For discrimination by way of victimization to have taken place, B needs to have been less favourably treated than 'other persons in the same circumstances' (Regulation 4(1)) for doing, intending to do, or suspected of doing a protected act. What constitutes less favourable treatment is anything a reasonable worker would think is a disadvantage; the test is the same as that for direct and indirect discrimination. The less favourable treatment may be dismissal, failure to give a promotion, or burdening a person with particularly unpleasant tasks, for example.

2.6.2.2 *Comparators*

The treatment must be less favourable than the treatment of others in the same situation for victimization to be established. Thus, it will be necessary for the person claiming he has been victimized to establish he was treated less favourably than the comparators, actual or hypothetical, that he identifies.

In cases of victimization, A does not have to compare members of the particular group he is in (eg, Humanists) with people in the same situation who are not in that group. That would be the test for discrimination under Regulation 3. Here, B compares himself with people who did not do a protected act (whatever their religion or belief/sexual orientation) but who are otherwise in the same situation. For example, B may himself be a Christian, but he may have given evidence in an employment tribunal for a Humanist colleague of his. B may then be suspended by his employer as a result of giving that evidence. B's comparators are other employees in the same circumstances (of whatever belief: Christians, Humanists, or others) who did not give evidence to support the Humanist worker.

2.6.2.3 *Reason for Less Favourable Treatment is Protected Act*

Naturally, B must establish the less favourable treatment is as a result of the protected act, A's knowledge that B intends to do a protected act, or A's suspicion that A has done, or intends to do, a protected act. Thus B must establish a causal link between his act and A's alleged victimization of him.

Whilst B must show that A's reason for treating him less favourably was that he did (or intended to do) a protected act, it is not necessary for B to show that A acted in 'bad faith'. As with discrimination generally, a malicious motive is not a requirement, although motive will usually be relevant to cases of victimization (see

Nagarajan v London Regional Transport [1999] ICR 877 (HL) for a consideration of this issue in relation to victimization under the RRA).

Often there may be 'mixed motives' for the less favourable treatment. For instance, the fact that B brought a claim against A for discrimination on grounds of his sexual orientation was one of the reasons A dismissed B, but the other reason was B's poor performance record. In a case of mixed motives, then, so long as the unlawful motive had 'sufficient weight', the conduct will be victimization (*O'Donoghue v Redcar and Cleveland BC* [2001] IRLR 615 (CA)). Note that an unlawful reason having 'sufficient weight' is not a particularly difficult thing to establish, once an unlawful reason has been identified; it should be distinguished from the test requiring a reason to be the 'principal reason' for dismissal, such as is required in relation to protected disclosures in whistle-blowing cases.

2.6.2.4 *Conduct Falling within Regulation 4(1)*
Defining the conduct that falls within Regulation 4(1) sub-paragraphs (a) to (c) is relatively straightforward.

2.6.2.4.1 *B brought proceedings against A or any other person under the Regulations*
Sub-paragraph (a) concerns the situation where B has brought any proceedings under the Regulations against A, or against any other person. For example, where an employee has brought a complaint in the employment tribunal alleging he has been discriminated against by co-workers contrary to the EE (Religion or Belief) Regulations, then if his employer subsequently transfers him to a job with a less favourable environment as a result of him having brought those proceedings this will be unlawful victimization contrary to Regulation 4(1)(a) of the EE (Religion or Belief) Regulations.

2.6.2.4.2 *B has given evidence in connection with proceedings brought by any person against A or any other person under the Regulations*
Sub-paragraph (b) concerns the situation where B has given evidence or information in connection with proceedings brought by any person against A or any other person under these Regulations. As with sub-paragraph (a) this relates to proceedings brought not only against A but also against any other person. So, where B gives evidence in an employment tribunal for his friend, an applicant 'C' who is bringing a claim of discrimination under the EE (Sexual Orientation) Regulations against C's employer D, then if A is unhappy about this because, for instance, D is a good customer of A's, and A thus dismisses B, this is victimization contrary to Regulation 4(1)(b) of the EE (Sexual Orientation) Regulations.

2.6.2.4.3 *B has done anything else under the Regulations in relation to A or any other person*
Sub-paragraph (c) concerns the situation where B does anything else under 'or by reference to' the Regulations in relation to A or any other person. This offers a particularly wide protection for the employee. Anything done by reference to the

Regulations can include all sorts of things. Similar wording under the RRA/SDA has been given a broad interpretation. A person does not have to focus his mind on the precise provision of the Regulations.

For example, if an employee (B) gathers information from fellow employees or from third parties relating to a suspicion he has that his employer (A) might be unlawfully discriminating against heterosexual job applicants, then this is conduct likely to fall within Regulation 4(1)(c) of the EE (Sexual Orientation) Regulations. This will even be the case if the conduct of the employee is otherwise open to sanction, for instance if B was secretly tape-recording the conversations of other employees or customers of A's business—but note if B is subsequently dismissed for the conduct where it is considered to be a serious breach of trust and confidence he will be unable to establish victimization where the reason for his dismissal is his breach of trust and not doing the act under the Regulations (see *Aziz v Trinity Street Taxis Ltd* [1988] ICR 534 (CA), concerning a case under the RRA, but see also the qualification of the decision in *Aziz* by the House of Lords in *Nagarajan*, above: if A treats B less favourably because B has done something with reference to the Regulations, this will be victimization even if A was not conscious of the discriminatory reason for his act).

2.6.2.4.4 *B alleged that A or any other person has committed an act contrary to the Regulations* Sub-paragraph (d) concerns situations where B has alleged A or any other person has committed an act which 'whether or not the allegation so states' amounts to a contravention of the Regulations. For example, if B tells his supervisor that he thinks the employer's dress code is unfair to a Sikh employee, and B is then not promoted to become a supervisor because he is considered a 'trouble maker', then this may be victimization contrary to Regulation 4(1)(d) of the EE (Religion or Belief) Regulations. It is not necessary that the employee brought, was bringing, or was even contemplating proceedings under the Regulations. Nor is it necessary that the allegation he makes complains of a breach of the Regulations—the question is whether it is an allegation that, if true, could amount to a breach of the Regulations. As with the other sub-paragraphs, B's allegation does not have to be against or in relation to his employer: if he is treated less favourably as a result of making an allegation against a completely different body, he may still be protected.

2.6.2.5 *Allegation must be in good faith*
Regulation 4(2) provides that the protection in Regulation 4(1) does not apply where the allegation made, or evidence/information given, was false and not made/given in good faith. So, if an employee (B) alleges a colleague is homophobic to his boss, knowing the allegation is not true, and motivated by a desire to get his colleague in trouble, for instance, then B will not be able to rely on the protection provided for in Regulation 4 if he is treated less favourably as a result.

2.7 HARASSMENT

2.7.1 Introduction

One of the most significant features of both sets of Regulations is that they specifically define and outlaw harassment on the prohibited grounds. This is a very important development in domestic discrimination law generally, as it marks a departure from the previous treatment of harassment by providing for explicit protection from harassment.

The explicit prohibition of harassment represents the European approach and is in contrast to the traditional domestic approach to discrimination law. Article 2 of the EC Framework Directive defines and outlaws discrimination on the grounds set out in Article 1 (including religion or belief and sexuality). By Article 2.3, harassment is deemed a form of discrimination and defined as 'any unwanted conduct related to the grounds referred to' that 'takes place with the purpose or effect of violating the dignity of a person and of creating an intimidating, hostile, degrading, humiliating or offensive environment'.

Previously, in domestic discrimination law, harassment has only been prohibited where the victim can prove it is direct discrimination. There was no explicit definition or prohibition of harassment in the RRA or the SDA. A victim of harassment had to show he had been the victim of less favourable treatment on grounds of his race/sex, and that that less favourable treatment caused him a detriment. One of the problems with this approach was demonstrating the treatment was less favourable. For instance, if a man regularly used unwanted 'gender-specific' insults to describe a woman this might be 'sexual harassment', but if he was able to demonstrate he treated men just as badly it would not necessarily be sex discrimination. Since the Scottish Court of Session, in *Porcelli v Strathclyde Regional Council* [1986] ICR 564, found that sexual harassment could be sex discrimination, a line of authorities adopted a relatively liberal approach to what constituted harassment. This reached its highpoint in *British Telecommunications plc v Williams* [1997] IRLR when Morison J held that it was no defence to a complaint of sexual harassment that a person of the other sex would have been similarly so treated. The House of Lords rejected this liberal approach in *Macdonald v Ministry of Defence & Pearce v Governing Body of Mayfield Secondary School* [2003] UKHL 34, [2003] ICR 937. Their Lordships confirmed that as harassment was a form of direct discrimination, it is always necessary to resort to a comparison: the complainant must show she was treated less favourably than a man was or would have been treated. For instance, Lord Nicholls held (at paragraphs 15–17 of his speech):

the expression 'sexual harassment' is ambiguous. The adjective 'sexual' may describe the form of the harassment; for instance, verbal abuse in explicitly sexual terms. Or it may be descriptive of the reason for the harassment; for instance, if a male employee makes office life difficult for a female employee because he does not wish to share his office with a woman. It is only in the latter sense that, although not as such prohibited by the Sex Discrimination Act 1975, sexual harassment may nevertheless be within the scope of the Act as less favourable treatment accorded on the ground of sex. A claim under the Act cannot get off the ground unless the claimant can show she was harassed because she was a woman . . . It has been suggested that if the form of the harassment is sexual, that of itself constitutes less favourable treatment on the ground of sex. When the gender of the victim dictates the form of the harassment, that of itself, it is said, indicates the reason for the harassment, namely, it is on the ground of the sex of the victim. Degrading treatment of this nature differs materially from unpleasant treatment inflicted on an equally disliked male colleague, regardless of equality of overall unpleasantness . . . Because the form of the harassment is gender specific, there is no need to look for a male comparator . . . I respectfully think some of these observations go too far. They cannot be reconciled with the language or the scheme of the statute. The fact that the harassment is gender specific in form cannot be regarded as of itself establishing conclusively that the reason for the harassment is gender based: 'on the ground of her sex.' It will certainly point in that direction. But this does not dispense with the need for the tribunal of fact to be satisfied that the reason why the victim was being harassed was her sex. The gender specific form of the harassment will be evidence, whose weight will depend on the form of the harassment and the sex of the victim.

The fact that harassment is explicitly prohibited in the Regulations, and the victim of harassment does not have to find a comparator, means that the Regulations go considerably further than the former position in domestic race and sex discrimination law.

However, the RRA has been amended to incorporate the European approach. By Regulation 5 of the Race Relations Act 1976 (Amendment) Regulations 2003 (SI 2003/1626), the RRA is amended to include a new s 3A prohibiting racial harassment in the same terms as used in the EE (Religion or Belief) & (Sexual Orientation) Regulations 2003. This amendment brought the RRA into line with EC Council Directive 2000/43/EC of 29 June 2000 implementing the principle of equal treatment between persons irrespective of racial or ethnic origin ('the Race Directive'). With respect to sex discrimination law, EC 2002/73/EC amended the Equal Treatment Directive and incorporated a similarly worded prohibition on sexual harassment into Article 2 of that Directive. However, as yet the SDA definition of harassment remains unchanged; the UK Government has until 5 October 2005 to amend the SDA to give effect to the Directive.

In short, the prohibition on harassment in Regulation 5 of both Regulations gives greater protection from harassment than had previously existed in relation to race and sex. Unlike the RRA (before amendment) and the SDA, it is not necessary for a victim of harassment to prove he was treated less favourably on prohibited grounds. For example, where a gay man is subject to name-calling about his sexual activities it is no defence for the harasser to say he engages in the same 'banter' with heterosexual colleagues about their sexual activities. The previous case law in harassment under the RRA/SDA therefore needs to be treated with caution. The amendments to the RRA mean that racial harassment will be treated in the same way as harassment under the Regulations, but it will be some time until the same can be said for sexual harassment.

Macdonald & Pearce was also an important case in that it demonstrated that, until the Regulations, harassment on grounds of sexual orientation, however serious, was not unlawful. The facts of the case involved a lesbian teacher being regularly subjected to homophobic abuse and name-calling by school pupils. She was called 'lesbian' 'lezzie', 'dyke', 'lesbian shit', and 'lemon' by the pupils. She reported the abuse to the head teacher who told her to 'grit her teeth'. In the end she went off sick and took early retirement on health grounds. As it was then not unlawful to subject a person to harassment on grounds of sexual orientation, she brought a claim under the SDA claiming the harassment was on grounds of her sex. Her case was unsuccessful because it was held the *reason* for the harassment was her sexual orientation and not her sex, and as sexual orientation discrimination was not unlawful she must fail. The EE (Sexual Orientation) Regulations will obviously have an important effect on many people in Ms Pearce's position who are subjected to homophobic abuse at work and previously had no remedy.

Protection from harassment is likely to be one of the parts of the Regulations most frequently relied on in employment tribunal cases. In many workplaces, 'banter' and other comments directed at a person's sexual orientation, or religion or belief is as common as racist or sexist jokes were some years ago. Whatever the efforts of employers, it is likely to take some time to eradicate the expression of such prejudices, stereotypes, or insensitivities. It may also be easier to demonstrate harassment on grounds of religion or belief, or sexual orientation than it is to demonstrate discrimination. In this regard it will be important employers take seriously their obligations to protect their employees from harassment. New policies and training programmes ought to be developed (see further, Chapters 8 and 9 below, and the ACAS guidance at Appendices 4 and 5).

2.7.2 Harassment Defined

According to Regulation 5(1) of both Regulations, harassment occurs where a person (A) subjects another person (B), on grounds of religion or belief/sexual orientation, to unwanted conduct which has the purpose or effect of:

(i)   violating B's dignity; or

(ii) creating an intimidating, hostile, degrading, humiliating or offensive environment for B.

The definition here goes further than that contained in the Framework Directive. In the latter it was necessary to show the harassment violated a person's dignity *and* created an offensive environment. Under the Regulations, unwanted conduct is unlawful where it violates B's dignity *or* creates an offensive environment. The Government thought it would be difficult to envisage a practical example of harassment which involves one without the other.

2.7.2.1 *Unwanted Conduct*

The words 'unwanted conduct' should be given a broad and literal meaning. They include both words and actions. It is any such conduct, on the prohibited grounds, which the receiver of the conduct does not want, or welcome. This might involve name-calling, 'jokes', or it might be that the receiver of the conduct is made to feel ostracized or is always picked on to do the worst jobs.

It is not necessary for the complainant to have previously indicated he did not want such conduct for it to be treated as unwanted. Nor does the fact that the word 'conduct' is used suggest that a series of incidents have to occur. In *Reed v Stedman* [1999] IRLR 299 (a sexual harassment case involving a man making remarks with a sexual connotation, and attempting to look up the complainant's skirt) the EAT held at paragraph 30:

Whether a single act of verbal sexual harassment is sufficient to found a complaint is also a question of fact and degree. It seems to be the argument that because the Code refers to 'unwanted conduct' it cannot be said that a single act can ever amount to harassment because until done and rejected it cannot be said that the conduct is 'unwanted'. We regard this argument as specious. If it were correct it would mean that a man was always entitled to argue that every act of harassment was different from the first and that he was testing to see if it was unwanted: in other words it would amount to a licence for harassment. The evidence shows that what was said . . . was unwanted. If intention were relevant, and it is not, any sensible adult would know that the remark made would be unwanted, unless there were very exceptional circumstances. The word 'unwanted' is essentially the same as 'unwelcome' or 'uninvited'. No one, other than a person used to indulging in loutish behaviour, could think that the remark made in this case was other than obviously unwanted.

It will usually be a question of fact for a tribunal to determine whether the conduct was indeed unwanted. Often, a respondent to a harassment complaint claims that the complainant's own conduct demonstrates he did not treat the conduct complained of as 'unwanted'. For instance, if a Sikh employee was to regularly engage in jokes about his Hindu colleagues' religion and eating habits, in part because his colleagues indicate they do not mind such jokes and they make similar ones about him, it may be difficult for the Sikh employee to show a similar joke made about his religion by one of his colleagues amounted to unwanted conduct. What is unwanted for one person may not be unwanted for another, and whilst it is for the person at the receiving end of the conduct to determine whether or not it is wanted or not, simply asserting it is after the event is not enough. The tribunal will consider the facts of the case to determine whether it was in fact unwanted by the complainant at the time.

2.7.2.2 *On Grounds of Religion or Belief/Sexual Orientation*

Contrary to what their Lordships said in *Macdonald & Pearce* (in relation to sexual harassment) the definition of harassment on grounds of religion or belief/sexual orientation must here mean that *both the reason and the form of the conduct is relevant*. For instance, where a gay man constantly complains about and derides a bisexual colleague of his because he dislikes bisexuals, the reason for the harassment will be the bisexual's sexual orientation and the conduct will thus be covered by Regulation 5 of the EE (Sexual Orientation) Regulations. Alternatively, where a Muslim doesn't like a colleague because he thinks he is too slow at his job and he therefore constantly makes jokes about the colleague in front of the other workers, including jokes about the fact the man is an 'atheist and therefore stupid', the reason for the harassment may well have nothing to do with the victim's belief, but the form of it does. It remains capable of amounting to unwanted conduct on grounds of the victim's belief under Regulation 5 of the EE (Religion or Belief) Regulations. The fact that the Muslim worker may be just as rude to another worker but limits his remarks to the fact that the other worker has no qualifications will not be an automatic defence. The important point is that the unwanted conduct may have an adverse affect on the victim's dignity or his working environment because he is made to look stupid for not believing in God.

2.7.2.3 *Purpose or Effect*
The use of the words 'purpose or effect' in Regulation 5 of both Regulations is important. It demonstrates that as with discrimination generally it is not necessary to prove the discriminator was motivated by discriminatory motives. Harassment does not have to be intended. Where the intention of the harasser is to demean, insult, drive out, or otherwise make uncomfortable the person to whom he directs his conduct, then the *purpose* of the conduct will be to violate the victim's dignity and/or create a hostile working environment for him. The conduct thus falls under Regulation 5(1). However, where the intention is simply to 'lighten' the working atmosphere, to 'bring humour' into the workplace by ridiculing people's sexual behaviour or religious dietary requirements, there may be no hostile intent but the *effect* of the conduct can still violate the victim's dignity or create a hostile working environment for him. In these circumstances the conduct also falls within Regulation 5.

2.7.2.4 *Violating B's Dignity or Creating an Intimidating, Hostile, Degrading, Humiliating, or Offensive Environment*
Whether or not a person's dignity is violated is primarily a question for the victim himself. If he feels his dignity has been violated because of harassment, it will be for the respondent to show otherwise. This will be difficult where there is no dispute about the conduct in question and that the conduct was unwanted. The most likely circumstances in which the respondent could be successful on this point is where the conduct is obviously not serious enough to have any adverse effect on the victim's dignity, and thus either the tribunal finds B is not being honest when he claims his dignity has been violated, or the tribunal finds that it is not reasonable to treat such conduct as having an adverse effect on B (see section 2.7.2.5, below).

Creating an intimidating, hostile, degrading, humiliating, or offensive environment again covers a wide range of things. In general, where a person is made to feel uncomfortable at work as a result of the unwanted conduct such an environment will have been created. Whether or not such an environment was created by the conduct will be a mixed subjective/objective question. The question is whether the environment is hostile to B, from B's standpoint. But if B's perception is unreasonable in the circumstances he cannot establish such an environment was created (see section 2.7.2.5, below).

An example of circumstances in which it should be easy to demonstrate the employer has subjected an employee to a hostile and degrading environment contrary to Regulation 5 of the EE (Sexual Orientation) Regulations could arise where the staff toilets have anti-gay graffiti on the walls, and a gay male employee is offended by this. If the employer does not remove and prevent such graffiti it will be strongly arguable that he has subjected the gay employee to harassment.

Whilst it may be unusual for a person's dignity to be violated without the working environment being made hostile, or a hostile environment created without the person's dignity being violated, it is not too difficult to envisage circumstances in which this could occur. For instance, an employee could be subject to a single particularly serious incident of harassment on grounds of his religion by an employee who left a few weeks later. The insult may have violated the victim's dignity without creating a hostile working environment. Alternatively, the failure of an employer to takes steps to eradicate homophobic abuse in the workplace may create a working environment that is offensive for a gay person, but a complainant, who is gay, cannot demonstrate that any particular incident of abuse has violated his dignity. Instead he relies on the combined effect of the conduct on his working environment. Thus, the wording of the Regulation 5, in going further than the Framework Directive on this point, confers particularly wide protection from harassment.

2.7.2.5 *Reasonableness*

According to Regulation 5(2), conduct shall be regarded as having the *effect* specified above 'only if, having regard to all the circumstances, including in particular the perception of B, it should reasonably be considered as having that effect'. This imports an objective test of reasonableness into the definition of harassment. Whether conduct is unwanted, and whether it violates B's dignity, is primarily a question of B's perception. But if B's perception is unreasonable in all the circumstances, there will be no harassment.

This sub-paragraph is supposed to deal with the over sensitive complainant who takes unreasonable offence at a perfectly innocent comment. It is based on the approach of the EAT in *Driskel v Peninsula Business Services Ltd* [2000] IRLR 151, that in determining whether sexual harassment took place, the tribunal must objectively assess all the facts including the applicant's subjective perception of the conduct and the alleged harasser's understanding, motive, and intention. If the facts disclose 'hypersensitivity' by the applicant to conduct which was reasonably not perceived by the alleged harasser as being to her detriment then no finding of discrimination can follow.

The problem with the wording of Regulation 5(2) is that it does not specify what circumstances can be taken into account by the tribunal. Of course this will depend on the facts of each case, but there are dangers if the tribunal takes account, or too much account, of the harasser's motives or intentions. Motive and intention are strictly speaking not relevant to any claim of discrimination or harassment. But this does not mean evidence of intention will always be irrelevant, rather that the victim of the alleged conduct does not have to show the alleged harasser was motivated by a prejudice, and the alleged harasser cannot rely on holding an innocent intent as a defence. Many who harass others explain their conduct was only meant as a joke, and the victim is overreacting to it. The words 'purpose or effect' in Regulation 5(1) (see section 2.7.2.3, above) are of particular importance here. Where the effect of the conduct is to violate B's dignity, a hostile intention (or purpose) of the harasser does not need to be proved. As Regulation 5(2) only concerns the *effect* of the conduct, it is strongly arguable that the alleged harasser's intention cannot be one of the relevant circumstances a tribunal should have regard to.

It is unlikely, however, that a tribunal will have no regard whatsoever to a person's intention when making the comments complained of. What is important is that any innocent explanation, even if believed, is not taken as determinative of the matter. The tribunal should consider whether it is reasonable in all the circumstances, including the nature of the things said or done, whether the victim made known he did not welcome such conduct, whether a reasonable person would consider the victim to have been over-sensitive to the complaint, the intention of the alleged harasser and whether such intentions were reasonably held or not, the steps taken by the employer to create a better working environment and remedy the potentially adverse effect of the conduct on the employee or his working environment, and *most of important of all, the victim's perception of the effect* of the conduct. Regulation 5(2) stresses the need to pay particular regard to the victim's perception of the effect of the conduct, and it should therefore be only in exceptional cases, where a Tribunal finds that, despite the victim's perception of the effect, the victim was so hypersensitive that no reasonable person could have held the perception he did, and the conduct is not harassment. The intention of the alleged harasser cannot be determinative of whether the conduct had the effect alleged; the tribunal's objective assessment of the effect the conduct would have on a reasonable person will be.

2.7.2.6 *Harassment by Third Parties*

Circumstances may often arise where the harassment complained of is not by the employer himself, or indeed other employees on behalf of whom the employer is liable, but by separate third parties. A good example of this is where a teacher is subjected to homophobic abuse by the school children, or a bus conductor to religious discrimination by passengers on the bus. The employer is not liable for the actions of the school children or bus passengers under the Regulations, but there may still be circumstances in which he is liable for harassment because he failed to protect the employer from the harassment.

This is another area where the existence of an explicit prohibition of harassment in the Regulations is significant. In *Burton v De Vere Hotels* [1996] IRLR 668, the EAT extended the protection of employees under the RRA to circumstances in which the employer subjected black staff to racial harassment. The facts involved a comedian telling racist 'jokes' at a hotel in which black waitresses worked and were offended. The EAT held that the hotel manager should have taken steps to protect the waitresses from the harassment involved, and his failure to do so was racial discrimination.

The House of Lords in *Macdonald & Pearce* disapproved of *Burton*. They found it was wrongly decided because, amongst other things, there was no finding that the hotel manager failed to protect the waitress on grounds of their race, and his activity was therefore not racial discrimination. However, the situation cannot be the same under the Regulations because of the explicit protection from harassment. Regulation 6(3), for example, prohibits an employer from subjecting an employee to harassment under Regulation 5. If an employer forces an employee to work in circumstances where the employee's dignity is violated and/or in circumstances that create an offensive working environment, the employer is in breach of Regulation 6(3). He has subjected the employee to harassment. Thus, if similar facts as those arising in *Burton* occurred but the comedian made anti-Islamic jokes, Muslim workers subjected to the harassment may indeed have a claim under the Regulations regardless of the House of Lords' disapproval of *Burton*.

2.7.3 Harassment Distinguished from Discrimination

As discussed above, the Regulations, in implementing the European approach, make explicit reference to a prohibition of harassment. It is not necessary to fit allegations of harassment into the definition of direct discrimination as it was previously under the RRA, and continues to be under the SDA.

This distinction is important for a number of reasons, not only those listed above. The availability of the Genuine Occupational Requirement defence, for instance, which allows an employer to exempt himself from the obligation not to discriminate in the Regulations in certain exceptional circumstances, *does not* exempt the employer from his obligation not to harass, or subject to harassment, his employees or applicants for employment.

However, the flip side of this is that it will generally be impossible for a person who complains of harassment to argue in the alternative that he has been discriminated against. The Regulations clearly distinguish between harassment and discrimination. In particular, Regulation 2(3) of both sets of Regulations, which deals with interpretation, provides that the word 'detriment' used in the Regulations 'does not include harassment within the meaning of regulation 5'. This is contrary to the approach under the RRA and SDA where harassment has only been covered by the prohibition on discrimination because harassment was capable of being a detriment. Regulation 6(2)(d) of the Regulations makes it unlawful for an employer to discriminate against a person, 'by dismissing him, or subjecting him to any other detriment'.

It is clear that 'subjecting him to any other detriment' does not include subjecting him to harassment. This is covered by Regulation 6(3) in any event (which prohibits an employer from subjecting a person to harassment).

It will therefore be important that complaints clearly identify the nature of the conduct they complain about, in particular, whether it is harassment or discrimination. If a complainant or his legal advisor believe that the conduct could be both or either, it would be sensible to plead both discrimination and harassment in an originating application. Whilst there is no case law on the question so far, it should not be assumed that simply pleading discrimination, where the real complaint is harassment, is satisfactory. Contrary to the previous situation under the RRA, and the current one under the SDA, harassment is not a form of discrimination for the purposes of the Regulations.

3

THE SCOPE OF THE PROTECTION

3.1 INTRODUCTION

The purpose of the Regulations and the parts of the Framework Directive upon which they are based, is to prohibit the discrimination defined and promote equality within the sphere of employment. Their aim is to 'fill the gap' in employment discrimination law, by which discrimination on grounds of race, sex, and disability were prohibited but discrimination on grounds of religion or belief, or on grounds of sexual orientation were not. That gap meant that, for example, a Muslim employee had no protection from discrimination where he was sacked for his religion and a lesbian could not complain where her employer failed to protect her from harassment at work on grounds of her sexual orientation, unless their complaints could be made to fit into the RRA/SDA (as to which see sections 1.2 and 1.3, above).

However, the fact that the Regulations are primarily aimed at outlawing discrimination in employment means their scope is narrower than the RRA, SDA, and DDA, all of which prohibit discrimination in broader fields of society, for instance in education or the provision of housing. The narrow scope of the Regulations can create anomalies. For instance, if an employer dismissed a person for being black or Catholic, he could be liable under the RRA and the EE (Religion or Belief) Regulations respectively; if a school expelled a pupil on the same grounds, the black pupil would have a remedy under the RRA, but the Catholic pupil could not rely on the Regulations. Other legislation can fill some of the gaps. For instance, since the HRA, public authorities cannot discriminate in relation to, amongst other things, a person's home or private life on grounds of religion or sexual orientation (Articles 8, 9, and 14 of the European Convention of Human Rights, as to which, see sections 1.2 and 1.3, above). However, as the HRA only applies to public authorities (or bodies carrying out a public function), anomalies will continue to exist where the discriminator is a private body or person.

The fact that discrimination on grounds of religion or belief, and on grounds of sexual orientation, is for the first time prohibited in an area as important as employment is, however, highly significant. Taken together with other legal developments, particularly since the HRA came into force, it is likely to add considerable momentum towards the prohibition of these forms of discrimination in other fields. But these Regulations cannot be applied beyond the strict scope to which they are intended.

Like the RRA/SDA, and in order to give effect to the Framework Directive, the Regulations apply to employment broadly. Thus, it is not just traditional employees who can rely on them; agency workers, partners, and those applying for training or vocational qualifications are covered. In fact, the extension of the Regulations to cover institutions of further and higher education, included to prevent discrimination in relation to access to employment, has the important side-effect of creating rights under the Regulations for many students.

Part II of the Regulations contains most of the provisions relating to their scope. This chapter reviews that Part and considers to whom the Regulations apply and how their application may differ from one group to another. Chapter 4 considers other unlawful acts under the Regulations, which make employers responsible for acts of discrimination by their employees, and which give the victim of discrimination a right to bring an action against a co-worker as well as his employer.

Regulation 6 is the most important of the Regulations concerning scope. It covers the vast majority of people to whom the Regulations apply: employees and applicants for a job. The other Regulations have a narrower scope, but are based on Regulation 6.

3.2 EMPLOYEES AND APPLICANTS

Regulation 6 of both Regulations concerns discrimination in employment. Regulation 6 prohibits discrimination and harassment on grounds of religion or belief/sexual orientation in a wide variety of circumstances, from the arrangements made for the purposes of deciding to whom an offer of employment is made and the offering or refusal to offer employment (Regulation 6(1)), to the terms of employment, the affording or refusal to give the employee benefits or other opportunities, and dismissal (Regulation 6(2)).

3.2.1 Applicants for Employment

Regulation 6(1) makes it unlawful for an employer to discriminate against a person in the arrangements he makes for the purpose of determining to whom he should offer employment (Regulation 6(1)(a)), the terms on which he offers that person employment (Regulation 6(1)(b)), or by refusing to offer, or deliberately not offering, him employment (Regulation 6(1)(c)). The wording of Regulation 6(1) is virtually identical to that used in s 4(1) RRA, and s 6(1) SDA: case law under those provisions should therefore be of assistance.

Discrimination in relation to the arrangements made to determine who should be offered a job can arise in many different ways. For instance, advertising a job vacancy can involve discrimination. If the employer places an advert in a Christian journal or a gay newspaper it may indirectly discriminate against non-Christians or heterosexuals respectively, since those groups are less likely to buy the paper than Christians or gays. The ACAS guidance suggests advertising is best undertaken in a form accessible to a diverse audience to avoid the dangers of such discrimination. This could either be done by advertising in newspapers or journals which have a diverse audience, or by advertising in a range of specialist journals, each of which is directed at a particular group, and ensuring the range covers a diverse audience. There may be special situations, however, where it is appropriate to target groups, such as Muslims or lesbians, for employment either because there is a Genuine Occupational Requirement (GOR) for a person from one of those groups to hold the post (see Chapter 5 on the GOR), or because the employer seeks to take positive action to redress the fact that a disproportionate number of people from one of those groups is employed by him (see section 6.3 on positive action, below).

The ACAS guidance provides other useful examples of situations where discrimination in relation to recruitment may arise. For instance, it is recommended good practice to avoid questions about a job applicant's marital status in job interviews or on application forms. It is unlikely that such information would be relevant to the applicant's ability to do the job, but it could be perceived as intrusive and/or discriminatory by a lesbian or gay applicant.

Another interesting example in relation to sexual orientation discrimination at recruitment stage is in relation to previous convictions. Laws relating to gay men have changed significantly over time, and it is quite possible that an applicant has obtained a criminal conviction from many years before for conduct which is no longer unlawful (for example, certain forms of 'public indecency' or consensual sex with a man older than 16 but younger than 21). The conviction may have no relevance to the applicant's skill and competence for the job vacancy. Because it is a sexual offence, it would not become 'spent' unlike other non-sexual offences about which the employer may never know under the Rehabilitation of Offenders Act 1974. A blanket rule that nobody who enters a criminal conviction on their application form will be selected for interview may therefore indirectly discriminate against gay men.

In relation to discrimination on grounds of religion or belief it is important that interview questions, for instance, do not dwell on a person's belief or whether they attend church on Sundays. The ACAS guidance warns employers to be careful that where the recruitment process involves a social gathering care should be taken to avoid disadvantaging anybody for whom alcohol is prohibited on the grounds of religion or belief, and invitations should make clear that reasonable dietary requirements (associated with religion or belief) will be provided for.

Regulation 6(3) makes it unlawful for an employer to subject to harassment a person who has applied to him for employment.

3.2.2 Employees

Regulation 6(2) makes it unlawful for an employer to discriminate against an employee in the terms of employment which he affords him (Regulation 6(2)(a)); in the opportunities which he affords him for promotion, transfer, training, or receiving any other benefit (Regulation 6(2)(b)); by refusing to afford him, or deliberately not affording him, any such opportunity (Regulation 6(2)(c)); or by dismissing him, or subjecting him to any other detriment (Regulation 6(2)(d)).

3.2.2.1 *Terms of Employment must not Discriminate*

Regulation 6(2)(a) is straightforward. The terms of the contract must not discriminate on the prohibited grounds. Thus, to give a crude example, somebody should not be paid less because he is a Quaker than a person doing the same job who is of another (or no) religion. Nor should entitlement to notice periods, holiday pay, work-related bonuses and any other contractual terms covered by this sub-paragraph be applied in a discriminatory manner.

Religious holidays provide an example of how indirect discrimination may arise in relation to Regulation 6(2)(b). Where an employer has as a term of the employment the requirement that 5 days of the employees' annual entitlement of 25 days holiday be taken over the Christmas period, and 3 days over Easter, this may discriminate against non-Christians. For instance, a Muslim employee may want to use his annual holiday entitlement to make a pilgrimage to Mecca, but is unable to if he is required to take part of his holiday entitlement during the Christian religious festival. If it is reasonably practicable for the employer to make other arrangements, allowing a degree of flexibility in relation to when holidays are taken, or allowing the employee to take unpaid leave for some of the time off, then it may be indirect discrimination if the employer refuses to take such steps. On the other had, where it is a business necessity that the employee takes holiday when allocated by the employer, perhaps because it is a small company, or because of cycles in sales, then the disadvantage may be justifiable and there would be no indirect discrimination. Terms relating to the timing of breaks for tea or coffee and lunch provide another example. Where the employer can be flexible about this, so as to facilitate those who need to pray during the day, then they should do so (see, for further discussion in Chapter 8, below).

3.2.2.2 *Discrimination in Opportunities for Work-Related Benefits*

Regulation 6(2)(b) and (c) cover two sides of the same question. It is unlawful to discriminate in opportunities afforded to the employee in relation to, for example, promotion (Regulation 6(2)(b)) and it is unlawful to discriminate by refusing such an opportunity (Regulation 6(2)(c)) (note that in other fields of discrimination law the two sides are combined in one single sub-paragraph, see: s 4(2) RRA and s 6(2)(a) SDA).

Discrimination in the opportunities an employer affords for promotion, transfer, or training is quite straightforward. Discrimination in relation to the receiving of 'any other benefit' is particularly broad. Allowing a person more holiday, breaks, or even unpaid time off to observe religious holidays or prayer times than an atheist employee is allowed could discriminate in the opportunity afforded to an employee to receive 'any other benefit'. However, a 'trivial' disadvantage will not be regarded as a disadvantage to the complainant or a benefit to the discriminating group (see, for an example of a case decided on this under the SDA, *Peake v Automotive Products Ltd* [1978] 1 All ER 106 (CA): women being allowed to leave work five minutes before men not a 'benefit').

The prohibition on discrimination in relation to the opportunity an employer affords an employee to receive a benefit in Regulation 6(2) does not apply if the employer is concerned with the provision of benefits of the same description to the public, or a section of the public which includes the employee in question, unless that provision differs in a material respect from the provision of the benefits by the employer to his employees, or the provision of the benefits to the employee in question is regulated by his contract of employment, or the benefits relate to training (Regulation 6(4)). So, for instance, if an insurance company discriminates against gay men in relation to the provision of life insurance services then an employee of that company, who is discriminated against in relation to his application to it for life insurance, is discriminated against as a member of the public and not as an employee. He therefore cannot claim discrimination under Regulation 6 by virtue of Regulation 6(4). However, if employees of the company are entitled to special discounts when applying for insurance from their employment, then the discrimination the employee suffers on grounds of his sexual orientation would be discrimination in relation to an employment-related benefit, and would thus fall within Regulation 6.

3.2.2.3 *Discrimination in Relation to Dismissal or any other Detriment*
Regulation 6(2)(d) concerns dismissal or subjecting the employee to any other detriment. Naturally, it is contrary to the Regulations and unlawful discrimination if an employer dismisses an employee because of his religion or belief, or because of his sexual orientation. However, it is unlikely that an employer would give as his reason for dismissal the employee's religion, for instance. It will therefore be more common that the employee will have to try to prove the real reason for dismissal was the employer's dislike of his religion or belief/sexual orientation.

For instance, where a shop worker who is an observant Jew is dismissed when he tells his boss he cannot work on Saturday because it is the Sabbath, the employer is likely to say the reason for dismissal was the employee's failure to work when instructed to do so. However, it is clear that the dismissal resulted from the employee's failure to work on a day that his religion or religious belief prevented him from working on. So the question becomes whether the requirement to work on a Saturday was indirect discrimination. If it was, then the dismissal will be indirect discrimination, as the reason for it was the refusal of the employee to follow an instruction that discriminated against him on grounds of his religion or belief.

Dismissal is given a wide meaning. Whereas it was not certain under the RRA whether dismissal covered the expiry without renewal of a fixed-term contract, or constructive dismissal, Regulation 6(5) makes it clear that the Regulations cover both situations. Thus, the term 'dismissal' in Regulation 6(2)(d) includes termination of a person's employment 'by the expiration of any period (including a period expiring by reference to an event or circumstance), not being a termination immediately after which the employment is renewed on the same terms' (Regulation 6(5)(a)); and constructive dismissal, ie the termination of a person's employment 'by any act of his (including the giving of notice) in circumstances such that he is entitled to terminate it without notice by reason of the conduct of the employer' (Regulation 6(5)(b)).

The inclusion of constructive dismissal is particularly important in discrimination cases. Where, for instance, an employee feels his employer's failure to act to prevent a campaign of harassment he has been subjected to by his colleagues on grounds of his sexual orientation has made his working environment impossible, and he subsequently resigns as a response to this, this may be constructive dismissal and fall within Regulation 6.

Regulation 6(2)(d) also covers situations where the employee is subject to a 'detriment' on grounds of his religion or belief/sexual orientation. The word 'detriment' means the employee takes the view that he has been disadvantaged in the circumstances in which he has to work. The disadvantage should amount to something more than an unjustified sense of grievance, but need not have physical or economic consequences (see *Shamoon v Chief Constable of the RUC* [2003] UKHL 11; [2003] ICR 337: two male police chief inspectors entitled to carry out appraisals of constables, female complainant was not, this was a 'detriment'; the case concerned the Sex Discrimination (Northern Ireland) Order 1976, but the House discussed the meaning of the word 'detriment' in discrimination legislation generally).

Unlike other areas of discrimination law, however, 'detriment' does not include harassment within the meaning of Regulation 5. The reason for this is obvious: harassment is explicitly outlawed by Regulation 5, so there is no need to try and fit the concept into discrimination by describing certain acts of harassment as a detriment—which is the approach of the RRA/SDA (see further section 2.7 on harassment, above).

3.2.2.4 *Harassment*
It is unlawful for an employer to subject an employee to harassment by virtue of Regulation 6(3). What constitutes harassment is covered in section 2.7, above. As

harassment will often occur by other work colleagues or third parties (for instance pupils towards a teacher in a school) it is important to note that the prohibition on harassment is not limited to situations in which the employer harasses the employee, but includes any situation in which the employee is subjected to harassment.

3.3 PERSONS COVERED BY THE REGULATIONS

All employees of, and applicants for employment to, an establishment in Great Britain are covered by the Regulations. The Regulations do not extend to Northern Ireland (see Regulation 1(2) of the Regulations); separate Regulations will apply to Northern Ireland.

However, other groups of workers who might not be categorized as ordinary employees are also covered by the Regulations. So are various persons who might normally be described as self-employed, and so are civil servants who do not have contracts of employment. The Regulations are intended to cover all aspects of employment, including training and qualifications for employment. As such their scope is wide, and indeed applies to many students in further and higher education, amongst others.

The genuine occupational requirement ('GOR') exception to the Regulations contained in Regulation 7 of both Regulations, exempting employers from the protection from discrimination provided by the Regulations where there is a genuine occupational requirement to employ a person of a particular religion or belief, or sexual orientation, applies to many of the other Regulations considered below, as well as to employment under Regulation 6. The GOR applies as an exception to Regulation 8 (contract workers), Regulation 14 (partnerships), Regulation 16 (qualifications bodies), Regulation 17 (providers of vocational training), Regulation 18 (employment agencies), and Regulation 20 (institutions of further and higher education). The GOR is considered in Chapter 5, below.

3.3.1 Meaning of 'Employment' and 'Employment at an Establishment'

Employment is defined in both Regulations as 'employment under a contract of service or of apprenticeship or a contract personally to do any work' (Regulation 2 (3)). All employees are covered by Regulation 6. The inclusion of the words 'contract to do any work' means many self-employed people who may be engaged to do a specific job for someone for a specific time will be protected under the Regulations. So long as the work is done under a contract, it falls within the category of employment, and the self-employed can be treated as 'employees' for the purposes of Regulation 6.

For the purposes of Regulations 6 (employees) and 8 (contract workers), 'employment at an establishment' means the employee does his work 'wholly or partly' in Great Britain (Regulation 9(1)(a)), or where he works wholly outside Great Britain but the employer has a place of business at an establishment in Great Britain, the work is for the purposes of the business carried on at that establishment, and the employee is ordinarily resident in Great Britain when he applied for or was offered the employment, or during the course of the employment (Regulation 9(1)(b) and 9(1)(2)).

Thus, for example, if an employee is a citizen of the USA who works for a multinational corporation based in Seattle for nine months of the year, and at the London office of the corporation for three months of the year, he will be able to rely on the Regulations if the discrimination he complains of occurs whilst he is working in the London office by people at that office. The fact that he is not a British national and normally works in the USA, the corporation is foreign, and his contract of employment may say that any disputes must be determined by the law of the state of Washington, will not preclude his right to rely on the Regulations. Alternatively, where a British national works for an oil company based in Britain, for example, but is himself based in Saudi Arabia where he works full time, he will be covered by the Regulations if he applied for the job in Britain. Note also that if an employee is wholly employed in another EC member state and cannot rely on the Regulations because, for instance, the company he works for does business solely in France and Belgium, then he should still have some protection from discrimination on grounds of religion or belief or on grounds of sexual orientation by virtue of the Framework Directive.

The meaning of 'employment at an establishment' applies to contract workers (about which see section 3.3.2, below) as it does to employees (Regulation 9(7)).

3.3.2 Contract Workers

'Temps' and other agency workers are covered by Regulation 8 which deals with 'contract workers'. Contract workers are employees of a third party (B) who supplies them to a principal (A) under a contract B has with A.

Where a temp is employed by an agency, he is able to bring an action against the agency for discrimination in relation to that employment under Regulation 6 of the Regulations. But where it is the company he is 'lent' to as a temp that discriminates against him, he would normally have no remedy as the company is not his employer. Therefore Regulation 8 gives him protection by describing the company he is lent to as 'a principal' and then treating the principal, for all intents and purposes, as if it was the employer.

Furthermore, the contract worker can rely on the Regulation where he has been discriminated against by employees of the company he is 'lent to', and not just where he has been discriminated against by fellow contract workers or by the employer (see *Allonby v Accrington and Rossendale College* [2001] IRLR 364, CA, on the parallel provision under the SDA). Otherwise, Regulation 8 is very closely modelled on Regulation 6.

3.3.3 Office Holders

Regulation 10 covers 'office holders'. An office holder is a person holding any office or post to which persons are appointed to discharge functions personally under the directions of another person in respect of which they are entitled to receive remuneration, or a person holding any office or post appointed by a Crown Minister, a Government department, or the National Assembly of Wales or the Scottish Assembly (Regulation 10(8)).

The rights and duties of an office holder are defined by the office he holds, not by a contract of employment. One of the best examples of an office holder is a police constable. He is not employed by the police force in the usual way but has been appointed to and holds the office of constable. However, the Regulations make specific separate provision for police to ensure they are covered by the Regulations (see section 3.3.5, below). Clergymen or Company Directors are probably better examples of office holders for the purposes of Regulation 10.

Regulation 10 does not apply to any person to whom Regulations 6 (employees), 8 (contract workers), 12 (barristers), 13 (advocates), and 14 (partnerships) apply. Nor does it apply to persons holding a 'political office' (Regulation 10(8)). 'Political office' is defined in Regulation 10(10) and basically includes such offices as offices of a member of the House of Commons, the Scottish Assembly, or a local council. Otherwise, Regulation 10 provides similar protection to Regulation 6.

3.3.4 Civil Servants and Members of the Armed Forces

The Regulations apply to civil servants and members of the armed forces. Both of these groups are not employed under contracts of employment, and thus fall outside the definition of employment in Regulation 2(3) of the Regulations. Therefore, Regulation 36 applies the Regulations to acts by Government ministers and departments and other Crown bodies. By Regulation 36(2) persons working for such bodies are deemed to be employees for the purposes of the Regulations, and therefore Regulation 6 applies to them (civil servants are covered by Regulation 36(2)(a), members of the armed forces by Regulation 36(2)(c)).

Special provision is, however, made for members of the armed forces in the Regulations. By Regulation 36 paragraphs (7)–(10), a member of the armed forces who wishes to make a complaint under the Regulations is first required to submit that complaint under the internal service procedures before presenting it to an employment tribunal (but note, the complainant is not required to await the determination of his complaint under the internal procedures before bringing a complaint in the employment tribunal; see Regulation 36(10)).

3.3.5 Police

Regulation 11 provides that the Regulations apply to police officers. Police officers are to be treated as employees, and the chief officer of the police and police authority are to be treated as the officer's employer in relation to any act done by either body (Regulation 11(1)). Regulation 6 therefore applies to the police. Regulation 11 applies to police cadets as it does to police officers generally, and to members of the National Criminal Intelligence Service and the National Crime Squad.

3.3.6 Barristers and Advocates

Barristers and pupil barristers are protected by the Regulations. Regulation 12 makes it unlawful for a barrister or barrister's clerk to discriminate in relation to any offer of a pupillage or tenancy (Regulation 12(1)), or generally in relation to a pupil or tenant in a set of chambers (Regulation 12(2)), or to subject a pupil or tenant barrister (or an applicant for either) to harassment (Regulation 12(3)). The language here is much the same as contained in Regulation 6, and the extension of protection from discrimination to barristers is similar to that found in s 26A of the RRA and s 35A of the SDA.

It is also unlawful for 'any person'—thus including instructing solicitors and lay clients—to discriminate against a barrister on the prohibited grounds in relation to the 'giving, withholding or acceptance' of instructions to a barrister, or to subject him to harassment (Regulation 12(4)). A barrister who refused to accept instructions from a client on the grounds of the client's religion, for instance, would be in breach of this Regulation.

Regulation 13 provides for the same protection for the parallel profession of Advocates in Scotland, with slight variations in the wording to reflect the different ways in which the professions in Scotland and England are organized.

3.3.7 Partnerships

As with race and sex discrimination legislation, discrimination on grounds of religion or belief/sexual orientation within a firm of partners is unlawful in relation to the offering or refusing to offer a partnership to a person, in the affording of benefits to an existing partner, or in the expulsion of a partner from a partnership, or in causing a partner any other detriment (Regulation 14(1)). Protection from harassment within partnerships is provided by Regulation 14(2).

3.3.8 Trade Organizations

'Trade organizations' may not discriminate in the terms applied to admit members of the organization, and may not discriminate against or harass members (Regulations 15(2) and 15(3)). A trade organization is any organization of workers or employers or similar employment-related organization. For instance, trade unions or professional bodies such as the British Medical Association or the Royal Institute of British Architects are trade organizations. Employers' organizations, such as the Confederation of British Industry, are covered by Regulation 15.

As with discrimination law generally, the extension of the protection in this sphere is of great importance. Under the Regulations, it will be possible for a trade union member to bring an action against his union because it did not properly pursue his claim for harassment on grounds of sexual orientation, for instance, as vigorously as the union would have pursued a claim based on the same circumstances but for sexual harassment. The union member may be able to show that the less favourable treatment, in terms of union representation, was on grounds of sexual orientation. So, for example, if a postal worker is regularly ostracized and called a 'queer' by co-workers, and the postal workers' union does not treat his harassment as seriously as it would a woman subjected to similar treatment but called a 'bitch', the worker may be able to show that the reason his union did not pursue his case so seriously was his (real or perceived) sexual orientation. If an employer's organization refuses to accept an applicant's application to join because of his previous record in supporting complaints made in employment tribunals against other employers in relation to discrimination on grounds of religion, for example, then the employer's organization will be liable under Regulation 15(2).

Many trade unions and professional bodies offer their members a range of benefits including insurance and other financial services. There must be no discrimination in the way benefits of these kinds are offered (Regulation 15(2)(a)).

3.3.9 Qualifications Bodies

The Regulations extend to 'qualifications bodies' by Regulation 16. This is based on similar provisions in the RRA (s 12) and the SDA (s 13), and the case law under those acts will be relevant.

A 'qualifications body' is any body that can confer a professional or trade qualification, not including institutions of further and higher education (which are dealt with in section 3.3.13, below). A 'professional or trade qualification' is any qualification which is needed, or facilitates engagement, in a particular profession or trade (Regulation 16(3)).

Regulation 16 makes it unlawful for a qualifications body to discriminate against a person by refusing any application by him for such a qualification, in the terms on which it is prepared to confer a qualification, or by withdrawing such a qualification from him or varying the terms on which he holds it (Regulation 16(1)). Regulation 16(2) makes it unlawful for a qualifications body to subject a person who holds or applies for a qualification to harassment.

Thus, bodies as diverse as the Law Society (who confer qualifications needed to enter and remain in the profession of solicitor) and a local authority (who confer a variety of trade qualifications, such as a licence for a 'door supervisor' of a night-club) cannot discriminate as set out in Regulation 16(1).

In relation to the EE (Sexual Orientation) Regulations, Regulation 16(3) provides an exception from the general protection in relation to qualifications 'for purposes of an organized religion'. This exception mirrors the controversial exception in

Regulation 7(3) of the EE (Sexual Orientation) Regulations which extends the genuine occupational requirement exception broadly to employment for the purposes of organized religion. Regulation 16(3) exempts qualifying bodies from the prohibition on discrimination contained in Regulation 16(1) where a requirement related to sexual orientation is applied to the qualification so as to comply with the doctrines of the religion concerned or to avoid conflicting with strongly held religious convictions of a significant number of the religion's followers. It would thus appear that a church could refuse to confer the qualification necessary to become a preacher to an applicant who was gay or bisexual, because 'a significant number of the religion's followers' strongly believed to do so was wrong. Whilst the wording of this controversial exception appears to be written in even broader terms than the 'genuine occupation requirement' provision in Regulation 7(3), it essentially raises the same question and is discussed in detail in section 5.5, below.

3.3.10 Providers of Vocational Training

Regulation 17 of both Regulations provides similar protection as contained in Regulation 16, but this time in relation to providers of vocational training. A provider of vocational training is a person or body who provides training to help prepare people for employment.

The definition of training includes practical work experience provided by an employer to a person he does not employ (Regulation 17(4)(b)). So a company that agrees to take on a trainee for even a week, without agreeing to pay him or offer him any other employment rights, must recognize that it is liable for discrimination and harassment under the Regulations in relation to that training. The same will apply in relation to that company's decision of whether to offer training to a person.

Case law under the RRA/SDA will also be relevant here, as Regulation 17 is similar to s 13 RRA and s 14 SDA.

3.3.11 Employment Agencies and Careers Guidance

It is unlawful for an employment agency to discriminate in the way it offers or provides its services (Regulation 18(1)). It is also unlawful for that agency to subject a person who uses, or has applied to use, its services to harassment (Regulation 18(2)).

An employment agency's services include the services it offers people trying to find employment (for instance, 'temps' on an agency's books), and the supplying of workers to employers.

Regulation 18(4) creates a defence to a complaint brought against an employment agency under the Regulations where the agency acted in reliance on a statement made to it by the employer to whom the agency supplied a worker, to the effect that its action would not be unlawful because of the employer's genuine occupational requirement (Regulation. 18(4)(a)). So, if an employer told an employment agency it specifically required a lesbian for a particular job working in a 'women only' lesbian café, and that this was a lawful genuine occupational requirement, an employment agency would not necessarily be in breach of the Regulations if it discriminated against non-lesbians in supplying a worker to the employer. However, the reliance on the employer's statement by the employment agency must be 'reasonable' in the circumstances (Regulation 18(4)(b)); it is not enough for the agency to simply say, 'we were told it was lawful so we did it'. If a person knowingly or recklessly makes such a statement which is false or misleading, he commits a criminal offence and shall be liable on summary conviction to a fine not exceeding level 5 on the standard scale (Regulation 18(5)).

Regulation 18 is based on parallel provisions contained in s 14 RRA and s 15 SDA, so again the case law under those sections will be relevant to the interpretation and application of this Regulation.

3.3.12 Assisting Persons to Obtain Employment

Section 2 of the Employment and Training Act 1973 requires the Secretary of State to make arrangements for the purpose of assisting persons to select, train for, obtain, and retain employment suitable employment, and to help employers obtain suitable employees. The Secretary of State has power to make grants or loans to persons providing such facilities. By Regulation 19 of both Regulations, it is unlawful for the Secretary of State to discriminate against, or subject to harassment, any person in the provision of these facilities and services.

3.3.13 Further and Higher Education

Discrimination by institutions of further and higher education (including FE colleges, many Community Colleges and universities, but not including schools) is unlawful by virtue of Regulation 20. This is because qualifications essential for certain employment are conferred by these bodies (such as NVQs (National Vocational Qualifications) and university degrees). It is thus not surprising that 'vocational training' is covered by the Regulations. However, the consequence of this Regulation extends beyond the employment sphere and creates rights for many students.

The types of discrimination outlawed are broadly similar to elsewhere in the Regulations. Regulation 20(1) makes it unlawful for the governing body of an educational establishment to discriminate against a person in the terms on which it offers to admit him to the establishment as a student, by refusing his application, or where he is already a student treating him differently for the purpose of access to many benefits, or excluding him from the establishment, or subjecting him to any other detriment. Regulation 20(2) makes it unlawful for the governing body of an educational establishment to subject a student (or an applicant to become a student) to harassment.

3.3.13.1 *Application to Students*

Regulation 20 is one of the Regulations that implements Article 3.1(b) of the Framework Directive (in relation to discrimination on grounds of religion or belief and sexual orientation) which states that the Directive applies to:

access to all types and to all levels of vocational guidance, vocational training, advanced vocational training and retraining, including practical work experience.

In Case C-293/83 *Gravier v City of Liège* [1984] ECR 606 (concerning discrimination on grounds of nationality) the European Court of Justice held that 'vocational training' included any form of education preparing for a qualification or skills for a profession, trade, or employment. The ECJ indicated, in another case, that university courses are generally likely to be considered as vocational training (Case C-24/86 *Blaizot v University of Liège* [1988] ECR 355) not only in relation to a final examination required for qualification for a particular profession, trade, or employment,

but also in so far as the studies in question provide specific training and skills, that is where a student needs the knowledge so acquired for the pursuit of a profession, trade or employment.

The Government had these cases in mind in drafting Regulation 20; this is clear from the Office of the Deputy Prime Minister's Notes on the draft Regulations (see paragraph 63 of both the Notes on the draft EE (Religion or Belief) Regulations and the draft EE (Sexual Orientation) Regulations). However, the Office of the Deputy Prime Minister's Notes explain that Regulation 20 actually goes further than is required by the Framework Directive:

. . . most university studies and many further education courses will fall within the scope of the Directive. Courses of study which, because of their general nature, are intended for persons wishing to improve their general knowledge rather than prepare themselves for an occupation, do not fall within the scope of the Directive. Regulation 20 applies to all acts by further and higher education institutions in Great Britain, so as to establish a uniform regime in this regard. This includes those acts which relate to courses of study which fall outside the Directive's scope, as it can be said that those acts arise out of or are related to the Directive's obligations in relation to vocational training.

So whereas the Framework Directive might distinguish between a further education course in 'leisure and tourism' or a university degree in medicine on the one hand, (that is, courses that prepare students for qualifications or skills necessary for certain employment) and, on the other hand, an adult education course provided by an institution of further and higher education in jewellery making, for instance (that is, a course many attend simply to pursue a hobby), Regulation 20 does not. Regulation 20 prohibits discrimination by institutions providing further and higher education generally; there is no requirement that the education or guidance provided must be 'vocational'.

Regulation 20 obviously creates broad rights for many students. If a university student is subjected to a disciplinary process because he has participated in a religious fundamentalist organization or a meeting that has been banned on the university campus, Regulation 20 would appear to offer the student protection. Considering previous attempts by some universities and student unions to ban certain Jewish organizations accused of promoting Zionism and racism, or certain Muslim organizations accused of being anti-semetic and hostile to equal opportunities, Regulation 20 is likely to be of particular importance. Where a student can complain that the prohibition of such organizations or the disciplining of him as an individual for involvement in them discriminates against him on grounds of his religion or belief, university authorities will have to proceed with caution. On the other hand, the failure to protect students from harassment by fanatical religious organizations on college campuses may lead to claims that students have been subjected to harassment on grounds of their religion or belief, or indeed on grounds of their sexual orientation.

Educational establishments might also be vulnerable to claims by students who are bullied by classmates because of their (real or perceived) sexual orientation. Whereas the educational establishment is not vicariously liable for the acts of its students, it is liable where it subjects 'to harassment a person who is a student at the establishment' (Regulation 20(2)). If the establishment has not taken reasonable steps to prevent such harassment it may be in breach of the Regulations.

Other potential effects of Regulation 20 on students and educational establishment will be similar to those arising in employment situations. Religious holidays, prayer facilities, and the organization of social functions that do not discriminate on grounds of religion or belief/sexual orientation will all be important areas.

Whilst the Regulations have generated a considerable amount of discussion in relation to the effect they will have on employment, their effect on students has so far gone largely unnoticed. However, in making unlawful discrimination and harassment that has been rife in some educational establishments in the past, and in providing students with new rights, Regulation 20 alone is of enormous significance. It will be important for institutions of further and higher education to radically review their equal opportunities, harassment, and disciplinary programmes to take into account these potential pitfalls. Student unions and other student groups should also take particular note of Regulation 20 and the effect it might have on their members.

It should be noted that complaints under Regulation 20 must be brought in a county court (or a sheriff court in Scotland) and not in an employment tribunal. The usual county court rules of procedure will apply in the same way as any other claim in tort (or in reparation in Scotland) for breach of statutory duty (see Regulation 31 of both Regulations) (see further section 7.3, below).

3.3.14 Relationships that have Come to an End

Regulation 21 of the Regulations makes discrimination or harassment by a person (A) of another (B) after the end of their relationship, where that discrimination or harassment 'arises out of or is clearly connected to that relationship'. A 'relationship' is any relationship covered by the Regulations.

The most obvious example is an employment relationship. Where employer, A, subjects a previous employee, B, to discrimination, for example in relation to a provision of a reference, A may be liable under Regulation 21.

Another important example relates to post-termination appeals by ex-employees. Where the contract of employment provides that a person who is dismissed can appeal against their dismissal, after their contract has been terminated by the dismissal, Regulation 21 will be of importance because the employment relationship has come to an end. So if the ex-employer discriminates (or subjects to harassment) the ex-employee in relation to the post-termination appeal, then provided the discrimination arises out of or is clearly connected to the relationship (which is most likely) the ex-employee can complain under Regulation 21.

Regulation 21 of the Regulations provides greater protection for workers than was previously provided under the RRA in relation to discrimination on grounds of race. However, the RRA was amended in July 2003 and a new s 27A provides protection similar to Regulation 21. It had previously been the case that complaints by an employee or a person employed under the RRA could not include complaints by a former employee appealing or seeking re-instatement (see *Adekeye v Post Office* (No 2) [1997] IRLR 105, but *cf Rhys-Harper v Relaxion Group plc* [2003] UKHL 33, [2003] ICR 867). The SDA was also amended in July 2003 to reflect this approach (as required by European law); the new s 20A of the SDA adopts similar language to Regulation 21 of the Regulations. In considering whether a person has a cause of action under Regulation 21, and the relevant time limits, old case law under the RRA and SDA should be treated with caution.

The wording of Regulation 21 is sufficiently broad to allow a complaint to be brought after the end of a relationship even where an allegation of discrimination was never brought during the relationship. Consider, for example, that a student is excluded from a university after he was arrested for having sexual intercourse in a public place. The disciplinary action against him may not have involved any discrimination at all and the relationship between the student and the university ended at the time of the student's expulsion. However, if during a later appeal against the expulsion to the board of governors the student is subjected to discrimination or harassment on grounds of his sexual orientation relating to the disciplinary offence, then he might have a claim under Regulation 21 regardless of the fact that he would not have had one at the time of his expulsion.

For the purposes of time limits (see generally Chapter 7, below) the date from which the time limit for bringing a complaint will run where the complaint is brought under Regulation 21 is the date of the last act of post-termination discrimination, not the date of termination. Thus, for the purposes of complaints brought under Regulation 34 to an employment tribunal, a complaint to an employment tribunal must be brought within three months of the last act of post-termination discrimination. The Office of the Deputy Prime Minister's Notes (paragraph 65) point out that the further removed the alleged act of discrimination is from the termination of the working relationship, the less likely it is that a person will be able to establish the necessary close connection to the former relationship.

3.3.15 Occupational Pension Schemes

The Regulations also apply to members of occupational pension schemes. Before the Regulations came into force they were amended to include a new Regulation 9A and Schedule 1A for this purpose. Regulation 9A makes it unlawful for trustees or managers of occupational pension schemes to discriminate against, or to subject to harassment, the members or prospective members of the scheme in carrying out any of their functions. The Regulation does not apply retrospectively, ie 'in relation to rights accrued or benefits payable in respect of periods of service prior to the coming into force' of the Regulations. Regulation 9A cross-refers to Schedule 1A which introduces a new 'non-discrimination rule' into all occupational pension schemes.

According to the Schedule, where a complainant wants to bring a complaint against the trustees or managers of the occupational pension scheme that he has been discriminated against or harassed contrary to Regulation 9A he does so in the employment tribunal under the normal procedure set out in Regulation 28 of the Regulations (see section 7.2, below).

It should be noted that, in relation to the EE (Sexual Orientation) Regulations, the inclusion of Regulation 9A must be read subject to the controversial Regulation 25 of the EE (Sexual Orientation) Regulations which allows an exception from the Regulations where the access to a benefit is by virtue of marital status (see further section 6.5, below).

4

OTHER UNLAWFUL ACTS

4.1 INTRODUCTION

Part III of both sets of Regulations provides protection from what is called 'other unlawful acts'. Two principal areas are covered:

(i) what is often called vicarious liability, that is an employer's liability for the acts of his employees (Regulation 22); and

(ii) liability which is extended to people who help others commit unlawful discrimination (Regulation 23).

The wording of this Part of the Regulations is based on the approach in the RRA and SDA to these issues. Thus Regulation 22 is similar to s 32 of the RRA and s 41 of the SDA; and Regulation 23 is similar to s 33 of the RRA and s 42 of the SDA. The case law under the RRA/SDA on these matters will therefore be of assistance.

4.2 EMPLOYERS' AND PRINCIPALS' LIABILITY

An employer is liable for any unlawful act under the Regulations that is committed by an employee of his, 'in the course of his employment', whether or not the employer knows or approves of the act (Regulation 22(1)). Thus, where an employee subjects another to harassment on grounds of the other's religion, for example, the employer will be liable under the Regulations for his employee's harassment.

4.2.1 Whether Act Done in the Course of Employment

The most common issue to arise in relation to employer's liability is whether the act complained of was done in the course of a person's employment. There is substantial case law on this issue under the RRA/SDA, and the approach the courts have laid down there should be followed. In short, the words 'in the course of [his] employment' should be given a broad interpretation, and not one similar to the narrower common law test of 'vicarious liability' (see *Jones v Tower Boot Co Ltd* [1997] IRLR 168, CA). Conduct outside the hours and/or premises of the employment may be in the course of employment in certain circumstances, for instance a work Christmas party organized by the employer and attended mostly by employees; but conduct at social events organized by the employer outside working hours where the majority of those in attendance are families and friends of employees, and not the employees themselves, is unlikely to be conduct in the course of employment (*Sidhu v Aerospace Composite Technology Ltd* [2000] IRLR 602, CA).

So, for example, if an employee is subjected to homophobic abuse in the work canteen, during his lunch hour, by other employees, the employer should be liable for harassment under Regulation 22 of the EE (Sexual Orientation) Regulations. The harassment will have been perpetrated by employees in the course of their employment and the fact that the employer may not have known, controlled, or approved of the conduct will be no defence.

4.2.2 Defence where Employer took Reasonable Steps to Prevent Act

By Regulation 22(3) of both Regulations, an employer has a defence if he can show he took 'such steps as were reasonably practicable' to prevent the employee responsible for the act of discrimination/harassment from doing that act. Having a comprehensive equal opportunities policy, anti-harassment procedures, and proper disciplinary and grievance procedures that make clear that employees are prohibited from discrimination/harassment will be important for employers to demonstrate they have taken some steps to prevent discrimination. In this respect it is most important that employers review their equal opportunities and other policies to ensure they reflect the changes in the law brought about by the Regulations. Equal opportunities and anti-harassment policies will need to ensure that discrimination and harassment on grounds of religion or belief, and on grounds of sexual orientation, will not be tolerated. However, the existence of paper policies is unlikely to be enough to prove that reasonably practicable steps have been taken by the employer. The employer should be able to demonstrate that he has taken steps to inform the employees of those policies, and has provided adequate training in them. Naturally, where the employee responsible for the discrimination/harassment complaint occupies a managerial or supervisory position within the employer's undertaking, it will be more difficult for the employer to rely on this defence, particularly where there is evidence of a record of similar behaviour by, or allegations against, the employee responsible. Generally, where an employee has made previous complaints, whether formal or informal, about discrimination and harassment, and the employer has not taken reasonable steps to resolve those complaints, it will be difficult for the employer to rely on this defence.

In terms of the quality of the employer's procedures and training, the larger the employer, the greater the scrutiny an employment tribunal can be expected to put them under. A very small employer, without a personnel manager or department, might not be expected to have comprehensive procedures and training in equal opportunities. The Regulations will still apply to them, and the employer will still need to demonstrate he has taken reasonably practicable steps to prevent discrimination. But what is reasonably practicable for a small or family business will be different from what is reasonably practicable for a large business. Employers with existing equal opportunities policies, a number of employees (for instance 20 or more), and a personnel officer or department, will need to be particularly scrupulous to ensure they take stock of the new Regulations (see further Chapters 8 and 9).

4.2.3 Importance of Employer's Liability

Employer's liability is particularly important in discrimination cases. Whereas in other areas of employment law there is often little question about who is liable for the act complained of, because there can be no doubt that the employer must be responsible for it (for instance in cases of unfair dismissal) discrimination cases raise more difficulties. It will very often be the complainant's colleagues that are directly responsible for the discrimination or harassment the complainant suffers. Parliament has nevertheless decided that it is particularly important in discrimination cases that the employer has a special burden of responsibility. There are a number of reasons for this. First, employer's liability reflects society's specific disapproval of discrimination. The employer ought to take positive steps to prevent discrimination in the workplace and to guarantee a comfortable working environment where individuals are not subjected to degrading or hostile treatment for arbitrary reasons, such as their religion or sexual orientation. Secondly, discrimination and harassment often take place in insidious ways; they often involve more than one person, and can be caused by the working environment or culture. The employer is ultimately responsible for the working environment and it will often be more difficult to pin the blame on a specific individual, or set of individuals. Thirdly, a victim of unlawful discrimination is compensated by a monetary award. The award will reflect, amongst other things, the injury to his feelings caused by the discrimination. It can run into large amounts of money. If the employee could only bring a complaint in the employment tribunal against the individual directly responsible for the discriminatory treatment, he may not be able to recover the compensation the tribunal awards. The employer, on the other hand, will usually have sufficient funds to satisfy such complaints.

4.2.4 Principal's Liability

Regulation 22(2) extends the same regime of vicarious liability that applies to employers to principals. A principal will be liable for the discriminatory acts of his agent. Rather than having to act in the course of his employment, the agent must be acting with the 'express or implied authority' of the principal 'whether precedent or subsequent'. Thus, where one agency worker discriminates against another, the principal will be liable for the discrimination if the discriminating agency worker is acting with the principal's express or implied authority. The concept of express or implied authority should be treated broadly, as with the concept of 'in the course of employment'. It does not mean the principal authorized the specific act of discrimination, rather that he authorized the agent's act which was conducted in a discriminatory way (see, for a case decided in relation to the same wording of principal's liability under the SDA, *Lana v Positive Action Training in Housing (London) Ltd* [2001] IRLR 501, EAT). So, where one agent has the principal's authority to give instructions to two other agents, for example, and he treats one agent less favourably than the other because that agent is a Buddhist, he will have been acting with the express or implied authority of his principal.

The employer's defence discussed above (Regulation 22(3) where the employer has taken reasonably practicable steps to prevent the discrimination) does not apply to a principal.

4.3 AIDING UNLAWFUL ACTS

Regulation 23 provides that it will be unlawful for a person to 'knowingly aid' another person do an act which is unlawful under the Regulations.

4.3.1 Knowingly Aiding an Unlawful Act

The words 'knowingly aid' also appear in s 33 RDA and s 42 SDA. The House of Lords held in *Anyanwu v South Bank Students' Union* [2001] UKHL 14; [2001] IRLR 305, HL (a case under the RRA) that the word 'aid' should be given a broad and ordinary meaning: a person aids another if he helps, assists, cooperates, or collaborates with him, and whether or not his help is substantial and productive, provided it is not so insignificant as to be negligible.

In terms of knowledge, the person liable must have either wanted the discrimination or harassment that the other committed, or he must have known that the other was contemplating discrimination or harassing the victim (see *Hallam v Cheltenham Borough Council* [2001] UKHL 15; [2001] IRLR 312, HL).

Consider an employer does not want to employ anybody wearing overtly religious dress and an employee, who knows this, throws away an application form submitted by a Muslim woman job applicant because he thinks there is no chance she will be employed due to her religious dress, then that employee should be liable under Regulation 23. However, if the employee does not realise that the act he is assisting is discriminatory (perhaps he thinks it is just a health and safety requirement), and if he does not want the discrimination that results, he probably did not 'knowingly' aid the discrimination that occurred, and will thus not be liable under Regulation 23.

A common situation in which Regulation 23 will come into play is where the employee is, in fact, the person directly responsible for the discrimination or harassment. This is because, in relation to employment, the Regulations only provide that the employer can be liable for discrimination (see Regulation 6, discussed in Chapter 3, above). So if one employee discriminates against another then, so long as the employer is liable under Regulation 22, the employee who actually does the act is treated as aiding the employer's unlawful act under Regulation 23. This route, relying on the legal fiction that the perpetrator of the discrimination is treated as assisting the employer's discrimination, at least ensures that it is possible to bring an action against individual discriminators as well as their employers.

It will often be important for a complainant to bring his complaint in an employment tribunal against the individuals responsible for the discrimination as well as against the employer. The two most frequent reasons for doing so are, first, that the complainant's real grievance is against the individual discriminator—it is important for the complainant that the individual concerned is subject to some sanction; and secondly, it will often be the best or only way for the complainant to elicit the evidence he requires—for instance, he may know that the individual discriminator will give evidence under cross-examination that will help his case whereas the employer would be more cautious.

4.3.2 Defence to Knowingly Aiding an Unlawful Act

Regulation 23(3) provides a defence to an allegation of knowingly assisting an unlawful act. A person will not knowingly assist another's unlawful act where he acts in reliance on a statement made by that other to the effect that the act complained of is not discriminatory by reason of another provision of the Regulations. So, taking the example given in section 4.3.1, above: an employee is told that it is a genuine occupational requirement not to employ any person who covers their head, due to health and safety reasons, and he therefore fails to process the application form of a Muslim woman who tells him she must always wear a hijab for religious reasons; he may be able to rely on the defence in Regulation 23(3)(a). However, as with the similar defence in Regulation 18(4) (see, section 3.3.11, above), it must be reasonable to rely on the statement; it is not enough to just say 'I was only doing what I was told' (Regulation 23(3)(b)).

If a parish priest refused to employ an openly gay church organist in reliance on a policy from the local bishop stating that, in reliance on Regulation 7 of the EE (Sexual Orientation) Regulations (the GOR, see section 5.5, below), so as not to offend the deeply held convictions of the congregation, the church would not appoint any known homosexual to a position that participated in the service, the priest may have a defence under Regulation 23(3), even if the policy itself falls foul of Regulation 7. This is because the priest may be able to show he reasonably relied on the policy. However, if the Archbishop issued a more recent statement that warned priests not to follow the local Bishop's previous policy as it was thought it might be in breach of the Regulations, then it would be very difficult for the priest to show he reasonably relied on the Bishop's statement, and the Regulation 23(3) defence is unlike to assist him.

A person who knowingly or recklessly makes a Regulation 23(3) statement (that the act is justified under the Regulations) which is false commits an offence by virtue of Regulation 23(4), and is liable on summary conviction to a fine (not exceeding level 5 on the standard scale).

5

THE GENUINE OCCUPATIONAL REQUIREMENT

5.1 INTRODUCTION

One of the most important provisions in both sets of Regulations is the general exception to many of the Regulations provided by Regulation 7, the Genuine Occupational Requirement (GOR). Generally this provides an employer with a defence to claims of both direct and indirect discrimination. Where the employer can show that it is a genuine occupational requirement for him to employ a person from a particular religion or belief/sexual orientation, or where he can show the requirement means he cannot employ a person from one of those groups, it will not be discriminatory if he refuses to do so. Considering Regulation 7 allows acts that would otherwise be discriminatory, it is both a particularly controversial area, and one which demands particularly close scrutiny. The GOR will generally have to be construed and applied restrictively, although it is arguable that the Framework Directive provides for a more restrictive approach than the Regulations. In particular, Regulation 7(3) of the EE (Sexual Orientation) Regulations, giving a particularly wide GOR in relation to employment for the purposes of organized religion, has been the subject of much criticism.

The GOR closely resembles a similar concept in domestic discrimination law, the 'genuine occupational qualification' in the RRA/SDA. The development of the genuine occupational qualification within the RRA/SDA is considered in brief to assist in comprehending the meaning and scope of the GOR in these Regulations.

Two further general points need to be made about the GOR. First, the GOR only exempts the employer from complaints of direct and indirect discrimination under Regulation 3 of the Regulations—the employer who establishes a GOR will still be liable for any victimization or harassment he or his employees commit. Secondly, the burden of proving a particular job is covered by the GOR exception falls on the employer.

5.2 THE GENUINE OCCUPATIONAL QUALIFICATION IN DOMESTIC LAW GENERALLY

By s 7 of the SDA, the prohibition on discrimination on grounds of sex under the SDA does not apply to employment where to be, eg a man, is a 'genuine occupational qualification' of the job. Section 7 of the SDA sets out an exhaustive list of eight situations in which there may be a genuine occupational qualification. Broadly speaking these are:

(i) the nature of the job calls for a man for reasons of physiology or authenticity;

(ii) the job needs to be held by a man to preserve decency or privacy;

(iii) the job involves work, or living, in a private home and needs to be held by a man because objection might be taken to allowing a woman physical or social contact with a person living in the home, or knowledge of intimate details of such a person's life;

(iv) the nature or location of the establishment makes it impracticable for the holder of the job to live elsewhere than in premises provided by the employer, and the only premises available for persons holding it are lived in by men and are not equipped with separate sleeping/sanitary facilities for women;

(v) the nature of the establishment, or of the part of it within which the work is done, requires the job to be held by a man because it is a hospital, prison, or other establishment for persons requiring special care, supervision, or attention, those persons are all men;

(vi) the holder of the job provides individuals with personal services promoting their welfare or education, or similar personal services, and those services can most effectively be provided by a man;

(vii) the job needs to be held by a man because it is likely to involve the performance of duties outside the United Kingdom in a country whose laws or customs are such that the duties could not, or could not effectively, be performed by a woman; and

(viii) the job is one of two to be held by a married couple (note that where the word 'man' is used in these examples the word 'woman' can be substituted).

Under s 5 of the RRA there are four situations in which a job could be given to a person of a particular race. These are:

(i) the job involves acting or other entertainment where authenticity demands a person of that racial group (eg a part in a play needs to be played by a black actor for authenticity);

(ii) the job involves being an artist's/ photographic model in the production of a work of art/visual image where a person of a particular colour, race, etc, is required for authenticity;

(iii) the job is in a public restaurant, bar, or similar establishment where the setting is such that authenticity demands that that particular job be filled by a person of a particular racial group (a common textbook example given is a preference for Chinese waiters in an 'authentic' Chinese restaurant);

(iv) the job involves welfare services which can be most effectively provided by someone of a particular racial group (eg it may be preferable to have an Afro-Caribbean social worker to deal with Afro-Caribbean adopted children with identity problems).

However, as a result of the amendments to the RRA caused by the Race Directive, which uses similar words to describe the GOR as does the Framework Directive, a new s 4A of the RRA imports the GOR test into the RRA. The starting point for courts and tribunals will now be to first consider whether or not there is a GOR under the RRA, and only if this fails will it be necessary to consider the genuine occupational qualification test.

It should be noted that, in contrast to these sections of the RRA and the SDA, the GOR in the Regulations does not set out narrowly defined examples of situations in which it may apply, the language is more general.

The GOR is a different test to the genuine occupational qualification test in the RRA and SDA. Nevertheless, it is likely that courts and tribunals will turn to the case law and principles established under those tests for assistance in applying the GOR. In particular, the GOR ought to be applied restrictively. The limited circumstances in which it might be possible to advertise to employ a man, or a black person, under the SDA and the RRA, for instance, may provide useful examples by analogy of similar situations that may arise in relation to religion or belief/sexual orientation discrimination.

5.3 THE GOR IN THE FRAMEWORK DIRECTIVE

Article 4.1 of the Framework Directive on which both Regulations are based, provides that Member States may allow a difference of treatment (and that such difference will not be discrimination) based on a characteristic related to religion or belief/sexual orientation where:

by reason of the nature of the particular occupational activities concerned or of the context in which they are carried out, such a characteristic constitutes a genuine and determining occupational requirement, provided that the objective is legitimate and the requirement is proportionate.

There are therefore three conditions for the GOR under the Directive. First, the difference in treatment must be by reason of a *genuine and determining* occupational requirement. Secondly, the objective that the requirement seeks to meet must be *legitimate*. Thirdly, the requirement must be *proportionate*.

In addition, recital (23) of the Framework Directive makes clear that such difference in treatment, as defined above, will be justifiable in '*very limited circumstances*'.

Justifying differential treatment under the GOR in the Framework Directive is thus a difficult and exceptional exercise. It will only be in rare cases that such differential treatment is capable of being justified, and the requirement for proportionality means that even when it is capable of justification, it can only be actually justified where the differential treatment is proportionate to (eg does not exceed) the legitimate objective it seeks to pursue.

Other than the controversial difference between the GOR in the Framework Directive and that in Regulation 7(3) of the EE (Sexual Orientation) Regulations (reviewed in some depth below (see section 5.5), the Regulations largely transpose Article 4(1) of the Directive in full. One difference is that, whereas Article 4(1) of the Directive specifies that there must be a 'genuine and determining occupational requirement, *provided that the objective is legitimate*', Regulation 7 does not provide that the objective must be legitimate. The Government explains this difference as unimportant because the necessity to show a genuine and determining requirement is enough, a requirement cannot be genuine and illegitimate at the same time (see Office of the Deputy Prime Minister's Notes on the Draft Regulations, paragraph 23). This must be right, and in any event, considering the Government's explanation for not transposing the words directly, it would be wrong for courts or tribunals to distinguish between the Directive and the Regulations on the basis that the latter does not include the word 'legitimate'.

5.4 THE GOR AND RELIGION OR BELIEF DISCRIMINATION

Regulation 7 of the EE (Religion or Belief) Regulations provides for a GOR exception in relation to discrimination on grounds of religion or belief (contrary to Regulation 3) in the fields of employment (covered by Regulation 6). The exception therefore only applies to discrimination as set out in Regulation 3; it does not make lawful either victimization (Regulation 4) or harassment (Regulation 5).

Regulation 7(2) provides that where, 'being of a particular religion or belief is a genuine and determining occupational requirement' and it is 'proportionate to apply that requirement in the particular case', then the GOR exception will apply 'whether or not the employer has an ethos based on religion or belief'. Thus, for instance, if a local authority wishes to employ an 'outreach worker' to assist in finding out and meeting the needs of a religious community, for instance Muslim women, it may be arguable that the particular circumstances of the job require a Muslim (and perhaps, indeed, a Muslim woman), and that such requirement is the decisive one to be taken into account when determining who is suitable to do the job. The employer local authority has no religious ethos, but it can rely on the GOR in Regulation 7(2).

Regulation 7(3) of the EE (Religion or Belief) Regulations provides that where an employer 'has an ethos based on religion or belief' and 'being of a particular religion or belief is a genuine occupational requirement' and it is 'proportionate to apply that requirement in the particular case', then the GOR will apply. It will be apparent that Regulation 7(3) is very similar to Regulation 7(2). The only difference is that the requirement in Regulation 7(3) does not have to be 'determining'. This means the employer will not have to show the requirement is decisive, only that it is a genuine requirement. Not surprisingly, then, religious employers have a broader discretion in terms of the GOR. However, the fact that, under this paragraph it is still necessary to show a 'requirement' means that it will not be enough for the employer to say, for instance, that being of a particular religion is one of the factors it takes into account and therefore it is entitled to apply the GOR. The employer must show that being of a particular religion is a requirement of the job. The broader approach in Regulation 7(3) reflects the wording in Article 4(2) of the Framework Directive: the requirement must be 'genuine, legitimate and justified . . . having regard to the organization's ethos'. The burden will be on the employer to prove he has an ethos based on religion or belief.

Obvious examples of an employer with a religious ethos who is entitled to require an employee to be a member of the same religion will arise where the employers are churches, mosques, temples, or synagogues and they seek to employ preachers of their respective religions. There can be no doubt that it will be a genuine requirement of a synagogue that the Rabbi is Jewish. But there are more difficult examples where the issues are not so clear-cut. Consider a Halal or Kosher butcher or restaurant. Is it a justifiable requirement that everybody who works in such premises and handles food has to be, respectively, Muslim or Jewish? These questions cannot be answered in the abstract but will depend on the precise circumstances of each case. Where borderline cases such as this arise the employer would obviously be better off if the case is considered under Regulation 7(3) and not Regulation 7(2), as he will not be faced with the burden of proving the requirement was determinative of whom he employed. However, it will not always be clear whether the employer has an ethos based on religion or belief. Does a Halal chicken and chips take-away restaurant have 'an ethos based on religion or belief' or is it primarily a fast-food business that happens to present itself as Halal as this draws more customers, and which thus has an 'ethos' based on commercial principles?

The Government has indicated that it is committed to continuing the position whereby certain state-maintained religious schools can employ teachers of the same religious denomination (see ss 58–60 and new ss124A and 124B of the School Standards and Framework Act 1998), and it is most likely that religious schools will be allowed to rely on Regulation 7(3).

Both Regulation 7(2) and (3) allow the employer to rely on the GOR exception where either the person to whom the requirement is applied does not meet it, or the employer is not reasonably satisfied that the person meets it. So, if a person does in fact meet the requirement but has not made this clear in their application form and interview, then the employer should still be able to rely on Regulation 7.

5.5 THE GOR AND SEXUAL ORIENTATION DISCRIMINATION

Regulation 7(1) and (2) of the EE (Sexual Orientation) Regulations are identical in material terms to Regulation 7(1) and (2) of the EE (Religion or Belief) Regulations discussed above. An employer who can show that being of a particular sexual orientation is a genuine and determining requirement of the job, and that it is proportionate to apply that requirement in the particular case, is entitled to rely on the GOR exception in relation to discrimination under Regulation 3. The explanation of the general GOR in Regulation 7(1) and (2) is not repeated here and the reader is referred to section 5.3 above for a fuller explanation of how these parts of the general GOR work.

5.5.1 The GOR and Sexual Orientation Generally

It is suggested that examples of cases that might fall within the general GOR under Regulation 7(2) may be found in health and entertainment contexts. Consider an NHS trust employs health advisors to go out into the community and give people detailed and intimate advice on the transmission of sexual diseases. Where the Trust is concerned about a specific sexually transmitted disease that bisexual women are at greater risk of developing, it may be that a bisexual woman is best suited for the advisory role. If the 'target' community was gay men, it might be that a gay man would be best qualified for the job. If the Trust could show that it was a determinative requirement that a person of those sexual orientations was employed for those specific roles then it could rely on Regulation 7(2) as a defence to a claim by an aggrieved heterosexual job applicant that he had been discriminated against under Regulation 3 of the Regulations because the Trust had advertised for a 'gay man', for instance.

A more difficult example might arise in relation to a gay bar or nightclub. The club owner may be keen that the bar or club retained its gay identity and catered specifically for its gay customers. Under the RRA it is arguably lawful for a Chinese restaurant to insist on employing Chinese waiters, or a West Indian club to have black barmen, to maintain the identity and authenticity of the establishment. It is arguable that Regulation 7(2) could provide a similar exception to sexual orientation discrimination in the circumstances described. However, such an argument would face considerable difficulties. For the employer to be successful he would have to show that the authenticity of his establishment would be damaged if he employed a heterosexual barman, or that this would put off customers in some way, but considering it is most unlikely that most customers would know the sexuality of the person who sold them a beer this would be a difficult thing to show. This difference between sexual orientation and race means that, other than in welfare, health, and social-work type examples it is difficult to contemplate obvious examples of situations in which Regulation 7(2) might apply. Apart from these types of employment, and those referred to in Regulation 7(3), discussed at section 5.5.2, below, it is just as difficult to conceive of situations where a particular job would have to be filled by a heterosexual as opposed to a bisexual or homosexual. This is not surprising, though, since the GOR is meant to provide for limited and exceptional situations only.

5.5.2 Regulation 7(3) of the EE (Sexual Orientation) Regulations

Regulation 7(3) is the most controversial part of both Regulations. It has prompted specific criticism by a Parliamentary select committee, a lively debate in the House of Lords, and a legal challenge. The reason for this is the potentially wide scope of the GOR exception in Regulation 7(3), and the fact it departs from, and appears to go much further than, the words of Article 4 of the Framework Directive.

Regulation 7(3) concerns employment for the purposes of 'organized religion'. It provides that an employer can rely on the GOR when he applies a requirement related to sexual orientation:

(i) so as to comply with the doctrines of the religion, or

(ii) because of the nature of the employment and the context in which it is carried out, so as to avoid conflicting with the strongly held religious convictions of a significant number of the religion's followers.

The wording of Regulation 7(3) departs from the wording of Article 4 of the Framework Directive and the wording of the rest of Regulation 7 of both Regulations. There is no condition that the requirement has to be 'genuine' or even a 'requirement' of the job, never mind a determining requirement. There is no condition that the requirement must be applied proportionately. The paragraph uses vague and imprecise terminology not found or defined elsewhere in the Regulations, something that is of particular concern considering the GOR is supposed to be interpreted and applied restrictively.

The term 'organized religion' (Regulation 7(3)(a)) is not defined, and no explanation is given as to why it is used. Elsewhere in the Regulations a religion, or an organization with an ethos based on a religion or belief, is entitled to rely on the GOR exception in specific circumstances. Why does the wide exception contained in Regulation 7(3) of the EE (Sexual Orientation) Regulations only apply to 'organized religion'? It is arguable that to give greater protection to 'organized religion' than to religion that is not regarded as 'organized' is itself discrimination based on religion or belief.

One of the justifications for the this part of the GOR, withdrawing protection from discrimination on grounds of sexual orientation, is that it is done to avoid conflicting with the convictions of a 'significant number of the religion's followers' (Regulation 7(3)(b)(ii)). No explanation is given as to how this vague test will be determined. What constitutes a significant number? It does appear clear, however, that there is no requirement that the convictions of the 'significant number' must be reasonable—it is simply a question of what offends a 'significant number'.

It is true, as the Government have pointed out, that recital (24) of the Framework Directive recognizes that the EC respects and does not prejudice the status of churches and religious communities in national law and allows Member States to 'maintain or lay down specific provisions on genuine, legitimate and justified occupational requirements which might be required for carrying out an occupational activity'. But this has not satisfied the critics of Regulation 7(3).

In particular, the Parliamentary Joint Committee on Statutory Instruments expressed concern about the reach of Regulation 7(3) in their Twenty-First Report (13 June 2003). They were concerned that Regulation 7(3) went beyond the strict requirements applied to the GOR by Article 4 of the Framework Directive. In paragraph 1.11 of their Report the Joint Committee expressed concern that Regulation 7(3) might allow employers to permit difference of treatment on grounds of sexual orientation where there was no genuine and determining requirement which was proportionate. They also commented, in paragraph 1.14 of their Report, that Article 4 of the Directive must be construed strictly, and apply, as stated by Recital (23) of the Directive, to very limited circumstances. The Directive did not afford special protection to religious organization in the context of sexual orientation discrimination. Finally, in paragraph 1.17 of their Report, they concluded that there was 'doubt about the compatibility of Regulation 7(3) with the Directive'.

This concern, and criticism from other quarters, prompted a debate in the House of Lords on the Regulation. Lord Lester of Herne Hill QC moved a motion inviting the Lords to withdraw Regulation 7(3). The motion was defeated, but the debate is of assistance in clarifying the reach of the Regulation. In response to criticism of Regulation 7(3), the Government Minister, Lord Sainsbury of Turville, made a number of remarks that should assist courts and tribunals to construe the Regulation (HL Hansard, 17 June 2003, col 779–780):

When drafting Regulation 7(3), we had in mind a very narrow range of employment: ministers of religion, plus a small number of posts outside the clergy, including those who exist to promote and represent religion . . . The rule only applies to employment for the purposes of 'organised religion', not religious organisations . . . A care home run by a religious foundation may qualify as a religious organisation, for example. I do not wish to make light of differences which the involvement of a church, mosque or synagogue can make to the culture of an organisation, but I believe that it would be very difficult under these regulations to show that the job in a care home exists, 'for the purposes of an organised religion'. I would say exactly the same in relation to a teacher at a faith school. Such jobs exist for the purposes of health care and education . . . Even if an employer can show that the job exists for the purposes of an organised religion . . . two further tests [must be] met . . . In the first test the requirement must be applied with the doctrines of the religion. We do not believe that that test would be met in relation to many posts. It would be difficult for a church to argue that a requirement related to sexual orientation applied to a post of cleaner, gardener or secretary . . . If the first test is not met [the second is that] the church will have to show that the requirement related to sexual orientation is necessary, 'because of the nature of the employment and the context in which it is carried out, so as to avoid conflicting with the strongly held religious convictions of a significant number of the religion's followers'. . . . It is neither sufficient for the requirement to be imposed simply because of the nature of the work and the context in which it is carried out, nor may the requirement be imposed simply because of the religious convictions of the followers of the faith. Both elements have to be satisfied before the second test can be met. They are strict tests and will be met in very few cases.

Regulation 7(3) has also prompted a legal challenge, by way of judicial review brought by various trade unions who challenge its *vires*. At the time of writing this book the claim for judicial review has yet to be heard. Considering the arguments above surrounding this section it is quite likely that either the Court will strike down Regulation 7(3) for being *ultra vires* the Framework Directive, or it will narrowly construe the Regulation. In the meantime, or in the absence of either, the Regulation ought to be construed narrowly, in line with the ministerial statements quoted above.

5.6 EFFECT OF THE GOR ON OTHER REGULATIONS

The GOR allows for an exception from Regulation 3 in respect of Regulation 6, rights to employment. In particular, it creates an exception in relation to Regulation 6(1)(a) or (c) (arrangements made by the employer for the purpose of determining to whom he should offer employment and refusing or not offering employment), 6(2)(b) or (c) (opportunities for promotion or transfer to, or training for, any employment or refusing the same) and 6(2)(d) (dismissing or subjecting employee to any other detriment).

However, the GOR has an effect on a number of other Regulations. It can apply in certain circumstances to persons in the following situations: contract workers (Regulation 8(3)); office holders (Regulation 10(5)); partnerships (Regulation 14(4)); vocational training (Regulation 17(3)); employment agencies (Regulation 18(3)); and educational establishments (Regulation 20(3)) of both Regulations. Regulation 7(3) of the EE (Sexual Orientation) Regulations also applies to Regulation 16(3) (qualifications bodies) of those Regulations.

6

GENERAL EXCEPTIONS FROM PROTECTION

6.1 INTRODUCTION

In addition to the exception to Regulation 3 contained in Regulation 7, the Genuine Occupation Requirement (see Chapter 5, above), there are a number of other general exceptions to the Regulations. These are all contained in Part IV of the Regulations 'General Exceptions from Parts II and III'. Note that the GOR does not appear in this Part concerning general exceptions, rather it is contained in Part II, 'Discrimination in Employment and Vocational Training'.

The effect of Part IV is that any act done in pursuance of the various exceptions will not be regarded as unlawful under Parts II and III of the Regulations. Two of the exceptions apply to both Regulations, the exception for national security and positive active; the other two apply only to each separate Regulation: the exception concerning Sikhs and safety helmets is found in the EE (Religion or Belief) Regulation, whereas the exception regarding benefits related to marital status only applies to the EE (Sexual Orientation) Regulations.

The exception relating to national security and Sikhs and safety helmets will be known from other legislation and needs little discussion here, whereas the exceptions relating to positive action, and benefits related to marital status merit greater consideration.

6.2 NATIONAL SECURITY

Regulation 24 of both Regulations provides that the Regulations do not make unlawful any act that is done 'for the purpose of safeguarding national security', so long as that act was 'justified by that purpose'. Article 2(5) of the Framework Directive provides that the prohibition of the discrimination contained in the Directive shall be without prejudice to measures laid down by national law that are, amongst other things, necessary for public security. The exception in Regulation 24 is thus compatible with the Directive.

This Regulation reflects the exceptions to the RRA contained in s 42, and to the SDA in s 52(1), although the amended s 42 of the RRA adds the important limitation to the exception, that the act done for the purpose of safeguarding national security must be *'justified by that purpose'*, which is also contained in Regulation 24.

6.3 POSITIVE ACTION

The exception for positive action is one of the most significant factors in the Regulations. Regulation 25 of the EE (Religion or Belief) Regulations and Regulation 26 of the EE (Sexual Orientation) Regulations provide that positive action, or positive discrimination, is lawful in certain circumstances. Positive action has generally been unlawful in Great Britain, with some narrow exceptions. The exception for positive action in the Regulations goes beyond many of those narrow exceptions.

Broadly speaking, the exception allows employers and other persons to *discriminate in favour* of members of a particular religion or belief/sexual orientation in terms of access to training or encouragement to apply for particular work where such positive discrimination reasonably appears to prevent or compensate for disadvantages linked to religion or belief/sexual orientation suffered by persons of that religion or belief/sexual orientation doing that work or likely to take up that work (Regulation 25(1) of the EE (Religion or Belief Regulations) and Regulation 26(1) of the EE (Sexual Orientation) Regulations). Paragraph 2 of both Regulations allow trade organizations to discriminate in favour of the particular group in terms of making training for posts or encouragement to apply for posts *only* available to members of that particular group on the same basis.

6.3.1 Positive Action and European Law

Positive action to alleviate discrimination is in many respects a 'foreign' concept. Apart from the limited exceptions in domestic discrimination law, reviewed below (see section 6.3.2), positive action has been broadly unlawful under domestic law. Other jurisdictions take a different approach. The United States, for instance, allows for forms of 'affirmative action' in relation to a variety of spheres of society. Positive action is also permissible under various international law instruments, such as Article 26 of the International Covenant on Civil and Political Rights. It is European law, however, that has had the most important influence in the development of concepts of positive action in domestic employment discrimination law, and the Regulations in particular.

The European Court of Justice has held that the Equal Treatment Directive allows Member States to take measures that positively discriminate to ensure full equality in practice between men and women; and the amended Article 141 of the EC Treaty specifically allows Member States to take positive measures to 'make it easier for the under-represented sex to pursue a vocational activity or to prevent or compensate for disadvantages in professional careers'. Likewise, Article 5 of the Race Directive (EC Directive 2000/43/EEC) allows Member States to adopt 'specific measures to prevent or compensate for disadvantages linked to racial and ethnic origin'.

It is thus not surprising that the Framework Directive, on which the Regulations are based, makes specific provision for positive action. Article 7(1) of the Directive provides that:

With a view to ensuring full equality in practice, the principle of equal treatment shall not prevent any Member State from maintaining or adopting specific measures to prevent or compensate for disadvantages linked to any of the grounds referred to in Article 1 [including Religion or Belief and Sexual Orientation].

The Directive enables Great Britain to adopt measures to prevent or compensate for discrimination on grounds of religion or belief or sexual orientation. If, for instance, Hindus are found to be under-represented in certain jobs, then measures taken to remedy that under-representation will not violate the Directive. Regulation 25 of the EE (Religion or Belief) Regulations and Regulation 26 of the EE (Sexual Orientation) Regulations give effect to Article 7(1) of the Directive by allowing individual employers and trade organizations to take such measures themselves.

What European law has not previously allowed is blanket 'quotas' which take no account whatsoever of a job candidate's qualifications or experience. For instance, in *Abrahamsson and Anderson v Fogelqvist* [2000] ECR I-05539, the European Court of Justice held that the Equal Treatment Directive allowed Member States to have legislation whereby a candidate belonging to the under-represented sex could be granted preference over a competitor of the opposite sex, provided that the candidates possess *substantially equivalent* merits and are subjected to an objective assessment taking account of the specific personal situations of all the candidates. It is unlikely the Framework Directive was intended to depart from this approach and allow for blanket quotas.

The European Convention of Human Rights also allows for positive discrimination, so it is unlikely that a disgruntled job applicant could claim that positive action amounted to an infringement of his right not to be discriminated against protected by Article 14 of the Convention. The European Court of Human Rights has held that positive discrimination does not violate Article 14 if it has an 'objective and reasonable justification' (see, eg, the *Belgian Linguistics Case* (No 2) (1979–80) 1 EHRR 252, ECtHR).

6.3.2 Positive Action in the Regulations and in Domestic Law Generally

The RRA and the SDA both allow for positive action in certain limited circumstances. For instance, s 37 RRA provides that it is lawful to take measures 'affording only persons of a particular racial group access to facilities for training which would help to fit them for that work', or 'encouraging only persons of a particular racial group to take advantage of opportunities for doing that work', but *only* where it reasonably appeared that no persons of that group were among those doing that work in Great Britain, or a disproportionately small number of that group were (s 37(1) RRA). Section 38 of the RRA adopts a similar approach. Sections 47 and 48 of the SDA have similar language.

The critical difference between the Regulations and the provisions under the RRA and the SDA is that under the Regulations it is not necessary to show that no members, or a disproportionately small number of members, of a particular group are represented in a particular job. Rather, it is only necessary to show it reasonably appeared to the person making them that the measures taken prevent or compensate for disadvantages. The lack of a requirement to provide evidence of under-representation makes it easier for employers to justify positive action under the Regulations than under the RRA/SDA. The Government explicitly recognized this important difference in paragraph 74 of the Office of the Deputy Prime Minister's Notes on the Draft EE (Religion or Belief) Regulations, and paragraph 76 of the Notes on the Sexual Orientation Regulations. Case law on positive action in relation to complaints of race or sex discrimination therefore needs to be treated with caution when applying the more liberal approach contained in the Regulations.

Other limited spheres of domestic discrimination legislation allow for positive action. For instance s 6 of the DDA imposes a duty on employers to take reasonable (positive) steps to prevent disabled people from being at a substantial disadvantage compared to non-disabled people as a result of the employer's arrangements. This has been held by the EAT to require positive discrimination in certain circumstances (see *Kent County Council v Mingo* [2000] IRLR 90, EAT). Moreover, the Fair Employment and Treatment (Northern Ireland) Order 1998 allows for direct discrimination in pursuit of affirmative action in limited circumstances to secure fair participation in employment by members of the Protestant or Roman Catholic communities. However, both these legislative provisions are concerned with highly specific areas and they do not assist in interpreting the EE Regulations.

6.3.3 Positive Action in Practice

The positive action provided for by the Regulations will allow an employer to discriminate in favour of his existing employees of, for instance, a specific sexual orientation, where it reasonably appears to the employer that such training would prevent or compensate for disadvantages linked with membership of that sexual orientation. So, for example, if the Police Commissioner of a regional police force reasonably believed it is particularly difficult for lesbian and gay police officers to receive promotion, or even to stay for any protracted period in their jobs as police officers, because of the discrimination they face, he would be entitled to afford preferential access to training, or even develop specific training programmes, for those officers aimed at assisting them in overcoming these disadvantages and putting them in a better position to apply for promotion.

The Regulations also allow employers to encourage members of, for instance, a particular religious group, to apply for work. So, for example, where a local authority housing department manager reasonably believes Muslims are disadvantaged in terms that make it less likely for them to apply for a job in the department, it would be lawful for him to organize a recruitment drive aimed at Muslims, perhaps involving giving talks in the local mosque or advertising in an Islamic local newspaper.

In relation to trade organizations, such as trade unions, similar steps can be taken, but positive steps can be applied so as to assist *only* members of the particular group. So, for instance if a manual trade union reasonably believed that lesbians and gay members of the union, or practising members of non-Christian religions, were disadvantaged in gaining positions as union officers it would be entitled to organize training aimed *exclusively* at members of those particular groups, to assist them in being appointed to such posts, and it would also be entitled to exclusively encourage members of those groups to apply for such posts.

6.4 SIKHS AND REQUIREMENTS TO WEAR SAFETY HELMETS

This exception is contained in Regulation 26 of the EE (Religion or Belief) Regulations. It provides that where a member of the Sikh religion is wearing a turban and is then required to wear a safety helmet on a construction site, this will be regarded as indirect discrimination which cannot be justified (unlike most indirect discrimination which can be justified, see section 2.5.2, above). The provision gives effect to s 11 of the Employment Act 1989, which exempts a Sikh who wears a turban and is working on a construction site from other statutory provisions which require the wearing of a safety helmet. It reflects s 12 of the Employment Act 1989 which provides that where a person requires a Sikh to wear a safety helmet on a construction site it will be indirect racial discrimination that cannot be justified under s 1(1)(b) of the RRA.

The exception, whilst welcome insofar as it protects the religious beliefs of Sikhs, is drawn narrowly. First, it only applies to Sikhs working on construction sites. A Sikh who is required to wear a safety helmet in other circumstances, such as in a factory warehouse or coal mine, could not rely on the Regulation 26 exception. Indeed, in *Dhanjal v British Steel plc* (24 June 1994, unreported, EAT), the

Employment Appeal Tribunal found that it was open for a Tribunal to find, in circumstances where a Sikh had been dismissed for not wearing a safety helmet where the s 11 Employment Act 1989 exception did not apply, that any indirect discrimination was justified. Secondly, the exception only applies to Sikhs who wear turbans, it does not extend to other religious communities who cover their heads for religious reasons. For instance, Hasidic Jews would have difficulties being forced to wear a safety helmet where such a requirement prevents them from covering their heads in the traditional religious fashion. In terms of religious discrimination, there can be no justification for treating Sikhs who wear turbans differently from any other religious community whose faith requires them to cover their heads in circumstances that preclude the wearing of a safety helmet. The situation was different before the Regulations came into force as Sikhs were recognized as a 'racial group' for the purposes of the RRA, and could thus rely on protection from racial discrimination (whereas Hasidic Jews, for instance, as opposed to the 'racial group' of Jews as a whole, were not).

The EE (Religion of Belief) Regulations are supposed to guarantee equal protection from discrimination on grounds of religion or belief to all. It would be indirectly discriminatory, under the Regulations, to impose a safety helmet requirement on followers of some religions. The issue will be whether that indirect discrimination can be justified on health and safety grounds. There will be a strong argument that it will in certain circumstances; the difference for Sikhs is that Regulation 26 provides that such indirect discrimination can *never* be justified in the first place.

It seems contrary to the purpose of the Regulations and the Framework Directive to provide specific protection for one particular religious group where members of other groups are in the same circumstances. However, Regulation 26(2) specifically provides that any special treatment to a Sikh in relation to safety hats 'shall not be regarded as giving rise ... to any discrimination'. It is possible to argue this Regulation is *ultra vires* the Framework Directive, the Directive does not provide that national governments can grant certain religious groups 'special treatment', certainly it does not provide for a blanket rule in relation to discriminatory treatment on grounds of religion that other groups may also experience.

6.5 BENEFITS LINKED TO MARITAL STATUS

6.5.1 The Exception

Regulation 25 of the EE (Sexual Orientation) Regulations provides an exception in relation to benefits linked to a person's marital status. It is not unlawful to prevent or restrict access to a benefit by reference to marital status, even though to do so might otherwise be discriminatory on grounds of sexual orientation.

Thus, any rules that link pensions and other benefits to marriage cannot be challenged as indirectly discriminatory on the basis that same-sex partners cannot get married under domestic law.

According to paragraph 75 of the Office of the Deputy Prime Minister's Notes on the EE (Sexual Orientation) Regulations, the exception for benefits based on marital status reflects the fact that marital status benefits are outside the scope of the Framework Directive:

Article 3 of the Directive states that it applies only 'within the limits of the areas of competence conferred on the Community'. Distinctions between the rights of married and unmarried people are outside the scope of Community competence, because marriage is a family law concept which is regulated by the laws of the Member States. This was recognised by the Advocate General of the ECJ in C-249/96 *Grant v South West Trains* [1998] ECR I-621 (at paragraph 28 of his opinion). Recital (22) of the preamble to the Directive confirms that it is 'without prejudice to national laws on marital status and the benefits dependent thereon'.

This does not mean that all discrimination on grounds of sexual orientation in survivor schemes (widow's allowances, etc) and occupational pension schemes will be lawful. Quite the contrary, such discrimination will be unlawful (see eg, Regulation 9A, section 3.3.15, above). Rather a specific exception is made where the basis for the differential treatment is a person's marital status. So, if a pension scheme provided better terms to a person where he is in a relationship with the opposite sex this would be directly discriminatory and contrary to the Regulations. Where a scheme provided better terms to persons in long-term stable relationships, it might be possible to demonstrate this was indirectly discriminatory if evidence existed to demonstrate that people of one sexual orientation were more likely to be in such a relationship than people of another. It is only where a person's marital status produces different treatment that this exception comes into play. However, since so many occupational pension and survivors' benefits schemes are based on marital status, this is of little comfort.

6.5.2 Criticism of the Exception

It is regrettable that the Government decided not to use the opportunity of bringing in the Regulations to outlaw discrimination on the grounds of sexual orientation in terms of benefits linked to marital status. There is little justification for the continuation of such discrimination which not only discriminates against non-heterosexuals, but also many heterosexuals who live together unmarried. It may have been difficult for the Government to prohibit discrimination in relation to benefits based on marital status by the route in which they introduced the Regulations. As the Regulations were introduced by the Government under powers conferred by s 2(2) of the European Communities Act 1972, which gives the Government the power to transpose a Directive faithfully into domestic law, it was only possible to extend the law compatibly with the Framework Directive. If the Government had wanted to legislate outside the areas of EC competence it would have been required to introduce the Regulations in Parliament as normal primary legislation, requiring a debate and Parliamentary scrutiny. But there was nothing to stop the Government adopting this course, and indeed many proponents of equality legislation argued for it to do so.

In any event, it is strongly arguable that nothing in the Framework Directive prevented the Government from outlawing discrimination on grounds of marital status in terms of occupational benefits. The Government correctly interpreted Article 3(1)(c) of the Framework Directive, prohibiting discrimination in relation to 'employment . . . including . . . *pay*' as including all types of remuneration, such as health insurance and occupational pensions. In order to transpose this, the Government introduced Regulation 9A of both Regulations, prohibiting discrimination in occupational pension schemes (see section 3.3.15, above). There is no doubt, then, that the Government had and exercised the power to prohibit discrimination on grounds of sexual orientation in relation to occupational pension schemes. Whilst recital (22) of the Framework Directive provided that the Directive was 'without prejudice to national laws on marital status and the benefits thereon', this in itself does not prevent the Government from prohibiting discrimination in this sphere; it only means that if they fail to do so they are not acting incompatibly with the Directive. Moreover, it is unlikely that the Government's reliance on paragraph 28 of the Advocate General's opinion in Case C-249/96, *Grant v South-West Trains Ltd* [1998] ICR 449 is of assistance. *Grant* concerned a challenge to an employer's benefit providing that an employee's 'common law opposite sex spouse' was entitled to travel concessions. It was a case brought before the Framework Directive came into being. Today it is likely the same benefit would be challenged, successfully, under the Framework Directive and/or the EE (Sexual Orientation) Regulations. As the applicant in *Grant* was trying to 'fit' the discrimination, which was really on grounds of sexual orientation discrimination, into a case of sex (gender) discrimination, the case involved arguments about the meaning of the word 'spouse'. The Advocate General was simply saying that the definition of the word 'spouse' was an issue of family law, for national courts to decide. The ECJ dismissed the applicant's claim finding, amongst other things, that discrimination on grounds of sexual orientation was not contrary to EC law. EC competence now includes discrimination on grounds of sexual orientation, and *Grant* is not a particularly helpful case for the Government to rely on. It is now difficult to argue that indirect discrimination on grounds of sexual orientation, based on marital status, is outside the competence of EC law.

Discrimination on grounds of marital status is recognized as being unlawful sex discrimination (see s 3(1)(a) SDA) and there is good reason to treat it as unlawful sexual orientation discrimination.

There are a number of important moves to outlaw sexual orientation discrimination based on marital status which may overtake the Regulations. Within the common law, the House of Lords held in *Fitzpatrick v Sterling Housing Association Ltd* [2001] 1 AC 27 that a same-sex partner of a tenant was to be recognized as capable of being a member of the tenant's 'family' for the purposes of Rent Act 1977. The word 'family' was not defined in the Act, and the House of Lords took into account changing social attitudes in giving the word a meaning that did not discriminate on grounds of sexual orientation.

Applying the HRA, and Article 14 of the European Convention on Human Rights, the courts have been able to go even further. Under Article 14 of the Convention it is unlawful for a public authority to discriminate against a person in relation to his civil rights on grounds of sexual orientation or on grounds of marital status (see eg, *Sahin v Germany* (2003) 36 EHRR 43, E Ct HR, in relation to discrimination on grounds of marital status). In *Ghaidan v Mendoza* [2002] EWCA Civ 1522; [2003] 2 WLR 478, CA (leave to appeal to House of Lords granted), the Court of Appeal found that to give the word 'spouse' in the Rent Act 1977 the meaning of a person living with another 'as his or her wife or husband' was discriminatory on grounds of sexual orientation (contrary to Articles 8 and 14). They were thus prepared to read into the 1977 Act (by means of s 3 of the HRA) words to make the Act compatible. The word spouse would mean a person living with another '*as if they were* his or her wife or husband'. This overcame the discrimination on grounds of marital status that, in turn, discriminated on grounds of sexual orientation. In Application 40016/98, *Karner v Austria*, E Ct HR, 24 July 2003, another tenancy case, the European Court of Human Rights found the Austrian Supreme Court's decision that the term 'life companion' could not include same-sex couples to be in breach of Articles 8 and 14 of the Convention. It will thus be arguable that Regulation 25 of the EE (Sexual Orientation) Regulations is in breach of the HRA.

There have also been attempts in Parliament to bring in a civil partnership law that would allow people of all sexual orientations to have a legally recognized partnership, and could thus outlaw at least some discrimination on grounds of marital status.

Finally, various trade unions have brought a claim for judicial review challenging the *vires* of Regulation 7(3) and Regulation 25 of the EE (Sexual Orientation) Regulations because of their discriminatory effect. At the time of writing this book that case has yet to be heard, but it is clear the controversy surrounding this particular exception is unlikely to go away.

Considering all the developments in the law away from discrimination on grounds of marital status, it would be surprising if the important and unfortunate exception to the EE (Sexual Orientation) Regulations included in Regulation 25 will survive in the long term.

7

ENFORCING THE REGULATIONS

7.1 INTRODUCTION

Part V of both sets of Regulations concern enforcement. The Regulations are primarily about rights in employment; employment tribunals are the main forum in which they will be enforced. Indeed, it is only in relation to claims against educational establishments, arising out of Regulation 20, that other tribunals have jurisdiction: county courts in England and Wales, sheriff courts in Scotland. That is because students, rather than employees or persons in analogous situations as employees, have rights under Regulation 20. The focus of this chapter, reflecting the focus of the Regulations, is enforcement in the employment tribunals.

The Regulations themselves restrict the proceedings which can be brought. Regulation 27 makes clear that, apart from the jurisdiction conferred by Part V of the Regulations, no proceedings, whether civil or criminal, can be brought against any person arising out of an act which is unlawful under the Regulations. This restriction is clear and unambiguous. Any complaints about unlawful acts under the Regulations must be brought either in the employment tribunals (in relation to most of the unlawful acts that could be committed), or in the county courts/sheriff courts in relation to issues arising out of Regulation 20.

Regulation 27(2) does, however, make clear that the general restriction on jurisdiction contained in Regulation 27 does not prevent a claim for judicial review being made. So, for instance, it might be possible in certain circumstances for a trade union or religious group to judicially review a public body employer on the basis that it had not properly applied the Regulations to its recruitment policies, or that it overstepped them in its development of a positive action programme. Whilst it does not say so explicitly, Regulation 27 does not preclude a tribunal from making a reference to the

European Court of Justice where a question arises as to the interpretation of European law under Article 234 of the EC Treaty. An employment tribunal has the power to make a reference under EC law and under its own rules of procedure (see rule 22 of the Employment Tribunals Rules of Procedure). The Employment Appeal Tribunal and other courts also have this power. Considering the Regulations transpose the Framework Directive, such references can be anticipated.

7.2 COMPLAINTS IN THE EMPLOYMENT TRIBUNAL

The vast majority of complaints under the Regulations will be brought in employment tribunals. The rules of procedure in employment tribunals are fairly informal compared with other courts, but there are important provisions relating to such matters as time limits and costs. Many of these are outside the scope of the Regulations and of this book, but those contemplating bringing, or defending, a claim in the employment tribunals who do not have experience in employment tribunal claims should refer to specialist texts on procedure; reference should be made, in particular, to the Employment Tribunals Rules of Procedure, contained in Schedule 1 to the Employment Tribunals (Constitution etc) Regulations 2001 (SI 2001/1171) (for complaints brought in Scotland, see the Employment Tribunals Rules of Procedure (Scotland), contained in Schedule 1 to the Employment Tribunals (Constitution etc) (Scotland) Regulations 2001 (SI 2001/1170)).

The provisions in the Regulations concerning complaints in the employment tribunals broadly reflect those standard to other complaints in the tribunal, and to discrimination complaints in particular. The case law on procedural issues arising out of other discrimination complaints will therefore provide a useful guide to the way in which tribunals will consider complaints under the Regulations.

7.2.1 Jurisdiction of Employment Tribunals

Regulation 28 of the Regulations confers jurisdiction on the employment tribunals to consider complaints made by a person, referred to as the complainant, against another, the respondent, in relation to unlawful acts under the Regulations. The tribunal has jurisdiction to consider most complaints in relation to Part II of the Regulations (see Chapter 3, above), other than those mentioned in Regulation 28(2). Employment tribunals also have jurisdiction to consider complaints against a person who, by virtue of Regulation 22 (liability of employers and principals) or Regulation 23 (aiding unlawful acts), is to be treated as committing the act complained of (see Chapter 4, above). This allows a complainant to bring a complaint in an employment tribunal against an employer where the act complained of was committed by one of the employer's employees, and/or against the employee who actually committed the act along with the employer.

Employment tribunals do not have jurisdiction, by virtue of Regulation 28(2) to consider three types of complaints:

(a) where a statutory appeals procedure is available in relation to Regulation 16 qualifications bodies;

(b) where the complaint arises out of Regulation 20 (institutions of further and higher education); and

(c) where the complaint arises out of Regulation 21 (relationships that have come to an end) taken with Regulation 20.

7.2.1.1 *Statutory Appeals*

This provision is similar to those in s 54(2) of the RRA, and s 63(2) of the SDA. If a statutory appeal or proceedings in the nature of an appeal of some kind is available in relation to an act done by a qualifications body, then even though that act might be unlawful under the Regulations, the employment tribunal does not have jurisdiction to consider it (Regulation 29(2)(a)). This restriction on the employment tribunal's jurisdiction only arises where the appeal or proceedings in the nature of an appeal is provided for by an enactment in or instrument made under an Act of Parliament or (by virtue of Regulation 28(4)) an Act of the Scottish Parliament. The purpose of this restriction is that Parliament has decided a specialist qualifications body, such as the Law Society in relation to solicitors, is best qualified to determine complaints.

An example of the justification for this restriction on jurisdiction can be found in the case law of the RRA. Section 54(2) of the RRA is in similar terms to Regulation 29(2)(a) of the Regulations. By s 54(2) of the RRA, a person cannot bring a complaint before an employment tribunal under the section in the RRA concerning qualifications bodies (s 12(1) RRA) about an act in respect of which an appeal, or proceedings in the nature of an appeal, may be brought under any enactment. In *Khan v General Medical Council* [1996] ICR 1032, CA, Hoffmann LJ (as he then was) explained the rationale for this rule:

[Section 12(1) of the RRA] concerns qualifications for professions and trades. Parliament appears to have thought that, although the industrial tribunal is often called a specialist tribunal and has undoubted expertise in matters of sex and racial discrimination, its advantages in providing an effective remedy were outweighed by the even greater specialisation in a particular field or trade or professional qualification of statutory tribunals such as the review board, since the review board undoubtedly has a duty to give effect to the provisions of section 12 of the Act of 1976 . . . This seems to me a perfectly legitimate view for Parliament to have taken. Furthermore, section 54(2) makes it clear that decisions of the review board would themselves be open to judicial review on the ground that the board failed to have proper regard to the provisions of the Race Relations Act 1976. In my view, it cannot be said that the Medical Act 1983 does not provide the effective remedy required by Community law.

The same approach must apply to Regulation 29(2)(a) of the Regulations. An effective remedy is provided to the complainant by reason of the statutory appeals procedure and, to the extent that the relevant body does not properly have regard to the Regulations, by judicial review of that body. This should thus be compatible with the complainant's right to an effective remedy under both European law and the HRA.

It will therefore be important, where a complaint arises in relation to a qualifications body, for the complainant to ensure that no statutory appeals procedure is open to him before he presents a complaint to an employment tribunal. A failure to check this may leave the complainant out of time for bringing the appeal and out of pocket in terms of the wasted expense of bringing a complaint before an employment tribunal that does not have jurisdiction to hear it.

7.2.1.2 *Educational Institutions*

The remaining two restrictions are both concerned with institutions of further and higher education under Regulation 20—jurisdiction is restricted in relation to acts done under Regulation 20 itself (Regulation 28(2)(b)), and acts done arising out of Regulation 20 after the relationship has come to an end, ie Regulation 20 taken with Regulation 21 (Regulation 28(2)(c)). The reason for this is obvious. Regulation 20 complainants are not employees of further and higher education institutions; they will be students, applicants to study, or former students. There is no employment relationship and no employment law issues to be resolved. Thus, it is more appropriate for the normal civil courts, as opposed to specialist employment tribunals, to consider complaints brought under these Regulations. Regulation 31 confers jurisdiction on county courts and sheriff courts in this regard.

7.2.2 Bringing a Complaint in the Employment Tribunal

Regulation 34 of the Regulations sets down time limits for bringing a complaint under the Regulations. The Regulation is very closely modelled on s 68 of the RRA and s 76 of the SDA, and the interpretation of those sections, including guidance on the relevant principles for extending time limits, will be applied to Regulation 34.

7.2.2.1 *General Rule: Complaint must be Brought within Three Months*

A complaint must be presented to the employment tribunal before the end of the period of three months beginning when the act complained of was done (Regulation 34(1)(a)). Thus, if the complaint relates to a refusal to offer employment on grounds of religion or belief, or an act of harassment by fellow employers on grounds of sexual orientation, the complaint must be brought within three months of that refusal or act of harassment. A complaint is presented to an employment tribunal when it receives the complainant's originating application (IT1 form). Where the complaint is made under Regulation 36(7) (armed forces), the period for bringing the complaint is six months from the act complained of (Regulation 34(1)(b)).

7.2.2.2 Tribunal's Discretion to Consider Complaints Brought Out of Time

Although the rule is that the complaint must be brought within three months of the act complained of, the employment tribunal may consider any complaint that is made after this time if it considers it just and equitable to do so (Regulation 34(3)). This provision is similar to that contained in s 68(6) of the RRA and s 76(5) of the SDA.

The tribunal has a broad discretion to determine whether it is just and equitable to consider a complaint made out of time. Factors relevant to this discretion include: whether the respondent is prejudiced if the complaint is allowed to proceed (ie whether the passing of time makes it particularly burdensome for it to defend the claim); whether alternative remedies are available to the complainant; the conduct of the parties since the act complained of; the length of time by which the complaint is out of time (the more time that has passed since the end of the three month period, the more difficult it will be to persuade a tribunal to consider the complaint); the complainant's medical condition, particularly whether any condition prevented the complainant from bringing the complaint within time; and whether the complainant had legal or other professional advice since the act complained about (where a complainant is legally advised but is outside the time limit it will be difficult for him to persuade the tribunal it is just and equitable to extend time, except where the complainant reasonably relies on advice and such reliance caused the delay in bringing the complaint).

Generally employment tribunals are far more prepared to exercise their jurisdiction to consider complaints of discrimination that are made out of time than they are other complaints (such as unfair dismissal). However, where there is no good reason for the delay in bringing a complaint, or where the delay is particularly long, the tribunal should not be expected to exercise their jurisdiction in favour of the late complainant. As with any other decision on a procedural matter of this nature, if either party believes the tribunal has not exercised its discretion properly in relation to time, an appeal lies to the Employment Appeal Tribunal; but it will only be in exceptional cases that the EAT will interfere with a tribunal's decision on this issue. For further consideration of the case law and principles in relation to the tribunal's discretion on this point, the reader should refer to the case law under s 68(6) of the RRA and s 76(5) of the SDA.

7.2.2.3 Time Limits in Special Circumstances, Continuing Discrimination, etc

Regulation 34(4) sets out how time is calculated in a series of specific situations which can be quite common in discrimination cases.

Regulations 34(4)(a) concerns the situation where the contract of employment itself, because of any of its terms, is unlawful, the act of discrimination shall be taken as extending throughout the duration of a contract. So, for example, if a term of a Sikh employee's contract of employment requires him to wear a safety helmet whilst working on a construction site, that contract will be unlawful by reason of Regulation 26 of the EE (Religion or Belief) Regulations. Even though the employee may have been made to wear the hat from January 2004, but did not resign from his employment until December 2004, the three-month time limit would begin to run from the date he resigned in December: the contract itself is an unlawful act, and so the act extends throughout the duration of the contract.

A more common situation is what is commonly described as *continuing act discrimination*. This is where the discrimination or harassment complained of extends over a period of time. By Regulation 34(4)(b) the three-month time limit will begin to run from the end of that period. So, where a lesbian worker has been subjected to a series of offensive and degrading remarks by her colleagues over a period of two years of employment, and those remarks are capable of constituting unlawful harassment under Regulation 5 of the EE (Sexual Orientation) Regulations, the three-month time limit will begin to run from the date of the last of these remarks.

Where the matter complained of is an *omission* rather than an act, time runs from the date the omission occurred (Regulation 34(4(c)). For instance, if the allegation is that the employer appointed a Muslim applicant for a job instead of a Hindu applicant because he did not want Hindus to work for him, then time will run from the omission to employ the Hindu applicant.

7.2.2.4 *Employment Tribunal Complaints Generally*
Apart from those matters specifically mentioned in the Regulations, the normal rules of the employment tribunals will apply. Thus, on receipt of the Applicant's Originating Application (IT1) the Respondent must enter its Notice of Appearance (IT3) within 21 days. Either party can apply to the tribunal for a preliminary ruling on any matter, including an application to strike out the other party's originating application/notice of appearance where appropriate. The tribunal will usually lay down directions as to the hearing date, time for disclosure, exchange of witness statements, etc. Where there are numerous factual allegations and issues, as often arise in discrimination claims, it will be useful for the parties to try and agree a list of issues to submit to the tribunal before the hearing.

Guides about how to present a complaint to the employment tribunal, including IT1 forms, and how to resist a claim, including the respondent's notice of appearance form (IT3), are now all available to download from the employment tribunal's website: www.employmenttribunals.gov.uk.

7.2.3 The Questionnaire Procedure

As with other discrimination complaints, the Regulations make specific provision for a questionnaire. This is a useful procedure by which the complainant can find out further information to assist his complaint. By Regulation 33 of the Regulations, it is available in relation to both employment tribunal complaints (under Regulation 28), and to complaints in the county courts/sheriff courts (under Regulation 31). A questionnaire can be served before a complaint is brought, as it may assist the complainant in deciding whether to bring a complaint.

A complainant who has brought a complaint of discrimination or harassment under the Regulations can serve a questionnaire on the respondent in the form that is helpfully set out in Schedule 2 of the Regulations, or forms to like effect. The respondent is not obliged to respond to the questionnaire, since it is a voluntary procedure, but he may respond to all or any of the questions he so wishes in the form set out in Schedule 3 to the Regulations.

The questions sent to the respondent, and any reply to them by the respondent shall be admissible as evidence before the tribunal (or court) (Regulation 33(2)(a)) so long as the questionnaire is served on the respondent within three months of the act complained of where it is served before a complaint is presented to the tribunal (Regulation 33(4)(a)) or within 21 days after a complaint to the tribunal has been presented where it is served after (Regulation 33(4)(b)(i)), or at such later date as the tribunal directs (Regulation 33(4)(b)(ii)). A questionnaire and its reply is served on the respondent or complainant if it is delivered to him; sent in the post to his usual or last-known address; delivered or posted to the secretary or clerk of the body, union, or association at its registered office where the respondent is one of these bodies; served, delivered, or posted to the party's solicitor where he is represented by one in the proceedings; and, where it is a reply to the questionnaire, delivered or posted to the address for reply stated on the questionnaire (Regulation 33(5)).

Although the questionnaire procedure is voluntary, if it appears to the tribunal (or court) that the respondent has deliberately and without reasonable excuse omitted to reply to the questionnaire within eight weeks of its service, or it appears that the reply is evasive or equivocal, the tribunal (or court) may draw any inferences from that fact as it considers just and equitable (Regulation 33(2)(b)). This includes inferences that the respondent committed the unlawful act of discrimination/harassment complained of. It is this provision that makes the questionnaire a powerful weapon in discrimination cases. If the respondent accurately and honestly answers all the questions this may provide useful information for the complainant to rely on. If he does not do so, it may be possible to draw inferences that the reasons for no reply, or an evasive reply, is that he did indeed commit the act of discrimination complained of.

Questionnaires can be particularly useful in indirect discrimination claims when the complainant seeks a breakdown of the religion or belief/sexual orientation of the respondent's staff, or applicants for employment. However, it will often be difficult for a respondent to honestly supply such information because he does not have it in the first place and to seek to elicit it from employees/job applicants may itself provoke complaints of discrimination. One way round this is for anonymous surveys to be done of the employer's staff and job applicants. This can be done without invading the privacy of those asked to complete such surveys, and without compulsion. Employer's should consider keeping such records on file so that they can provide them if a complaint is brought against them. Many employers already maintain such information in relation to race, sex, nationality, disability etc, so it would only be a necessary to add a few questions to existing forms. If the employer was unable to provide a complete breakdown of staff, the fact that it had taken reasonable steps to compile one should be sufficient to prevent any adverse inferences being made.

Another useful question to ask in questionnaires relates to previous or similar complaints received about an alleged harasser, and/or how such complaints were dealt with.

If a complainant is unable to serve a questionnaire for any reason, usually because he is out of time to do so, it is always possible to serve a request for further and better particulars of a respondent's Notice of Appearance (and a respondent can serve a request for further and better particulars of the complainant's Originating Application). In certain circumstances it is possible to get the tribunal to order further and better particulars to be provided. Whilst the provisions applying to questionnaires do not apply to such requests, in practical terms it is often possible to use them for the same result.

7.2.4 Burden of Proof in Employment Tribunals

At the hearing itself, once certain evidence is adduced by the complainant, the burden of proof will shift to the respondent. Regulation 29 provides that, where the complainant has proven facts from which the tribunal could conclude that, in the absence of an adequate explanation by the respondent, an act of unlawful discrimination or harassment had occurred, the tribunal shall uphold the complaint unless the respondent proves he did not commit the unlawful act. So if, for instance, a complainant proved he had been forced to work during a period he had requested he could have as a break for prayer, then this will shift the burden of proof onto the respondent. The complainant has proved a fact from which the tribunal could conclude that discrimination contrary to Regulation 3 of the EE (Religion or Belief) Regulations had occurred, so it would then be for the respondent to show the act was not discriminatory or, to the extent it was an act that could amount to indirect discrimination, it was justified in the circumstances.

The shifting of the burden of proof is highly significant and can be of great importance for the complainant. Discrimination cases are notoriously difficult to prove and inferences often have to be made. If the burden of proof shifts from the complainant to the respondent, it will be much easier for the complainant to succeed in his claim.

The burden of proof provision in Regulation 29 is necessary to give effect to the Framework Directive. Article 10(1) of the Directive provides that when a complainant proves

. . . facts from which it may be presumed that there has been direct or indirect discrimination, it shall be for the respondent to prove that there has been no breach of the principle of equal treatment.

Similar provisions shifting the burden of proof have been added to the RRA (s 54A) and the SDA (s 63A) as a result of EC Directives. The case law under s 63A of the

SDA in particular has demonstrated that the shifting of the burden of proof is by no means a straightforward or uncontroversial matter. However, the following observations will generally be true. The complainant must first prove the facts from which the tribunal could conclude discrimination—if he cannot he will fail. In deciding whether the complainant has proved the relevant facts, the question will usually be, 'what inferences can be drawn from primary facts?'. As the Regulations use the word 'could' ('from which the tribunal could . . . conclude'), the tribunal does not have to reach a definitive conclusion before the burden shifts. Inferences can be drawn from the response to questionnaires. Once facts have been proved from which the tribunal could infer discrimination/harassment, the burden shifts to the respondent (see eg, *Barton v Investec* [2003] IRLR 332, EAT, a case considering s 63A SDA).

7.2.5 Remedies in the Employment Tribunal

Regulation 30 provides that the employment tribunal has the power to order three types of remedy where the complainant has been successful in his claim under the Regulations. First, the tribunal can make an order declaring the rights of the complainant and respondent in relation to the complaint (Regulation 30(1)(a)). Secondly, the tribunal can make an order requiring the respondent to pay the complainant compensation (Regulation 30(1)(b)). Thirdly the tribunal may make a recommendation that the respondent take reasonably practicable steps to obviate or reduce the adverse effect on the complainant of any act of discrimination or harassment (Regulation 30(1)(c)).

7.2.5.1 *Compensation*
The vast majority of complaints will involve claims for compensation. The amount of compensation that will be awarded will be the same amount as the complainant would be entitled to receive in damages if he had brought the claim in a county court or sheriff court. The following heads of compensation are available:

(i) *Past loss.* This will be the amount the complainant lost up until the date of the hearing. It may include lost wages, the costs of looking for alternative employment, or any other loss caused by the unlawful act under the Regulations. So, if a complainant claims he was refused a Christmas bonus because he was not a Christian, his past loss will include the loss of that bonus.

(ii) *Future loss.* Again this covers loss of earnings, benefits, pensions etc. This can be a quite difficult head to calculate, and a number of factors will have to be taken into account. The approach to the calculation of future losses will be the same under the Regulations as it is under the RRA, SDA, and DDA. Where a complainant claims he has suffered personal injury as a result of the discrimination he has suffered that prevents him from working again, or working again in a similar environment, that claim will be dealt with under this head.

(iii) *Injury to feelings.* This is compensation for the hurt to a complainant's feelings that the discrimination has caused. It is a difficult head to predict exactly. Injury to feelings awards in RRA and SDA complaints have not always been the same, but nevertheless, the Court of Appeal decision in *Vento v Chief Constable of West Yorkshire Police (No 2)* [2002] EWCA Civ 1871, [2003] IRLR 102, CA provides useful guidance for the correct level of compensation for injury to feelings in complaints of race or sex discrimination. This guidance should be relevant to complaints of discrimination under the Regulations. In *Vento*, the Court said that for the most serious acts of discrimination/harassment, the top level of compensation would be between £15,000 and £25,000; the middle level award, appropriate for serious cases that did not merit the highest amount, would be between £5,000 and £15,000; the lowest award, appropriate for less serious cases, such as where the act of discrimination is an isolated or one-off occurrence, would be between £500 and £5,000.

(iv) *Aggravated damages.* These are available in discrimination claims. Generally they will be appropriate where a respondent's behaviour in defending a claim, perhaps by acting in an aggressive and dishonest way throughout the proceedings, has aggravated the damage done to the complainant by the original discrimination. The case of *Vento*, again, provides useful guidance as to how this ought to be calculated.

(v) *Exemplary damages.* In very exceptional cases, where the conduct complained of was oppressive, arbitrary, or unconstitutional action by servants of the Government, *and* where the respondent's conduct was calculated by him to make a profit for himself which may exceed the compensation to the claimant, then a tribunal has the power to award exemplary damages (see *Kuddus v Chief Constable of Leicestershire Constabulary* [2001] UKHL 29, [2001] 3 All ER 193).

Normal principles apply to awards of compensation. Thus, the complainant has a duty to take reasonable steps to mitigate his financial loss and if he fails to do so his compensation should be decreased accordingly.

Unlike some other areas of employment law, most obviously unfair dismissal, there is no statutory upper limit on the amount of compensation a tribunal can award in cases involving a breach of the Regulations.

By virtue of Regulation 30(4), where the tribunal makes an award of compensation it may include an award for interest on that amount in accordance with the provisions of the Employment Tribunals (Interest on Awards in Discrimination Cases) Regulations 1996 (SI 1996/2803).

Where the act complained of is indirect discrimination falling within Regulation 3(1)(b) of the Regulations and the respondent proves it was unintentional, the tribunal can only make an award of compensation if it has made a declaration or recommendation and it considers it just *and* equitable to do so. Where a recommendation has been made and has not been complied with, the tribunal can award compensation or increase any award of compensation it has already made (see Regulation 30(2)).

7.2.5.2 *Recommendations*

The tribunal can make a recommendation that the respondent take action, within a specified period, 'for the purpose of obviating or reducing the adverse effect on the complainant of any act of discrimination or harassment to which the complaint relates' (Regulation 20(1)(c)). This provision is similar to those found in s 56(1) of the RRA, s 65(1) of the SDA, and the slightly wider power under s 8(2)(c) DDA. It has been held that the similar provision in the SDA entitles a tribunal to recommend that a Deputy Chief Constable discuss the findings of a complaint of sexual harassment, in which the police were found liable, with the named officers (*Chief Constable of West Yorkshire Police v Vento* (No 2) [2002] IRLR 177, EAT). Thus, where a complainant is successful in a complaint arising out of sexual orientation harassment he has been subjected to by work colleagues, the tribunal ought to be able to make a recommendation, for instance, that the respondent provide for sexual orientation harassment and equality training for the workers involved.

Where a respondent fails to comply with a recommendation made by an employment tribunal without reasonable justification the tribunal can make an order of compensation against the respondent, or, where it has already made such an order, increase the amount of compensation the respondent must pay the complainant (Regulation 30(3)). It should be noted that the recommendation remedy is only available to employment tribunals; a county court or sheriff court does not have jurisdiction to make such recommendations.

7.3 COMPLAINTS IN THE COUNTY COURT/SHERIFF COURTS

Much of the structure of the Regulations concerning complaints to the county court in England and Wales or the sheriff court in Scotland is substantially the same as that considered in relation to employment tribunals. This section only focuses on the differences. The reader should refer to the section above if more detailed discussion is required.

7.3.1 Jurisdiction of the County and Sheriff Courts

Regulation 31 provides that where a person (the claimant) claims that another (the respondent) has committed against the claimant any act of discrimination or harassment, unlawful by virtue of Regulation 20 (institutions of further and higher education), or by virtue of Regulation 21 taken with Regulation 20 (where a Regulation 20 relationship has come to an end), he may bring civil proceedings against the respondent in a county court in England and Wales and in a sheriff court in Scotland. The civil proceedings will be a claim in tort or (in Scotland) in reparation for breach of statutory duty. The normal court rules (ie the Civil Procedure Rules in England and Wales) will apply to such a claim. It is apparent that only students in institutions of further or higher education, applicants to study, or former students in the same, may bring a claim under the regulations by this route.

7.3.2 When Proceedings Must be Brought

By Regulation 34(2) a county court or sheriff court shall not consider a claim brought under Regulation 31 unless the proceedings are brought before the end of the period of six months beginning when the act, or last act, complained of was done. This is a longer period than the time limit for employment tribunals. As with provisions for employment tribunals, a county court or sheriff court can consider a claim that is brought outside this period where it considers it just and equitable in the circumstances to do so (Regulations 24(3)). The principles discussed in section 7.2.2, above, will be relevant here.

7.3.3 The Questionnaire Procedure

The questionnaire procedure, discussed above (see section 7.2.3) also applies to county courts and sheriff courts. The only difference concerns time limits, and this reflects the longer time limit in which a claim in the county and sheriff courts can be made. Thus, if the questionnaire is served before court proceedings are instituted, it must be served within six months of the act complained of; if it is served after proceedings have been instituted, it must serve the questionnaire subject to, and within a period specified by, the court in question (Regulation 33(3)).

7.3.4 Burden of Proof in County Courts and Sheriff Courts

Regulation 32 provides that the burden of proof will shift from the claimant in exactly the same circumstances as it will shift in the employment tribunals, discussed above in section 7.2.4. There is no material difference between these provisions.

7.3.5 Remedies in County Courts and Sheriff Courts

There is no specific Regulation concerning remedies in the county courts and sheriff courts. The normal rules in relation to damages will apply. As this is the case with employment tribunal claims for discrimination in any event, the approach to compensation discussed above (section 7.2.5.1) applies to these courts as it does to employment tribunals. In particular, Regulation 31(3) makes clear 'for the avoidance of doubt' that damages awarded by these courts may include compensation for injury to feelings whether or not they include compensation for any other head of loss.

The only material difference in terms of remedy is that the county courts and sheriff courts do not have the jurisdiction to make the recommendations an employment tribunal can make under Regulation 30(1)(c) (see section 7.2.5.2, above).

7.4 THE COMMISSION FOR EQUALITY AND HUMAN RIGHTS

On 30 October 2003, the Government announced it was setting up a new Commission for Equality and Human Rights. The aim of the Commission is to 'promote an inclusive agenda, underlining the importance of equality for all in society as well as working to combat discrimination affecting specific groups'. It will also promote citizenship and human rights.

The Commission will replace the various existing anti-discrimination commissions, the Equal Opportunities Commission (which is concerned with sex discrimination), the Commission for Racial Equality (which is concerned with racial discrimination), and the Disability Rights Commission (which is concerned with disability discrimination). Instead of different Commissions to protect the interests of different groups, the aim is to create a single unified statutory Commission to promote equality and tackle discrimination across the board. In addition to continuing the work of the existing Commissions, the new Commission will promote sexual orientation, religion and belief, and age equality.

Under the RRA, SDA, and DDA, the existing Commissions have various statutory functions related to enforcement of the anti-discrimination acts. These include powers to assist complainants bringing complaints in the employment tribunal and, in some circumstances, the power to initiate investigations, issue statutory non-discrimination notices, and bring proceedings in their own name.

The new unified Commission can be expected to take on these functions, and thus, although the Regulations are currently silent on the matter, it is reasonable to assume that the new Commission will provide various further means by which the Regulations can be enforced. It is too early to speculate on exactly what these will be; the Government is embarking on a consultation process regarding the new Commission in spring 2004 and does not anticipate the new Commission will be up and running until late 2006 at the earliest. In the meantime, it would appear that religion or belief and sexual orientation discrimination is left in somewhat of a lacuna, being the only areas of anti-discrimination law which do not have the backing of a statutory body to promote the aims and assist in the enforcement of the Regulations.

8

SPECIFIC ISSUES IN RELATION TO RELIGION OR BELIEF DISCRIMINATION

8.1 INTRODUCTION

The aim of this chapter is to review the specific issues likely to arise in relation to the EE (Religion or Belief) Regulations. Much of this chapter will cross-refer to other chapters which deal with the Regulations in turn. Naturally there will be an overlap in some areas. In order to have a full understanding of how the Regulations work, and all the potential issues that may arise, the reader needs to read the general chapters on the Regulations (Chapters 1–7) in addition to this chapter.

This chapter hopes to be of use to newcomers to the Regulations, to those concerned to ensure their workplace complies with them, and to those who may wish to rely on them. It should also be of interest to specialist lawyers and representatives interested in examining situations in which religion or belief discrimination can arise.

8.2 THE SCOPE OF 'RELIGION OR BELIEF'

The EE (Religion or Belief) Regulations prohibit discrimination and harassment on grounds of religion or belief. Regulation 2(1) explains that 'religion or belief' means any religion, religious belief, or similar philosophical belief. What exactly is meant by this description is discussed in some detail in section 2.2 above. It is clear that members of all religions, and not just 'organized religions' are protected. So is the holding of any particular religious belief, whether or not it is connected with a religion. It is also clear that the words 'similar philosophical belief' are intended to include people who did not believe in religion or in God. In specific, atheists, humanists, secularists, and agnostics are protected by the Regulations.

Rather than produce a list of religions or religious beliefs that are protected, the Government preferred the general wording in the Regulations. Otherwise there might be disputes as to what religions or beliefs ought to be on such a list, and such a list could become out of date as soon as new beliefs develop. Nevertheless, the ACAS guidance to these Regulations has provided a useful list of the most commonly practised religions in Britain based on the most recent census information. This list has no legislative authority, as all religions and beliefs are covered by the Regulations. However, it demonstrates the wide number of different religions practised, and importantly it gives basic details of each one. Readers are referred to the list in Appendix 2 of the ACAS guidance, which can be found in Appendix 4 of this book. The religions listed there are as follows: Baha'i, Buddhism, Christianity, Hinduism, Islam, Jainism, Judaism, Rastafarianism, Sikhism, and Zoroastrianism. Of course, even within these generic groups there will be many different types of religions. Methodism and Presbyterianism are just two of many different denominations that call themselves Christians. Shi'ites and Sunnis are two of the largest different groups within the Muslim religion, but many smaller groupings exist. Each different religion or faction of a religion will often have different patterns of worship and observance so it is important to avoid stereotypes.

It is perhaps even more difficult to determine what a 'similar philosophical belief' is, except that ministerial statements appear to confirm that this phrase is intended to include atheists, agnostics, humanists, and secularists. According to the Office of the Deputy Prime Minister's Notes on the Draft Regulations, courts and tribunals will have to consider a number of factors when deciding what a 'religion or belief' is including 'collective worship, clear belief system, profound belief affecting way of life or view of the world'.

The absence of a religious belief should also fall within the definition of a 'similar philosophical belief' to religion. Whilst this sounds like an oxymoron, if 'similar philosophical belief' includes atheism, which is premised on the positive disbelief in a Supreme Being, then a 'belief system' that includes a rejection of all religions and similar strong beliefs must also fall within the same category. When one scrutinizes the meaning of the words here there is some danger of wandering into the realm of philosophy. Courts and tribunals should take a practical approach. The real issue is whether a person is being discriminated against on *grounds* of religion or belief. A religious person is quite capable of discriminating against an atheist on grounds of the atheist's religion, or lack of it. It is still religious discrimination.

8.3 WHETHER BELIEF IS 'PHILOSOPHICAL' OR 'POLITICAL'

The Regulations are not intended to protect political beliefs. This is clear in some of the consultative and draft guidance documents. Some political beliefs may be protected in other ways, for instance under the HRA, Article 10 of the European Convention of Human Rights protects freedom of expression from interference by a public authority, and Article 11 protects the right of freedom of assembly (including the right to belong to a political party). In Northern Ireland constitutional legislation prohibits discrimination on grounds of religion and 'political belief' (see section 1.2, above). Dismissing a person for their political beliefs may constitute unfair dismissal contrary to the Employment Rights Act 1996. But the EC Framework Directive, on which the Regulations are based, and the Regulations themselves, are not intended to protect political beliefs.

However, just as it is not easy to define religion or similar philosophical belief, so it is not always easy to distinguish 'political belief' from philosophical beliefs. This is discussed in section 2.2 above. It is likely that an employment tribunal will have to reach a decision on this issue at some point, for example in relation to a decision to prohibit members of the British National Party from employment in certain fields. It is most unlikely that such a decision would fall foul of the Regulations.

Some religions or philosophies can be described as political. Certain types of Islam can be understood both in terms of a religious belief and a political ideology. Secularism can be both a 'similar philosophical belief' and a political view about how best to organize society. It is suggested that the best approach to this issue is to accept that the Regulations may, at times, protect what could be described as political beliefs, but *only* where those beliefs are at the same time either religious or similar philosophical beliefs. What the Regulations do not do is protect mere political beliefs, such as the right to be a member or supporter of a particular political party, or to have a strong view on a 'political issue', such as opposition to identity cards.

8.4 DISCRIMINATION IN RECRUITMENT PRACTICES

The first stage in the employment context that discrimination is likely to occur is before the formal employment relationship even begins, at the recruitment or even pre-recruitment stage where an employer is deciding how to advertise his job vacancy or how to select the most appropriate candidate. Discrimination at this stage is covered by Regulation 6(1)(a) of the EE (Religion or Belief) Regulations prohibiting discrimination on grounds of religion or belief 'in the arrangements [an employer] makes for the purpose of determining whom he should offer employment' (see section 3.2.1, above).

One of the first things an employer should consider is how he advertises the vacancy. Where a vacancy is filled by word of mouth there is always a risk of discrimination. People in the same social circle, or friends and family, might be the only people to know about the vacancy. These people will often share the same religion or belief, or the same attitude to a particular religion or belief. It might be impossible for a Buddhist, who is not in this social circle, to ever hear about the job in the first place. Advertising should be aimed at the most diverse and wide audience possible. Employers need to give some consideration to whether their advertising will reach a diverse audience. For instance, if an employer only advertised by notice board in a pub he is likely to indirectly discriminate against Muslims, since proportionately Muslims are less likely to frequent alcoholic establishments than non-Muslims.

It will not necessarily be unlawful to advertise in religious newspapers aimed at specific communities. Apart from circumstances where there is a genuine occupational requirement to fill a vacancy with a person of a particular religion or belief, or where it is appropriate to take positive action to encourage members of a particular religion to apply for a job, this kind of advertising can still be acceptable if a number of different newspapers are targeted. For instance, in a particular neighbourhood it may be just as likely that local residents read a Sikh newspaper published in Punjabi as read the local English (secular) newspaper. To advertise in the Sikh paper would not necessarily discriminate against non-Sikhs, and to fail to do so may in fact discriminate against Sikhs; so long as the advertisement is also put in the English local newspaper there should not be discrimination.

The ACAS guidance to these Regulations correctly highlights the importance of ensuring that any recruitment process that includes a social gathering should avoid disadvantaging anyone who, for reasons of religion or belief, has special dietary requirements or abstains from alcohol (see paragraph 2.6 of the ACAS guidance, Appendix 4 below). This does not mean that employers need to provide a whole range of different foods catering for every potential applicant. The Regulations do not put unreasonable burdens on employers. Rather, it means that some elementary thought should go into ensuring that certain people are not excluded. Increasingly employers do use social gatherings to recruit from. Where those gatherings are dominated by alcohol, or where only meat is available to eat, there are real risks that certain individuals will feel unable to participate because of their religion or belief.

The ACAS guidance also stresses that the selection criteria and interview process should be focused on a person's skills and experience for the job, and not on irrelevant factors that may lead to discrimination. If, for instance, a particular employer was himself an enthusiastic Christian, he should avoid asking job applicants if they go to church, or send their children to a religious school, in the job interview. It is unlikely that the answers to such questions would have any relevance to the applicant's ability to do the job, but there is a real risk that asking them will lead to discrimination, however unintentional, or even harassment, on grounds of religion or belief.

8.5 PERCEPTION OF RELIGION OR BELIEF

The Regulations prohibit discrimination on grounds of religion or belief. It is the grounds of the discrimination that are important, not the religion of the discriminated person. Discrimination on grounds of religion or belief includes discrimination based on a person's perception of another's religion or belief, whether or not that perception is right (see section 2.5.1.4, above). It is the assumptions made by the discriminator/harasser that matter.

For example, consider an employer who did not want to employ any Muslims in his factory because he was concerned that this might lead to difficulties with some of the Hindu workforce. The employer receives some written application forms and two of the applicants have Islamic names. He decides not to invite these two applicants for an interview because he does not want to employ any Muslims. If one of the job applicants was in fact a Muslim, he would obviously have a claim for unlawful direct discrimination under the Regulations. But if the other was not a Muslim, and was in fact an atheist or a Hindu who had been given an Islamic name at birth but had stopped being Muslim at an early age, he has just the same claim as the Muslim applicant. The second applicant was discriminated against on grounds of religion, he was not invited to an interview because the employer perceived that he was Muslim. The employer's perception was wrong, but that does not matter. The *reason* for the discrimination was religion, and the second applicant has a claim for unlawful direct discrimination.

The same applies to cases of harassment. If a group of workers are told by someone that one of their colleagues is a practising Zoroastrian, and as a result they tease and mock this worker, then the worker may be able to bring a complaint to an employment tribunal that he has been unlawfully harassed on grounds of religion contrary to Regulation 5 of the Regulations. Whether or not he is in fact a Zoroastrian is irrelevant to his right to bring a claim. If he has been subjected to harassment on grounds of religion, then even though his work colleagues based their assumptions on incorrect assumptions, he will have a valid complaint.

This approach is obviously sensible. It focuses on the reason for the discrimination—religion or belief—and not the religion of the discriminated person. The aim of the Regulations is to outlaw discrimination on grounds of religion or belief in the workplace, whether or not that discrimination is based on correct assumptions. And discrimination based on incorrect assumptions can be as pernicious as discrimination based on 'correct' assumptions. The person who was not invited to a job interview because it was thought he was Muslim has suffered to the same extent as the person who was in fact Muslim. In the aftermath of the 11 September 2001 attack on the New York World Trade Centre there was a rise in attacks on, and harassment against, Muslims and people who attackers believed were Muslim. It is no less objectionable for a Sikh man to be attacked because his attackers thought he 'looked like a Muslim' than for a Muslim to be attacked. By focusing on the reason for the discrimination, and not the religion of the discriminated, the Regulations reflect society's disapproval of such irrational discrimination and hatred. It should be noted that in focusing on the 'reason' for the discrimination, however, it is not necessary to demonstrate that the discriminator was *motivated* by prejudice against a particular religion—he may unknowingly discriminate—it is the *grounds* of the discrimination that are important.

The other reason it is important the Regulations focus on the grounds of discrimination, and include discrimination where the discriminator's perception is that someone has a particular religion or belief, is that it could otherwise put unreasonable obstacles in the way of a person trying to prove discrimination. He would have to prove, not only that he was of a particular religion or held a particular belief, but also that the person who discriminated against him knew he held that religion or had that belief. Whilst this might often be straightforward, in some circumstances it might be difficult, and trying to prove this, or allowing an employer to rely on the defence of lack of knowledge, would not be a valuable way to spend the tribunal's time.

In terms of training and the development of anti-harassment programmes, managers and employees should have this feature of the Regulations explained to them. It needs to be clear that discrimination on grounds of religion and belief is prohibited, regardless of the actual religion or belief of the person discriminated against. It will be no defence for a person to say 'I could not have been harassing Mary for being a Catholic, because Mary is in fact not Catholic'.

8.6 DISCRIMINATION ON GROUNDS OF ANOTHER'S RELIGION OR BELIEF

Discrimination, or harassment, will also be unlawful where it is on the grounds of another person's religion or belief (see section 2.5.1.5, above). So, if a person is harassed at work because her husband is a Jehovah's Witness, this is capable of being harassment on grounds of religion or belief, albeit on grounds of another person's religion or belief. Likewise, if a Muslim man is sacked from a job in a small family-run company hostile to non-Muslims because the employer found out the man's daughter married a Christian or a Jew, this will be unlawful discrimination on grounds of religion or belief, even though the sacked man shared the same religion as his employer.

Again, in terms of training, it is therefore important to stress that it is discrimination on grounds of religion or belief that is banned in the workplace, and it does not matter whether the victim was discriminated against because of his own religion or because of the religion of others.

8.7 DIETARY REQUIREMENTS AND ALCOHOL

Many religions have particular dietary requirements. Within the main religions a variety of dietary requirements exist. The religions listed below have particular dietary requirements. The information is based on that set out in Appendix 2 to the ACAS guidance, which is in Appendix 4 of this book. ACAS rightly point out that not all members of each of these religions observe the 'requirements' set out.

Buddhists are vegetarian. So are most Hindus, and many Hindus tend not to eat fish or eggs. Muslims do not eat pork and this can extend to pork lard used in some bread or ice cream. Many Muslims will not eat meat from a carnivorous animal, or a 'scavenger', including most seafood. Where meat is eaten it needs to be slaughtered in the Halal method. During the festival of Ramadan (which falls on the ninth month of the Muslim lunar calendar), Muslims cannot eat (or drink) between sunrise and sunset. Jains are strict vegetarians and avoid eggs. Some will take some dairy products, others will not. Many avoid root vegetables, and Jains do not eat between sunset and sunrise. Many Jews will only eat kosher food, which has been treated and prepared in a particular manner. Observant Jews will not eat pork or seafood. Rastafarians tend to be vegetarian and avoid eggs; many Rastafarians only eat organic food products. Sikhs do not eat Halal meat, many don't eat beef, and many are vegetarian. Some people who are not religious but have a 'similar philosophical belief' may also have certain dietary requirements corresponding to their beliefs. For instance, a Humanist may object to eating meat, or meat that has been killed inhumanely.

Employers should take note of these requirements and take such steps as are reasonable to accommodate them. It will not be reasonable to expect every employer to facilitate for every religion's dietary requirement, but there are some basic steps that it will be reasonable for many employers to take. For instance, where an employer provides a 'work canteen' he should at least ensure there are vegetarian options on the menu. In addition, it would be good practice to ask employees if they have any special dietary requirements—an employer cannot be expected to cater for requirements that might remotely arise, but where he knows particular requirements do exist he should take reasonable steps to cater for them. The larger the employer the more important these issues are likely to be. Employers should also consider these matters when making arrangements for any work-related social activities or meals, and in arrangements made related to recruitment where food is on offer.

The ACAS guidance gives the example of a worker who for religious reasons does not wish to store her vegetarian lunch in the office fridge next to a meat sandwich belonging to a co-worker. In the example, following consultation, all staff are requested to store their food in sealed containers and on separate shelves within the fridge marked 'meat' and 'vegetarian'. This is the kind of sensible arrangement that it might be possible to make without unreasonably interfering in the employer's business.

Many religions abstain from alcohol. Muslims, Jains, most Baha'is, and some Christian churches prohibit alcohol. Traditionally, alcohol has played a central role in British cultural life. Most social events, including work-related social events have not only included alcohol but have in fact revolved around alcohol. From the office Christmas party or 'leaving do', to Friday night drinks, or a meal with clients, it is often commonplace to expect all employees who take part in work-social gatherings to take alcohol, and those who do not can feel quite ostracized. These attitudes and practices will clearly have to change, insofar as the employer, to avoid discrimination on grounds of religion or belief, sanctions them. This does not mean employers need to go to the other extreme and ban alcohol at work-related social functions. Rather, it means that all employees should be catered for. Social events should be devised so that people from all religions can participate. A meal in a restaurant, where some employees may drink and others choose not to is one thing, a night out in a pub, where the only real activity is drinking alcohol, is another.

Alcohol-related work/social events raise a number of potential problems. If the event is in a pub, many people from other religions will be uncomfortable or feel unable to attend. Official work functions, whether social gatherings as part of the recruitment process, or office parties, should wherever possible avoid such environments, which by their nature can exclude some employees by reason of their religion. Even where the employer does not officially sanction such activity, dangers can arise. In many trades and professions, much of the 'bonding' that goes on between employees takes place in the pub or a similar environment. Employees who do not take part in such activities may feel marginalized by their colleagues. Their colleagues may feel such employees do not 'fit in'. This may lead to discrimination or harassment. It is therefore important that employees are given equal opportunities and anti-harassment training that encourages them not to ostracize their colleagues merely because they do not join in alcohol-centred social activities, and to make clear that such treatment may in some circumstances be religious discrimination or harassment.

8.8 CLOTHING AND DRESS

Some religions have dress codes which may conflict with the dress codes of a particular employer. One of the best-known example of this, and one which has been included in legislation for some time, is the wearing of the turban by men in the Sikh religion. By Regulation 26 of the EE (Religion or Belief) Regulations, it is unlawful and unjustifiable indirect discrimination to require a Sikh who wears a turban to wear a safety helmet on a construction site. However, there are numerous other examples of situations in which an employee may be discriminated against on grounds of his religion because his religion's dress code conflicts with his employer's dress code. The difference here will be the employer is entitled to justify the indirect discrimination, whereas he cannot in relation to Sikhs and safety helmets on construction sites (for a discussion of the anomaly, in this regard, whereby one religious group is afforded special protection under the Regulations, see section 6.4, above).

In terms of clothing, Buddhists tend to have a preference for clothing that reflects their adherence to non-harm (eg, not wearing fur or leather goods). Some Christian churches forbid cosmetics and require female members to dress modestly. Hindu women often wear a *bindi*—a red spot on their forehead—denoting membership of the Hindu faith. Married Hindu women may wear a *mangal sutra*—necklace—placed around their necks during the marriage ceremony, in addition to a wedding ring. A few Hindu men will wear a *shikha*—a small tuft of hair similar to a pony tail and often hidden beneath the remaining hair—and some will wear a *tilak*—a clay marking on their foreheads. Muslim men will often wear beards. Muslims are generally required to cover the body. Muslim men may be unable to wear shorts. Many Muslim women cover their whole body, including their head, except their face, hands, and feet (and some will also cover their face). Orthodox Jewish men are required to keep their heads covered, and women to dress modestly and not wear trousers, short skirts, or short sleeves. Some Jewish women will also cover their heads. Rastafarians wear their hair in dreadlocks, often covered by a hat. In addition to the turban, Sikhs will often wear beards, metal bracelets on the right wrist, and a small ceremonial sword hidden under the shirt.

These are just some of the clothing requirements that some of the religions have. It is important to note that the fact that only some members of a particular religion choose to adopt these requirements is irrelevant to their right to do so. If a Jewish woman wishes to cover her head for religious reasons, discrimination against her for doing so will be on grounds of religion (directly or indirectly) regardless of the fact that most Jewish women do not cover their heads. Within each of the 'main' religions there is a wealth of different interpretations of the rules. In the eyes of the Regulations each interpretation is as valid as any other. A Jewish woman who chooses to cover her head has as much right to do so, under the Regulations, as a Muslim woman who chooses to cover her head. It will be no defence for a respondent to say, 'very few Jewish women cover their heads, so it cannot be religious discrimination to insist a Jewish woman does not cover her head'. Of course, if a person dishonestly invents a religious requirement to justify wearing or refusing to wear an article of clothing, this will not fall within the Regulations; they must wear the article for reasons of their religion or belief, and a dishonest invention is not a genuine belief, religious or otherwise. The fact that only a tiny minority of a particular religion choose to adopt a particular dress code does not mean they have no right to do so. However, the more difficult it is for the employer to accommodate a person's dress code—either because of a feature of that code, or because so few people adopt it—the easier it will be for the employer to justify a failure to do so. If he can show his refusal to allow a person to wear a specific article of clothing is reasonably necessary for his business, then the refusal will be justifiable.

There are many examples of circumstances in which religious discrimination could arise in relation to dress codes. Many fast-food outlets and supermarkets, for instance, require their staff to wear a uniform that includes a baseball cap and a T-shirt. Of the religious groups listed above, it is a quite common requirement for some followers to cover their heads. This is sometimes possible to do under a baseball cap, but will not be in all circumstances. Showing bare arms will also be contrary to some of the religious dress codes described. Other working environments do not allow employees to wear hats or beards, sometimes ostensibly for health and safety reasons. This would affect a variety of different religions described above, Muslims, Sikhs, and orthodox Jews in particular.

Rules that a person cannot have a beard or cannot cover his head will be indirectly discriminatory against those who cannot comply with them for religious reasons unless the employer can justify the rule (for justification of indirect discrimination, see section 2.5.2.6, above). It will be difficult to justify such rules. The fact that it is the employer's preference that all employees wear the same uniform will not be enough. Some cases decided under the RRA in relation to Sikhs and beards demonstrate the type of approach the tribunals will take. In *Panesar v Nestlé Co Ltd* [1980] IRLR 64, CA, a Sikh was refused a job in a chocolate factory because he would not shave off his beard. The employer's justification was based on expert evidence about hygiene and succeeded (see also *Singh v Rowntree Mackintosh Ltd* [1979] ICR 554, EAT). So, if the employer can show evidence that the requirement is for genuine health reasons he may be successful at the justification stage, but it is difficult to think of many, general, justifications of a less serious nature that would succeed.

8.9 RELIGIOUS HOLIDAYS AND FESTIVALS

Different religions have holidays and festivals on different calendar days. Lists of the principal festivals of the main religions are contained in Appendix 2 of the ACAS guidance, (Appendix 4 of this book, below). If employees wish to take days off to observe a particular religious festival, they should generally be allowed to do so, providing they have the requisite available annual leave, and provided taking that particular day off would not unreasonably interfere with the employer's business. A refusal to allow an employee to take a day off to observe a religious festival could be direct or indirect discrimination unless the employer can justify the refusal.

In some circumstances where the employee does not have the requisite annual leave left to observe the festival it may be possible to allow him to take the time off as unpaid leave. This will generally depend on business practicalities.

The ACAS guidance gives an example of a small toy shop employing four staff being unable to release one of them to attend a religious festival in the busy pre-Christmas period. The employer will probably be able to justify refusing a request for leave in these circumstances. But where the employer employs 250 staff it will probably be able to cover the same absence of one person, and a refusal would not be justifiable.

8.10 PRAYER FACILITIES

Employees may wish to pray during the working day. For instance, observant Muslims are required to pray five times a day in a quiet and clean place. Prayer times are at dawn (*Fajr*), midday in winter or mid-afternoon in summer (*Zuhr*), mid-afternoon in winter and late afternoon in summer (*Asr*), after sunset (*Maghrib*), and late evening (*Isha*). Three to four of these prayer times could fall within the normal working day. Before prayer Muslims undertake a ritual act of purification that involves the use of running water. Prayer times will take about ten minutes each. Baha'is say between one and three obligatory prayers during the day, in a quiet place, and after washing their hands and face.

Where possible it will be good practice for an employer to consider providing facilities for employees who wish to pray during working hours. There is no requirement to provide a prayer room under the Regulations, but if an employer, particularly a large employer is asked to do so and he has capacity, ie, he has a quiet room that can be used for limited periods as a prayer room, then he should consider doing so. If the room does not include washing facilities it ought to be as close as possible to such facilities. An employer who refuses to provide an employee with facilities for prayer without justification, in circumstances such that the person feels they are unable to express their religious belief, may be found to have indirectly discriminated against a person on grounds of his religion or belief. It should usually be adequate justification if he cannot spare the facilities.

The ACAS guidance suggests, where possible, that it is good practice for organizations to set aside a quiet room for prayer and private contemplation, in consultation with staff, rather than just a general rest room/staff room. This is sensible, and the emphasis on staff consultation is important.

One problem that arises with the issue of prayer rooms is that the provision of them can actually be religious discrimination. Consider a situation where employees share one staff room, and the employer takes it away from them so it can be a designated Muslim 'prayer room'. The employer may have done this in good faith, and/or to avoid being taken to the employment tribunal for religious discrimination under the Regulations. But if he does this without consultation and against the wishes of other employees, not only is this a recipe for an unsatisfactory working environment, but also he may have discriminated against non-Muslims who did not want a prayer room. The non-Muslim employees could argue that they have had a facility taken away from them and given exclusively to Muslims, and that they are therefore being treated less favourably than Muslims on grounds of religion. Consultation and arrangements that do not provide preferential treatment to one group over another is thus important. So are the practicalities of space. It would be most satisfactory if employees could have a normal rest room, where they could talk, eat, etc, and one for prayer and 'contemplation', but this might not always be possible. Even if it is, the 'prayer or contemplation room' ought to be one that atheists who just wish to sit and read, for instance, feel as welcome within as those who wish to use it for religious observance. Naturally, arrangements might need to be made so that the room is used in 'shifts' where different people wish to use it for different purposes.

In terms of allowing employees the time to take a break in order to pray, the ACAS guidance points out that those who wish to take this opportunity could do so instead of the other rest or tea breaks during the day, as prayer would take approximately the same time. This is a sensible approach where possible, although not all employees have such frequent breaks during the working day in the first place.

The issue of 'prayer rooms' can be quite a controversial one, and it will not necessarily be easy for employers to deal with. However, it is one that is likely to become an important one. In universities and further education colleges there have been various campaigns to provide such facilities, and ultimately authorities have tended to provide them where possible. This pattern is likely to be repeated in the sphere of employment, particularly within large organizations or ones with a significant number of employees from groups who require prayer facilities. Considering the difficulties that might arise, consultation with staff will be very important in this respect.

It should go without saying that an employer who, considering this or any of the other potential issues that might arise under the Regulations, decides to avoid offering a job to a person he believes is strongly religious and therefore might cause him trouble is a foolish employer. To do so would be direct discrimination under the Regulations, something the employer would not be able to justify.

8.11 WASHING AND SHOWERING FACILITIES

Where employees are obliged as part of their employment to wash or shower at the place of employment, the ACAS guidance recommends that it is good practice, where possible, to explore how this could be achieved without forcing an employee of a particular religion or belief to undress or shower in the company of others. This is because some religions do not allow individuals to undress in front of others. The provision of same-sex facilities will not necessarily resolve this issue, as some religions do not allow individuals to undress in front of others even of the same sex.

Whilst this might arise less frequently than the request for prayer rooms, and whilst it would appear to raise some similar issues (eg issues of space and physically available facilities), there are added risks for employers here. If a person has informed his employer that it is against his religion or belief to undress in front of others, and if that person is then forced to do so, this might be regarded as harassment on grounds of a person's belief and could certainly be regarded as indirect discrimination unless justified (it is more likely to be treated as indirect discrimination because the reason for the requirement, eg, 'health and safety', and the requirement, is applied equally to all). In any event, considering the distress it may cause an individual to force him to undress in front of others contrary to his religion, it will be difficult to justify. Where facilities are communal, therefore, it might be better to either exempt the employee from having to shower there at all, or make arrangements so that he can shower there on his own.

8.12 WHERE DIFFERENTIAL TREATMENT MIGHT BE ACCEPTABLE

Most of the examples considered above are incidents that could amount to indirect discrimination where the employer is unable to justify them. However, there are two general types of situation under the Regulations where what otherwise could be described as direct discrimination can be justified. These are where the employer positively discriminates in favour of a person of a particular religion or belief, or where the employer can show there is a genuine occupational requirement to employ a person of a particular religion or belief.

Positive action, ie discriminating in favour of a person on grounds of their religion or belief, is lawful under Regulation 25 of the EE (Religion or Belief) Regulations in certain circumstances. Regulation 25 is considered in section 6.3 above. An example is given in section 6.3.3 about advertising for a local authority housing officer in a Muslim newspaper to overcome the disproportionately small number of Muslims applying for that role. Another example could relate to training. If an employer found that Christian employees tended to be more likely to be promoted in their jobs than atheist, Hindu, and Sikh employees in the same company, it would not be unlawful for him to afford training to those disadvantaged groups in order to assist their chances of promotion, and therefore combat the discrimination they face, in the future.

In relation to the second area, the genuine occupational requirement, this is discussed in Chapter 5 above. Under Regulation 7 of the EE (Religion or Belief) Regulations, an employer has a defence to claims of both direct and indirect discrimination where he can show that it is a genuine occupational requirement for him to employ a person holding a particular religion or belief. Examples of this are provided in Chapter 5. A genuine occupational requirement will only arise in exceptional circumstances. An employer should take great care before deciding that a particular job vacancy must be filled by a person of a particular religion or belief. A genuine occupational requirement could apply to certain jobs in health and welfare, and nearly all jobs in religious instruction, but beyond this its application will be rare.

8.13 DISCIPLINARY, GRIEVANCE, AND ANTI-HARASSMENT POLICIES

It is very important that employers have clear procedures for dealing with discrimination and harassment on grounds of religion or belief. If religion or belief discrimination is not part of an employer's equal opportunities policy, the employer should revise and update the policy to include it. Employers should also consider developing anti-harassment procedures, whether as part of the equal opportunities, disciplinary, or grievance policies and procedures, or as a freestanding policy and procedure.

Broadly speaking, anti-harassment procedures should set out what is regarded as harassment, and the grounds on which harassment will be prohibited. For instance employers will want to prohibit racial, sexual, and sexual orientation harassment, and harassment on grounds of disability and religion or belief. The policy should explain that religion or belief harassment is generally defined as unwanted words or conduct based on or caused by a person's religion or belief, another person's religion or belief, or a person's perception about the victim's religion or belief, which has the effect of violating the victim's dignity, or of creating an intimidating, hostile, degrading, humiliating, or offensive environment for the victim. The unwanted conduct may consist of one particularly serious incident, or a series of less serious incidents. A discussion of the form and stages of such a procedure can be found below under section 9.12 (dealing with the comparable issue in relation to sexual orientation).

From October 2004, new measures to encourage employers and employees to resolve disputes before bringing complaints in the employment tribunal come into force. A new mandatory statutory disciplinary procedure is set to come into force (see Employment Act 2002, Sch 2, Part I). In addition, a new statutory grievance procedure should come into force. Under the standard procedure there will be three stages (see Employment Act 2002, Sch 2, Part II), which must be initiated by the employee:

(i) The employee sets down in writing the nature of the alleged grievance and sends the written complaint to the employer. He/she must inform the employee of the basis for his/her complaint.

(ii) The employer should invite the employee to at least one hearing at a reasonable time and place at which the alleged grievance can be discussed. The employee should take all reasonable steps to attend. After the meeting, the employer must inform the employee about any decision, and offer the employee the right of appeal.

(iii) If the employee considers that the grievance has not been satisfactorily resolved, he/she should inform the employer that he wishes to appeal against the employer's decision or failure to make a decision. The employer should arrange a meeting to discuss the appeal. After the meeting, the employer's final decision should be communicated to the employee.

If the employer or employee fails to comply with the procedures there will be serious implications for any subsequent complaint brought in the employment tribunal. Most importantly, if an employee does not submit a grievance under stage 1 of the standard procedure, where that procedure applies, his complaint to an employment tribunal will be inadmissible. Under the legislation proposed, this includes complaints of discrimination under the EE (Religion or Belief) Regulations. Failure to comply with procedures may also make dismissals automatically unfair and lead to an increase or decrease in the compensation awarded depending on which party is at fault.

It is therefore essential that employers revisit their procedures to see they comply with statutory developments and the EE Regulations, and that employees, their union representatives, or legal advisors familiarize themselves with these procedures and make sure that they are followed where appropriate.

8.14 CONCLUSION

The examples of discrimination that may arise under the Regulations discussed in this chapter are just some of the more obvious that are likely to arise. There are many other situations in which discrimination or harassment on grounds of religion or belief may arise. This area of discrimination law is a new one, and it will take some time to properly determine the limits and extent of the Regulations. Tribunals, lawyers, employers, and employees' representatives will have to think creatively about the circumstances in which religion or belief discrimination might arise, and about what is, and what is not, properly discrimination on these grounds. Many of the *principles* from race and sex discrimination cases will be of assistance in understanding and applying the Regulations, but the *type* of discrimination made unlawful under the Regulations is quite different. The discrimination is not based on a genetic or ethnic fact, but on a belief. People rarely agree about beliefs, and strong feelings can be provoked by religious beliefs. The underlying principle of these Regulations is that whatever a person thinks of another's fundamental belief, nobody should be discriminated against in relation to their employment for holding or observing that belief.

9

SPECIFIC ISSUES IN RELATION TO SEXUAL ORIENTATION DISCRIMINATION

9.1 INTRODUCTION

The aim of this chapter is to consider the specific issues likely to arise in relation to the EE (Sexual Orientation) Regulations. Much of this chapter will cross-refer to other chapters which deal with the Regulations in turn. There will be overlap in some areas. In order to have a full understanding of how the Regulations work, and all the potential issues that may arise, the reader is advised to read the general chapters on the Regulations (Chapters 1–7), in addition to this chapter.

This chapter hopes to be of use to newcomers to the Regulations, to those concerned to ensure their workplace conforms to them, and to those who may wish to rely on them. It should also be of interest to specialist lawyers and legal representatives interested in considering examples of the circumstances in which sexual orientation discrimination can arise.

9.2 SCOPE: SEXUAL ORIENTATION NOT OTHER SEXUAL PREFERENCE

Regulation 2(1) of the EE (Sexual Orientation) Regulations defines sexual orientation as meaning a sexual orientation towards persons of the same sex, the opposite sex, or the same sex and the opposite sex (see section 2.3, above). It thus prohibits discrimination on grounds that a person is (or is assumed to be) lesbian or gay, heterosexual, or bisexual. In that sense discrimination on grounds of any sexual orientation is prohibited. It is just as unlawful for a gay man to discriminate against a heterosexual or bisexual man as it would be for a heterosexual woman to discriminate against a lesbian woman.

This is, however, a limited definition of 'sexual orientation'. The term sexual orientation, as used in these Regulations, does *not* mean sexual preference. It only means the three orientations set out in Regulation 2(1). If a person has a preference for other types of sexual behaviour, such as sado-masochism or paedophilia, discrimination on grounds of such a preference will not necessarily be unlawful under the Regulations—even where the sexual preference or behaviour exhibited is itself lawful.

For example, in *Pay v Lancashire Probation Service* (Unreported, Appeal No EAT/1224/02/LA, 29 October 2003, EAT) the Employment Appeal Tribunal found that the decision of the respondent to dismiss a probation officer who ran an internet company selling bondage and sado-masochism merchandise in his spare time was not unlawful. The applicant dealt with sex offenders and the respondent decided his activities outside work were not compatible with his duties, and brought the service into disrepute. He claimed this infringed his rights under Article 8 (right to privacy) and Article 10 (freedom of expression) of the European Convention on Human Rights. The EAT found Article 8 was not engaged as he had put his activities into the public domain (via the internet) and that the respondent's interference in the applicant's right to freedom of expression was justified by the respondent's right to uphold its reputation. Mr Pay's activities were not unlawful and were an expression of his sexual preference but he was dismissed for them. Although this case was decided before the Regulations came into force, the result would probably be the same now. But, if a probation officer—including one who worked with sex offenders—advertised his sexual preference for men, perhaps over an Internet gay dating service, and was then dismissed, this would most probably be discrimination in breach of Regulation 3 of the EE (Sexual Orientation) Regulations. This demonstrates the difference between the prohibition on sexual orientation discrimination contained in the Regulations, and the wider issue of sexual preference discrimination which is outside of the scope of the Regulations.

The Regulations also do not cover discrimination against transsexuals. This is already unlawful by s 2A of the SDA, which prohibits discrimination against a person on grounds that the person 'intends to undergo, is undergoing or has undergone gender reassignment'. Furthermore, discrimination against a person on grounds of gender reassignment is contrary to Article 14 of the European Convention of Human Rights, and the implication of this in domestic employment law since *Goodwin v UK* [2002] 35 EHRR 447, E Ct HR and *Chief Constable of the West Yorkshire Police v A and another (No 2)* [2002] EWCA Civ 1584, [2003] ICR 161, HL, is that it is discrimination to treat an employee or applicant for employment who has undergone gender reassignment from, for instance, male to female, as a man. These issues fall outside the scope of the Regulations.

9.3 DISCRIMINATION IN RECRUITMENT PRACTICES

Regulation 6(1)(a) of the EE (Sexual Orientation) Regulations prohibits discrimination on grounds of sexual orientation in the arrangements an employer makes for the purpose of determining whom he should offer employment (see section 3.2.1, above).

It is important that employers advertise job vacancies to a broad and diverse spectrum of potential applicants. Job vacancies that are communicated by word of mouth are likely to discriminate on grounds of sexual orientation. In particular, where job vacancies are made known by employees informing their spouse or children of the vacancy, this will indirectly discriminate against lesbian and gay job applicants.

An advertisement in a gay newspaper or magazine might indirectly discriminate against heterosexual job applicants who do not read such publications. However, so long as the advertisement is not targeted exclusively at lesbians and gay men, advertising in a gay newspaper should not necessarily be unlawful. If the employer simply wants to encourage people from a variety of walks of life, including from different sexual orientations, to apply for a job he will often decide to advertise in the 'mainstream press' and newspapers aimed at particular communities, such as ethnic minorities, or lesbians and gay men. There should be nothing unlawful about this provided the advertising reaches a broad range of people of different sexual orientations.

If the employer is specifically aiming his advertisement at a lesbian, or gay man, or a heterosexual woman, for instance, he can only do so if it is in pursuance of either a genuine occupational requirement or a lawful measure of positive action under the Regulations (as to which, see section 9.11, below).

The ACAS guidance on the EE (Sexual Orientation) Regulations suggests it is good practice to avoid enquiring about marital status, number of children and arrangements for their care, sexual orientation, and social life (see Appendix 5, below). Some of these questions might seem quite innocuous, but they can make it particularly uncomfortable for a lesbian or gay job applicant. Heterosexual people often tend to make assumptions that other people are heterosexual. There is nothing malicious about such assumptions, but they can create difficulties for people who are not heterosexual. When a person applies for a job, it is unlikely he is going to want to discuss his sexual preferences with the person interviewing him—it would be largely irrelevant and potentially embarrassing. But as soon as he is asked if he is married or intends to marry, or if he has children, this can put a gay applicant in a position that forces him to either 'come out' as gay, to be dishonest, or to be evasive. This is likely to make the applicant ill at ease, even though that was never intended. In extreme circumstances, the applicant might feel he has been subjected to harassment, or, if he is unsuccessful in his application for the job, that he was discriminated against on grounds of his sexual orientation. Such questions should therefore be avoided in an interview, during the selection process, and generally where possible.

Similarly, as it is unlikely that a person's marital status is relevant to his application for a job, the once widespread and still relatively common practice of asking a job applicant about his marital status on an application form ought generally to be avoided.

Paragraph 2.7 of the ACAS guidance makes an interesting and novel point about previous convictions for 'sexual offences' that merits some consideration:

Employers may wish to consider that the laws relating to gay men have changed significantly over time. It is possible that applicants may have acquired a criminal conviction many years before for a matter no longer unlawful, (such as consensual adult gay sex). This is unlikely to have any bearing on the individual's skills and suitability for the job or training advertised. Generally a subsequent change in the criminal law does not affect whether an existing sentence becomes spent, the sentence still stands.

If all applicants are told, during the recruitment, interview, or selection process, that the employer welcomes applicants from different sexual orientations, and that discrimination or harassment on grounds of a person's sexual orientation is not tolerated by the employer, it should help encourage people who may otherwise feel they might not be welcome by a particular organization. Consider a lesbian applying for a job in the police service or as a postal worker, or a heterosexual man applying for a job in a gay pub, such assurances could help encourage the applicant to apply in the first place, and should assist in putting the applicant at ease, making him feel the recruitment process is fair and non-discriminatory, and that the working environment should be a good one. It may also help deter potential job applicants with prejudices based on sexual orientation from applying or expressing their prejudices at work.

9.4 IDENTIFYING A PERSON'S SEXUAL ORIENTATION

It is not normally easy to identify a person's sexual orientation. Most people assume others are heterosexual, and quite often people who are in fact not gay are assumed to be gay because of stereotyping. It is obviously much more difficult to identify a person's sexual orientation than it is to identify whether a person is black or female, and it will often be more difficult to identify a person's sexual orientation than it is to identify a person's religion. For many people, sexual orientation is a private matter and something they do not wish to disclose to their work colleagues or employer. There is nothing wrong with this and it is not generally necessary to identify a person's sexual orientation.

This is because, as explained below (sections 9.5 and 9.6) the discrimination and harassment prohibited in the Regulations is discrimination on *grounds* of sexual orientation, and a person does not have to have a particular sexual orientation to be discriminated against. If a heterosexual woman, for instance, is subject to harassment from male colleagues because they think she is a lesbian, then she has been harassed on grounds of sexual orientation. She does not have to prove she is a lesbian.

The fact that employers may find it difficult to identify their workforces' sexual orientation is therefore largely unimportant. Most cautious employers will assume that some of their employees, or applicants for employment, are not heterosexual, even if it appears that all of them are. To assume that all employees and applicants for employment are heterosexual may be factually incorrect and discriminatory itself, and may lead to unintentional discrimination or harassment, or to the failure to take steps to prevent the same.

However, there are certain circumstances in which it may be important for the employer to identify the sexual orientation of his workforce. The two most likely situations where this may arise is where the employer wants to consider whether it is appropriate to take any measures of positive action under the Regulations, or where he is defending a claim in the employment tribunal.

In relation to the first example, positive action in favour of persons from a particular sexual orientation is permissible under Regulation 26 of the EE (Sexual Orientation) Regulations if it reasonably appears to the employer that the action 'prevents or compensates for disadvantages linked to sexual orientation suffered by persons of that sexual orientation doing that work or likely to take up that work' (see section 6.3, above). The number of people applying for, or holding jobs from the relevant sexual orientation may thus be relevant (though not essential) to the question of whether the employer's belief was reasonable (but see section 9.11, below).

It is more likely the employer will need to identify the sexual orientation of his employees/applicants for employment in order to properly defend a complaint against him. There may be an allegation that the employer's failure to prevent harassment on grounds of sexual orientation has created a hostile working environment in which it is impossible for lesbian and gay men to work. Or there may be a complaint that a particular practice of the employer in his recruitment process indirectly discriminates against job applicants on grounds of their sexual orientation, and that therefore a smaller proportion of people from that sexual orientation are offered employment by the employer. Alternatively, the employer may be in receipt of a questionnaire served on him under Regulation 33 (see section 7.2.3, above) which asks him to provide a breakdown of the number of employees from each sexual orientation. The employer may be in a stronger position to deal with these situations where he has got figures in relation to sexual orientation, or at least where he has taken reasonable steps to collate such figures.

Employers, and large employers in particular, are advised to consider asking their employees about their sexual orientation by means of an anonymous equal opportunities survey. Many employers already do this in relation to race, sex, and nationality. All that would be necessary is a form (or an addition to a form) that each employee and job applicant could be asked to complete. The form should make clear its purpose, in line with an equal opportunities policy that prohibits discrimination on grounds of sexual orientation, and the fact that all responses will be held in confidence. It should not request that the person completing the form enter his name, address, or other such identifying personal features. Nor should completion of the form be compulsory. Those filling in the form could be asked to identify which of the three sexual orientations covered by the Regulations would they regard as best describing their own sexual orientation. If a form was presented in this way it is most unlikely that asking an employee to fill it out could be described as discrimination or harassment, the employer would have taken reasonable steps to identify the sexual orientation of his employees, and he may have, as a result, useful figures on which he can rely to further develop his equal opportunities policy, apply positive action, or defend a complaint in the employment tribunal.

9.5 PERCEPTION OF SEXUAL ORIENTATION

A person is discriminated against or harassed on grounds of sexual orientation whether or not he actually has the sexual orientation assigned to him by the discriminator. Discrimination on grounds of sexual orientation includes discrimination based on a person's perception of another's sexual orientation, whether or not that perception is right (see section 2.5.1.5, above). It is the assumptions made by the discriminator/harasser that are important.

For example, where a student at university is subject to bullying and name-calling, such as 'queer', faggot', 'batty man' etc, by other students because they believe the student is gay, he is likely to have been subject to sexual orientation harassment by the university, in contravention to Regulation 20 of the Regulations (see section 3.3.13, above). It does not matter whether the student is in fact gay, bisexual, or heterosexual. It is the grounds for the harassment he suffered that are important.

As with discrimination on grounds of religion or belief, there are two important reasons for prohibiting discrimination on grounds of the perception of a person's sexual orientation. First, it expresses society's disapproval of sexual orientation discrimination. It is not of prime importance whether the victim of the irrational and often hurtful discrimination is actually gay, it is the treatment itself that is objectionable, and which the Government and the EC, have taken the decision to prohibit within the sphere of employment. Secondly, there are particular difficulties that can arise in relation to identifying a person's sexual orientation—as discussed above (section 9.4). If it was necessary for a person to establish his sexual orientation before bringing a claim for sexual orientation discrimination this could present him with difficulties and embarrassment; a person might end up being subjected to intrusive and unpleasant cross-examination about his sexual preferences. This could put off employees from relying on the Regulations, and defeat their purpose.

9.6 DISCRIMINATION ON GROUNDS OF ANOTHER'S SEXUAL ORIENTATION

Discrimination or harassment on grounds of sexual orientation is also unlawful where it is on the grounds of another's sexual orientation (see section 2.5.1.6, above). Again, it is the *grounds* for the discrimination/harassment that are important, not the sexual orientation of the person to which it is directed. Common examples of this type of discrimination or harassment occur where a person is teased because he has gay friends, or his son is gay, or he goes out to gay clubs with his girlfriend, for instance. If, for example, an employee is dismissed or subjected to another kind of detriment because her daughter is a lesbian, and the employer strongly disapproves of lesbianism, then this is unlawful discrimination—even if the mother also disapproves of her daughter's sexual orientation. The mother is being discriminated against because of another's sexual orientation.

It is important that employees and managers are made aware that the Regulations extend to these types of situations. Many will assume the prohibition on harassment and discrimination on grounds of sexual orientation only applies where the person discriminated against or harassed is of the relevant sexual orientation. Equal opportunities/anti-harassment policies and training programmes need to make clear that if an employer harasses a woman for having gay friends, for instance, it is no defence to say 'she's not gay, so I wasn't harassing her' [on grounds of sexual orientation].

9.7 STEREOTYPING

One of the most common expressions of discrimination and harassment on grounds of sexual orientation is stereotyping. 'Stereotyping' is a recognized concept in discrimination law. In many ways it forms the basis of much discrimination law because it is often on the basis of generalized assumptions (whether about race, sex, or sexual orientation) that a person is treated, not as an individual, but as a member of a particular group which is, in turn, treated less favourably than another. In *Nagarajan v London Regional Transport* [2000] 1 AC 512, HL, a race discrimination case, Lord Nicholls said:

I turn to the question of subconscious motivation. All human beings have preconceptions, beliefs, attitudes and prejudices on many subjects. It is part of our make-up. Moreover, we do not always recognise our own prejudices. Many people are unable, or unwilling, to admit even to themselves that actions of theirs may be racially motivated. An employer may genuinely believe that the reason why he rejected an applicant had nothing to do with the applicant's race. After careful and thorough investigation of a claim members of an employment tribunal may decide that the proper inference to be drawn from the evidence is that, whether the employer realised it at the time or not, race was the reason why he acted as he did. . . . Members of racial groups need protection from conduct driven by unrecognised prejudice as much as from conscious and deliberate discrimination. . . . [A] high rate of failure to achieve promotion by members of a particular racial group may indicate that 'the real reason for refusal is a conscious or unconscious racial attitude which involves stereotyped assumptions' about members of the group.

Stereotyping in relation to sexual orientation can take many forms. In section 9.4, above, assumptions about an employee's sexual orientation are discussed. These assumptions can arise in many circumstances. It might be common in a workplace for employees to share wedding photographs and discuss their children's schooling and development. Employees may assume that their colleagues all want to get married and have children too. Such assumptions and unwitting insensitivity may create a working environment that is not comfortable for lesbian and gay workers.

The ACAS guidance uses the example of social gatherings. Those organizing an office party should not assume all of the employees are heterosexual, and that if they bring a partner along the partner will be of the opposite sex.

Stereotypes are made by homosexual, bisexual, and heterosexual people about each other. Gay men are commonly stereotyped as sexually promiscuous and/or effeminate. Lesbians are commonly stereotyped as 'man-haters' and 'butch'. Bisexuals can be stereotyped by both heterosexual and homosexuals as being 'confused' or 'wanting the best of both worlds'. Heterosexuals can be stereotyped as 'boring' or prejudiced. Some people hold even more dangerous stereotypes than these. Irrational prejudices and stereotypes that gay men are prone to paedophilia, are likely to have HIV/AIDS, or are 'predatory' towards their heterosexual colleagues often leads to violence against gay people.

All of these stereotypes, however serious, can lead to unlawful discrimination or harassment. It is therefore very important that in devising or reviewing equal opportunities and anti-harassment policies and training, the issue of stereotyping is tackled.

9.8 PRIVACY

A person's sexual orientation is part of their private life. This is recognized by, amongst other things, the case law of the European Court of Human Rights on Article 8 of the Convention (the right to private and family life; see eg, *Dudgeon v*

United Kingdom (1981) 4 EHRR 149, ECtHR). Many people do not want to discuss their sexual orientation and may not want their employer or their colleagues to know about their sexual orientation. It is therefore important that people are allowed to keep their sexual orientation private. To force a person to disclose his sexual orientation can often lead to harassment and discrimination in any event.

Employers should avoid situations that force employees to disclose their sexual orientation. The most obvious example is asking an employee if he is gay. Other examples include asking unnecessary questions about his marital status, children etc (see section 9.3, above). If an employer wishes to find out how many employees he has of a particular sexual orientation he should do so by way of a voluntary, anonymous survey (see section 9.4, above). A person may also feel pressured about his sexual orientation when he is asked to provide the name of their partner for the purposes of an invitation to an office party, or for contacting in case of an emergency. Where a male worker gives the name of his male partner, and this is heard or is disclosed to his colleagues, this undermines the worker's privacy and could lead to harassment on grounds of sexual orientation. Employers should therefore avoid asking such questions unless absolutely necessary, and where such questions are necessary the answers to them should be treated in confidence.

9.9 BENEFITS AND PENSIONS

Discrimination in the terms on which occupational benefits and pensions are provided is unlawful by Regulation 9A of the Regulations, and generally as Regulation 6(2)(b) of the Regulations makes it unlawful for an employer to discriminate against an employee on grounds of sexual orientation in the opportunities he affords the employee for 'any other benefit'.

The whole range of employment-related benefits are covered by this prohibition on discrimination: private health insurance, pensions, travel concessions, or expenses, provision of a company car, eating and living expenses etc. However, it is unlikely that there will be many examples of overt discrimination against people on grounds of their sexual orientation in this respect. An employer is not likely to refuse to provide an employee with a company car because the employee is gay. Where this does happen, it will obviously be unlawful.

One example of direct discrimination that might arise in this respect is where a life or health insurance plan provided by the employer applied a different score, leading to a higher premium, for a gay man than for a heterosexual man, due to stereotyping about the risk of HIV/AIDS. This would directly discriminate against gay men.

What is far more widespread is indirect discrimination. The problem here is that most examples of indirect discrimination that would arise in this regard are caused by discrimination on grounds of marital status (see section 9.10, below) which is not unlawful under the Regulations.

9.10 DISCRIMINATION ON GROUNDS OF MARITAL STATUS

The fact that the Regulations allow for discrimination on grounds of marital status is a major weakness in their potential effectiveness. Most occupational benefits and pensions that indirectly discriminate against lesbians and gay men do so because they discriminate on grounds of marital status, and a disproportionately small number of lesbians and gays are married compared to heterosexuals.

The exclusion of the prohibition on discrimination on grounds of marital status, by virtue of Regulation 25 of the EE (Sexual Orientation) Regulations is a highly controversial matter. It is discussed and criticized in section 6.5, above. There is a strong prospect that, due to either a legal challenge or by amendment, the exclusion will eventually disappear.

It is good practice for employers to avoid discriminating on grounds of marital status in any event. Such discrimination is contrary to the HRA (Article 14 of the European Convention on Human Rights—prohibition of discrimination—which can only be applied where another Convention is engaged, such as Article 8). Discrimination on grounds of marital status requires the employer to enquire into the employees' marital status—something which can itself either be or lead to discrimination or harassment.

Whilst it is not currently unlawful to discriminate on grounds of marital status under the EE (Sexual Orientation) Regulations, a cautious employer should avoid doing so, unless it is necessary to comply with another legal requirement (such as an existing term in an employment contract).

9.11 WHERE DIFFERENTIAL TREATMENT MIGHT BE ACCEPTABLE

The EE (Sexual Orientation) Regulations permits what would otherwise be direct discrimination in two general types of situation. First, where the employer positively discriminates in favour of a person of a particular sexual orientation, and secondly, where the employer can show there is a genuine occupational requirement to employ a person of a particular sexual orientation.

Positive action, ie discriminating in favour of a person on grounds of his sexual orientation, is lawful under Regulation 26 of the EE (Sexual Orientation) Regulations in certain circumstances. Regulation 26 is considered in section 6.3 above. Apart from the examples of circumstances where positive action might be justified given there, one could argue that it is particularly important for public authorities to reflect the diversity in the community and not to discriminate. Public authorities are large employers who ought to have proper equal opportunity policies and practices. They should be in a position to conduct an anonymous audit of their staff to see if people from a particular sexual orientation are under-represented generally, or at a particular grade. If they find they are, they should consider taking measures, including the positive action measures they are entitled to take under Regulation 26, aimed at remedying this situation. It is also arguable that other bodies of a representative nature, such as trade unions, should take similar steps to ensure those employed in official posts reasonably reflect their membership.

In terms of positive action in relation to sexual orientation discrimination, it is particularly important to stress the broader discretion an employer has to take positive action measures that exist in other areas of discrimination law. As discussed in section 6.3.2 above, the critical difference between the Regulations and the provisions under the RRA and the SDA is that under the Regulations it is not necessary to show that no members, or a disproportionately small number of members, of a particular group are represented in a particular job. It is only necessary to show it reasonably appeared to the person making them that the measures taken prevent or compensate for disadvantages. This lower threshold obviates the necessity to produce statistics demonstrating the representation of persons from particular sexual orientations before taking positive action. All that is necessary is for the employer to show he reasonably believed a particular group suffered from disadvantages—and some objective evidence ought to be provided as the basis of this belief—and that he took the measure to try and compensate for those disadvantages. However, it is good practice, will help the employer establish his reasonable belief, and will assist in defending complaints in the employment tribunal brought by aggrieved unsuccessful job applicants, if such statistical information is collated before positive action is taken.

The genuine occupational requirement is discussed in Chapter 5 above. Under Regulation 7 of the EE (Sexual Orientation) Regulations an employer has a defence to claims of both direct and indirect discrimination where he can show that it is a genuine occupational requirement for him to employ a person with a particular sexual orientation. Examples of this are provided in Chapter 5. A genuine occupational requirement will only arise in exceptional circumstances. An employer should take great care before deciding that a particular job vacancy must be filled by a person of a particular sexual orientation. A genuine occupational requirement might apply to certain jobs in health and welfare, and it is arguable that it could apply to some jobs in the 'gay community', such as in gay bars or restaurants, but beyond this its application will be rare.

The most controversial area concerning the genuine occupational requirement is in relation to sexual orientation and religion. Under Regulation 7(3) of the EE (Sexual Orientation) Regulations, an employer involved in employment for the purposes of organized religion can apply a requirement related to sexual orientation to comply with the doctrines of the religion or to avoid conflicting with the strongly held religious convictions of a significant number of the religion's followers. This area is discussed in some detail in section 5.5 above. It appears to mean that a church or synagogue could legitimately refuse to employ a vicar or rabbi because of the latter's sexual orientation. The discrimination would be lawful. The vague wording, broad scope, and 'blanket ban' nature of Regulation 7(3) has caused much concern. It was the subject of Parliamentary debate and is, at the time of writing, the subject of judicial review proceedings.

9.12 DISCIPLINARY, GRIEVANCE, AND ANTI-HARASSMENT POLICIES

It is very important that employers have clear procedures for dealing with discrimination and harassment on grounds of sexual orientation. If sexual orientation discrimination is not part of an employer's equal opportunities policy, the employer should update the policy to include it. The employer should also consider developing an anti-harassment procedure, whether as part of the equal opportunities, disciplinary, or grievance policies and procedures, or whether as a freestanding policy and procedure.

Broadly speaking, anti-harassment procedures should set out what is regarded as harassment, and the grounds on which harassment will be prohibited. For instance employers will want to prohibit racial, sexual, religious, and sexual orientation harassment, and harassment on grounds of disability. The policy should explain that sexual orientation harassment is generally defined as unwanted words or conduct based on or caused by a person's sexual orientation, another's sexual orientation, or a person's perception about the victim's sexual orientation which has the effect of violating the victim's dignity, or of creating an intimidating, hostile, degrading, humiliating, or offensive environment for the victim. The unwanted conduct may consist of one particularly serious incident, or a series of less serious incidents.

Most anti-harassment procedures have various stages. The victim is usually given the option, and encouraged to first confront the harasser and tell him his conduct is unwanted and must stop. This informal first stage has a number of advantages. It can often resolve the situation and obviate the need for further formal action, it can assist the victim in feeling comfortable in his environment, and it can highlight to the alleged harasser that his conduct is unwanted—something he may not have realized. In addition, if the case ends up in an employment tribunal, it will be important for the complainant to rely on in order to show the conduct was unwanted and/or that it continues, and/or that the employer did not take reasonable steps to prevent it. If the victim is uncomfortable about confronting his harasser he may wish to do so with his trade union representative, a colleague, or by memo or email. Usually the next stage will be a complaint to the line manager or above if the line manager is involved in the harassment. If the harassment is not resolved at this stage it should be formally investigated by the employer, either under the anti-harassment procedure or the grievance procedure. Disciplinary measures should be taken if necessary. If the victim is still not satisfied he should have some right of appeal against the handling of his complaint/grievance.

Obviously, if he remains unsatisfied he should bring a complaint in the employment tribunal. In this regard, victims of harassment need to be careful about the three-month time limit for bringing an employment tribunal claim. Tribunals will not always extend time just because the victim is pursuing an internal grievance/complaint. It will be sensible to submit a 'protective' IT1 before the time limit from the last act of harassment has expired (for time limits etc, see section 7.2, above).

Grievance procedures should set out the remedies an employee has if he feels he has been discriminated against or harassed whether by his manager or by other employees. Disciplinary procedures ought to make clear that harassment and discrimination on grounds of sexual orientation are serious disciplinary offences that can, in certain circumstances and following an investigation, lead to dismissal.

From October 2004, new measures to encourage employers and employees to resolve disputes before bringing complaints in the employment tribunal come into force. A new mandatory statutory disciplinary procedure comes into force (see Employment Act 2002, Sch 2, Part I). In addition, a new statutory grievance procedure comes into force. Under the standard procedure there will be three stages (see Employment Act 2002, Sch 2, Part II), which must be initiated by the employee (these are set out in full in the chapter on religion or belief discrimination, section 8.13, above).

If the employer or employee fails to comply with the procedures there will be serious implications on any subsequent complaint brought in the employment tribunal. Most importantly, if an employee does not submit a grievance under stage 1 of the standard procedure, where that procedure applies, his complaint to an employment tribunal will be inadmissible. This includes complaints of discrimination under the EE (Sexual Orientation) Regulations. Failure to comply with procedures may also make dismissals automatically unfair and lead to an increase or decrease in the compensation awarded depending on which party is at fault.

It is therefore essential that employers re-visit their procedures to see they comply with statutory developments and the EE Regulations, and that employees, their union representatives, or legal advisors, familiarize themselves with these procedures and make sure that they are followed where appropriate.

9.13 CONCLUSION

The examples of discrimination that may arise under the Regulations discussed in this chapter are just some of the more obvious that are likely to arise. There are many other situations in which discrimination or harassment on grounds of sexual orientation may arise. This area of discrimination law is a new one, and it will take some time to determine properly the limits and extent of the Regulations. Tribunals, lawyers, employers, and employees' representatives will all have to think creatively about the circumstances in which sexual orientation discrimination might arise, and about what is, and what is not, properly discrimination on these grounds. Many of the *principles* from race and sex discrimination cases will be of assistance in understanding and applying the Regulations, but the *type* of discrimination made lawful under the Regulations is very different.

Sexual orientation discrimination, and particularly harassment, has been a relatively common experience for lesbian and gay employees in particular. A recent survey by the TUC suggested as many as 44 per cent of lesbians and gay men experienced some form of discrimination in the workplace, largely harassment. Employers will have to take bold steps to combat what in some industries and professions is a culture of sexual orientation discrimination. If they fail to do so, employees, and their representatives, can rely on these Regulations to challenge a form of discrimination that was previously allowed to flourish by the law.

Appendix 1
The Employment Equality (Religion or Belief) Regulations 2003

SI 2003 NO. 1660

Made	*26th June 2003*
Coming into force	*2nd December 2003*

ARRANGEMENT OF REGULATIONS

Whereas a draft of these Regulations was laid before Parliament in accordance with paragraph 2 of Schedule 2 to the European Communities Act 1972, and was approved by resolution of each House of Parliament;

Now, therefore, the Secretary of State, being a Minister designated for the purposes of section 2(2) of the European Communities Act 1972 in relation to discrimination, in exercise of the powers conferred by that section, hereby makes the following Regulations:

Part 1
General

1. Citation, commencement and extent

(1) These Regulations may be cited as the Employment Equality (Religion or Belief) Regulations 2003, and shall come into force on 2nd December 2003.

(2) These Regulations do not extend to Northern Ireland.

2. Interpretation

(1) In these Regulations, 'religion or belief' means any religion, religious belief, or similar philosophical belief.

(2) In these Regulations, references to discrimination are to any discrimination falling within regulation 3 (discrimination on grounds of religion or belief) or 4 (discrimination by way of victimisation) and related expressions shall be construed accordingly, and references to harassment shall be construed in accordance with regulation 5 (harassment on grounds of religion or belief).

(3) In these Regulations—

'act' includes a deliberate omission;

'benefits', except in regulation 9A (trustees and managers of occupational pension schemes), includes facilities and services;

'detriment' does not include harassment within the meaning of regulation 5;

references to 'employer', in their application to a person at any time seeking to employ another, include a person who has no employees at that time;

'employment' means employment under a contract of service or of apprenticeship or a contract personally to do any work, and related expressions shall be construed accordingly;

'Great Britain', except where the context otherwise requires in regulation 26 (protection of Sikhs from discrimination in connection with requirements as to wearing of safety helmets), includes such of the territorial waters of the United Kingdom as are adjacent to Great Britain;

'Minister of the Crown' includes the Treasury and the Defence Council; and

'school', in England and Wales, has the meaning given by section 4 of the Education Act 1996, and, in Scotland, has the meaning given by section 135(1) of the Education (Scotland) Act 1980, and references to a school are to an institution in so far as it is engaged in the provision of education under those sections.

3. Discrimination on grounds of religion or belief

(1) For the purposes of these Regulations, a person ('A') discriminates against another person ('B') if—

(a) on grounds of religion or belief, A treats B less favourably than he treats or would treat other persons; or

(b) A applies to B a provision, criterion or practice which he applies or would apply equally to persons not of the same religion or belief as B, but—

(i) which puts or would put persons of the same religion or belief as B at a particular disadvantage when compared with other persons,

(ii) which puts B at that disadvantage, and

(iii) which A cannot show to be a proportionate means of achieving a legitimate aim.

(2) The reference in paragraph (1)(a) to religion or belief does not include A's religion or belief.

(3) A comparison of B's case with that of another person under paragraph (1) must be such that the relevant circumstances in the one case are the same, or not materially different, in the other.

4. Discrimination by way of victimisation

(1) For the purposes of these Regulations, a person ('A') discriminates against another person ('B') if he treats B less favourably than he treats or would treat other persons in the same circumstances, and does so by reason that B has—

(a) brought proceedings against A or any other person under these Regulations;

(b) given evidence or information in connection with proceedings brought by any person against A or any other person under these Regulations;

(c) otherwise done anything under or by reference to these Regulations in relation to A or any other person; or

(d) alleged that A or any other person has committed an act which (whether or not the allegation so states) would amount to a contravention of these Regulations,

or by reason that A knows that B intends to do any of those things, or suspects that B has done or intends to do any of them.

(2) Paragraph (1) does not apply to treatment of B by reason of any allegation made by him, or evidence or information given by him, if the allegation, evidence or information was false and not made (or, as the case may be, given) in good faith.

5. Harassment on grounds of religion or belief

(1) For the purposes of these Regulations, a person ('A') subjects another person ('B') to harassment where, on grounds of religion or belief, A engages in unwanted conduct which has the purpose or effect of—

(a) violating B's dignity; or

(b) creating an intimidating, hostile, degrading, humiliating or offensive environment for B.

(2) Conduct shall be regarded as having the effect specified in paragraph (1)(a) or (b) only if, having regard to all the circumstances, including in particular the perception of B, it should reasonably be considered as having that effect.

Part II
Discrimination in employment and vocational training

6. Applicants and employees

(1) It is unlawful for an employer, in relation to employment by him at an establishment in Great Britain, to discriminate against a person—

(a) in the arrangements he makes for the purpose of determining to whom he should offer employment;

(b) in the terms on which he offers that person employment; or (c) by refusing to offer, or deliberately not offering, him employment.

(2) It is unlawful for an employer, in relation to a person whom he employs at an establishment in Great Britain, to discriminate against that person—

(a) in the terms of employment which he affords him;

(b) in the opportunities which he affords him for promotion, a transfer, training, or receiving any other benefit;

(c) by refusing to afford him, or deliberately not affording him, any such opportunity; or

(d) by dismissing him, or subjecting him to any other detriment.

(3) It is unlawful for an employer, in relation to employment by him at an establishment in Great Britain, to subject to harassment a person whom he employs or who has applied to him for employment.

(4) Paragraph (2) does not apply to benefits of any description if the employer is concerned with the provision (for payment or not) of benefits of that description to the public, or to a section of the public which includes the employee in question, unless—

(a) that provision differs in a material respect from the provision of the benefits by the employer to his employees; or

(b) the provision of the benefits to the employee in question is regulated by his contract of employment; or

(c) the benefits relate to training.

(5) In paragraph (2)(d) reference to the dismissal of a person from employment includes reference—

(a) to the termination of that person's employment by the expiration of any period (including a period expiring by reference to an event or circumstance), not being a termination immediately after which the employment is renewed on the same terms; and

(b) to the termination of that person's employment by any act of his (including the giving of notice) in circumstances such that he is entitled to terminate it without notice by reason of the conduct of the employer.

7. Exception for genuine occupational requirement

(1) In relation to discrimination falling within regulation 3 (discrimination on grounds of religion or belief)—

(a) regulation 6(1)(a) or (c) does not apply to any employment;

(b) regulation 6(2)(b) or (c) does not apply to promotion or transfer to, or training for, any employment; and

(c) regulation 6(2)(d) does not apply to dismissal from any employment,
where paragraph (2) or (3) applies.

(2) This paragraph applies where, having regard to the nature of the employment or the context in which it is carried out—

(a) being of a particular religion or belief is a genuine and determining occupational requirement;

(b) it is proportionate to apply that requirement in the particular case; and

(c) either—

(i) the person to whom that requirement is applied does not meet it, or

(ii) the employer is not satisfied, and in all the circumstances it is reasonable for him not to be satisfied, that that person meets it,
and this paragraph applies whether or not the employer has an ethos based on religion or belief.

(3) This paragraph applies where an employer has an ethos based on religion or belief and, having regard to that ethos and to the nature of the employment or the context in which it is carried out—

(a) being of a particular religion or belief is a genuine occupational requirement for the job;

(b) it is proportionate to apply that requirement in the particular case; and

(c) either—

(i) the person to whom that requirement is applied does not meet it, or

(ii) the employer is not satisfied, and in all the circumstances it is reasonable for him not to be satisfied, that that person meets it.

8. Contract workers

(1) It is unlawful for a principal, in relation to contract work at an establishment in Great Britain, to discriminate against a contract worker—

(a) in the terms on which he allows him to do that work;

(b) by not allowing him to do it or continue to do it;

(c) in the way he affords him access to any benefits or by refusing or deliberately not affording him access to them; or

(d) by subjecting him to any other detriment.

(2) It is unlawful for a principal, in relation to contract work at an establishment in Great Britain, to subject a contract worker to harassment.

(3) A principal does not contravene paragraph (1)(b) by doing any act in relation to a contract worker where, if the work were to be done by a person taken into the principal's employment, that act would be lawful by virtue of regulation 7 (exception for genuine occupational requirement).

(4) Paragraph (1) does not apply to benefits of any description if the principal is concerned with the provision (for payment or not) of benefits of that description to the public, or to a section of the public to which the contract worker in question belongs, unless that provision differs in a material respect from the provision of the benefits by the principal to his contract workers.

(5) In this regulation—

'principal' means a person ('A') who makes work available for doing by individuals who are employed by another person who supplies them under a contract made with A;

'contract work' means work so made available; and

'contract worker' means any individual who is supplied to the principal under such a contract.

9. Meaning of employment and contract work at establishment in Great Britain

(1) For the purposes of this Part ('the relevant purposes'), employment is to be regarded as being at an establishment in Great Britain if the employee—

(a) does his work wholly or partly in Great Britain; or

(b) does his work wholly outside Great Britain and paragraph (2) applies.

(2) This paragraph applies if—

(a) the employer has a place of business at an establishment in Great Britain;

(b) the work is for the purposes of the business carried on at that establishment; and

(c) the employee is ordinarily resident in Great Britain—

(i) at the time when he applies for or is offered the employment, or

(ii) at any time during the course of the employment.

(3) The reference to 'employment' in paragraph (1) includes—

(a) employment on board a ship only if the ship is registered at a port of registry in Great Britain, and

(b) employment on an aircraft or hovercraft only if the aircraft or hovercraft is registered in the United Kingdom and operated by a person who has his principal place of business, or is ordinarily resident, in Great Britain.

(4) Subject to paragraph (5), for the purposes of determining if employment concerned with the exploration of the sea bed or sub-soil or the exploitation of their natural resources is outside Great Britain, this regulation has effect as if references to Great Britain included—

(a) any area designated under section 1(7) of the Continental Shelf Act 1964 except an area or part of an area in which the law of Northern Ireland applies; and

(b) in relation to employment concerned with the exploration or exploitation of the Frigg Gas Field, the part of the Norwegian sector of the Continental Shelf described in Schedule 1.

(5) Paragraph (4) shall not apply to employment which is concerned with the exploration or exploitation of the Frigg Gas Field unless the employer is—

(a) a company registered under the Companies Act 1985;

(b) an oversea company which has established a place of business within Great Britain from which it directs the exploration or exploitation in question; or

(c) any other person who has a place of business within Great Britain from which he directs the exploration or exploitation in question.

(6) In this regulation—

'the Frigg Gas Field' means the naturally occurring gas-bearing sand formations of the lower Eocene age located in the vicinity of the intersection of the line of latitude 59 degrees 53 minutes North and of the dividing line between the sectors of the Continental Shelf of the United Kingdom and the Kingdom of Norway and includes all other gas-bearing strata from which gas at the start of production is capable of flowing into the above-mentioned gas-bearing sand formations;

'oversea company' has the same meaning as in section 744 of the Companies Act 1985.

(7) This regulation applies in relation to contract work within the meaning of regulation 8 as it applies in relation to employment; and, in its application to contract work, references to 'employee', 'employer' and 'employment' are references to (respectively) 'contract worker', 'principal' and 'contract work' within the meaning of regulation 8.

9A. Trustees and managers of occupational pension schemes

(1) It is unlawful, except in relation to rights accrued or benefits payable in respect of periods of service prior to the coming into force of these Regulations, for the trustees or managers of an occupational pension scheme to discriminate against a member or prospective member of the scheme in carrying out any of their functions in relation to it (including in particular their functions relating to the admission of members to the scheme and the treatment of members of it).

(2) It is unlawful for the trustees or managers of an occupational pension scheme, in relation to the scheme, to subject to harassment a member or prospective member of it.

(3) Schedule 1A (occupational pension schemes) shall have effect for the purposes of—

(a) defining terms used in this regulation and in that Schedule;

(b) treating every occupational pension scheme as including a non-discrimination rule;

(c) giving trustees or managers of an occupational pension scheme power to alter the scheme so as to secure conformity with the non-discrimination rule;

(d) making provision in relation to the procedures, and remedies which may be granted, on certain complaints relating to occupational pension schemes presented to an employment tribunal under regulation 28 (jurisdiction of employment tribunals).'.

10. Office-holders etc

(1) It is unlawful for a relevant person, in relation to an appointment to an office or post to which this regulation applies, to discriminate against a person—

(a) in the arrangements which he makes for the purpose of determining to whom the appointment should be offered;

(b) in the terms on which he offers him the appointment; or

(c) by refusing to offer him the appointment.

(2) It is unlawful, in relation to an appointment to an office or post to which this regulation applies and which is an office or post referred to in paragraph (8)(b), for a relevant person on whose recommendation (or subject to whose approval) appointments to the office or post are made, to discriminate against a person—

(a) in the arrangements which he makes for the purpose of determining who should be recommended or approved in relation to the appointment; or

(b) in making or refusing to make a recommendation, or giving or refusing to give an approval, in relation to the appointment.

(3) It is unlawful for a relevant person, in relation to a person who has been appointed to an office or post to which this regulation applies, to discriminate against him—

(a) in the terms of the appointment;

(b) in the opportunities which he affords him for promotion, a transfer, training or receiving any other benefit, or by refusing to afford him any such opportunity;

(c) by terminating the appointment; or

(d) by subjecting him to any other detriment in relation to the appointment.

(4) It is unlawful for a relevant person, in relation to an office or post to which this regulation applies, to subject to harassment a person—

(a) who has been appointed to the office or post;

(b) who is seeking or being considered for appointment to the office or post; or

(c) who is seeking or being considered for a recommendation or approval in relation to an appointment to an office or post referred to in paragraph (8)(b).

(5) Paragraphs (1) and (3) do not apply to any act in relation to an office or post where, if the office or post constituted employment, that act would be lawful by virtue of regulation 7 (exception for genuine occupational requirement); and paragraph (2) does not apply to any act in relation to an office or post where, if the office or post constituted employment, it would be lawful by virtue of regulation 7 to refuse to offer the person such employment.

(6) Paragraph (3) does not apply to benefits of any description if the relevant person is concerned with the provision (for payment or not) of benefits of that description to the public, or a section of the public to which the person appointed belongs, unless—

(a) that provision differs in a material respect from the provision of the benefits by the relevant person to persons appointed to offices or posts which are the same as, or not materially different from, that which the person appointed holds; or

(b) the provision of the benefits to the person appointed is regulated by the terms and conditions of his appointment; or

(c) the benefits relate to training.

(7) In paragraph (3)(c) the reference to the termination of the appointment includes a reference—

(a) to the termination of the appointment by the expiration of any period (including a period expiring by reference to an event or circumstance), not being a termination immediately after which the appointment is renewed on the same terms and conditions; and

(b) to the termination of the appointment by any act of the person appointed (including the giving of notice) in circumstances such that he is entitled to terminate the appointment without notice by reason of the conduct of the relevant person.

(8) This regulation applies to—

(a) any office or post to which persons are appointed to discharge functions personally under the direction of another person, and in respect of which they are entitled to remuneration; and

(b) any office or post to which appointments are made by (or on the recommendation of or subject to the approval of) a Minister of the Crown, a government department, the National Assembly for Wales or any part of the Scottish Administration,

but not to a political office or a case where regulation 6 (applicants and employees), 8 (contract workers), 12 (barristers), 13 (advocates) or 14 (partnerships) applies, or would apply but for the operation of any other provision of these Regulations.

(9) For the purposes of paragraph (8)(a) the holder of an office or post—

(a) is to be regarded as discharging his functions under the direction of another person if that other person is entitled to direct him as to when and where he discharges those functions;

(b) is not to be regarded as entitled to remuneration merely because he is entitled to payments—

(i) in respect of expenses incurred by him in carrying out the functions of the office or post, or

(ii) by way of compensation for the loss of income or benefits he would or might have received from any person had he not been carrying out the functions of the office or post.

(10) In this regulation—

(a) appointment to an office or post does not include election to an office or post;

(b) 'political office' means—

(i) any office of the House of Commons held by a member of it,

(ii) a life peerage within the meaning of the Life Peerages Act 1958, or any office of the House of Lords held by a member of it,

(iii) any office mentioned in Schedule 2 (Ministerial offices) to the House of Commons Disqualification Act 1975,

(iv) the offices of Leader of the Opposition, Chief Opposition Whip or Assistant Opposition Whip within the meaning of the Ministerial and other Salaries Act 1975,

(v) any office of the Scottish Parliament held by a member of it,

(vi) a member of the Scottish Executive within the meaning of section 44 of the Scotland Act 1998, or a junior Scottish Minister within the meaning of section 49 of that Act,

(vii) any office of the National Assembly for Wales held by a member of it,

(viii) in England, any office of a county council, a London borough council, a district council, or a parish council held by a member of it,

(ix) in Wales, any office of a county council, a county borough council, or a community council held by a member of it,

(x) in relation to a council constituted under section 2 of the Local

Government etc (Scotland) Act 1994 or a community council established under section 51 of the Local Government (Scotland) Act 1973, any office of such a council held by a member of it,

  (xi) any office of the Greater London Authority held by a member of it,

  (xii) any office of the Common Council of the City of London held by a member of it,

  (xiii) any office of the Council of the Isles of Scilly held by a member of it,

  (xiv) any office of a political party;

 (c) 'relevant person', in relation to an office or post, means—

  (i) any person with power to make or terminate appointments to the office or post, or to determine the terms of appointment,

  (ii) any person with power to determine the working conditions of a person appointed to the office or post in relation to opportunities for promotion, a transfer, training or for receiving any other benefit, and

  (iii) any person or body referred to in paragraph (8)(b) on whose recommendation or subject to whose approval appointments are made to the office or post;

 (d) references to making a recommendation include references to making a negative recommendation; and (e) references to refusal include references to deliberate omission.

11. Police

(1) For the purposes of this Part, the holding of the office of constable shall be treated as employment—

 (a) by the chief officer of police as respects any act done by him in relation to a constable or that office;

 (b) by the police authority as respects any act done by it in relation to a constable or that office.

(2) For the purposes of regulation 22 (liability of employers and principals)—

 (a) the holding of the office of constable shall be treated as employment by the chief officer of police (and as not being employment by any other person); and

 (b) anything done by a person holding such an office in the performance, or purported performance, of his functions shall be treated as done in the course of that employment.

(3) There shall be paid out of the police fund—

 (a) any compensation, costs or expenses awarded against a chief officer of police in any proceedings brought against him under these Regulations, and any costs or expenses incurred by him in any such proceedings so far as not recovered by him in the proceedings; and

 (b) any sum required by a chief officer of police for the settlement of any claim made against him under these Regulations if the settlement is approved by the police authority.

(4) Any proceedings under these Regulations which, by virtue of paragraph (1), would lie against a chief officer of police shall be brought against the chief officer of police for the time being or, in the case of a vacancy in that office, against the person for the time being performing the functions of that office; and references in paragraph (3) to the chief officer of police shall be construed accordingly.

(5) A police authority may, in such cases and to such extent as appear to it to be appropriate, pay out of the police fund—

(a) any compensation, costs or expenses awarded in proceedings under these Regulations against a person under the direction and control of the chief officer of police;

(b) any costs or expenses incurred and not recovered by such a person in such proceedings; and

(c) any sum required in connection with the settlement of a claim that has or might have given rise to such proceedings.

(6) Paragraphs (1) and (2) apply to a police cadet and appointment as a police cadet as they apply to a constable and the office of constable.

(7) Subject to paragraph (8), in this regulation—

'chief officer of police'—

(a) in relation to a person appointed, or an appointment falling to be made, under a specified Act, has the same meaning as in the Police Act 1996,

(b) in relation to a person appointed, or an appointment falling to be made, under section 9(1)(b) or 55(1)(b) of the Police Act 1997 (police members of the National Criminal Intelligence Service and the National Crime Squad) means the Director General of the National Criminal Intelligence Service or, as the case may be, the Director General of the National Crime Squad,

(c) in relation to a person appointed, or an appointment falling to be made, under the Police (Scotland) Act 1967, means the chief constable of the relevant police force,

(d) in relation to any other person or appointment means the officer or other person who has the direction and control of the body of constables or cadets in question;

'police authority'—

(a) in relation to a person appointed, or an appointment falling to be made, under a specified Act, has the same meaning as in the Police Act 1996,

(b) in relation to a person appointed, or an appointment falling to be made, under section 9(1)(b) or 55(1)(b) of the Police Act 1997, means the Service Authority for the National Criminal Intelligence Service or, as the case may be, the Service Authority for the National Crime Squad,

(c) in relation to a person appointed, or an appointment falling to be made, under the Police (Scotland) Act 1967, has the meaning given in that Act,

(d) in relation to any other person or appointment, means the authority by whom the person in question is or on appointment would be paid;

'police cadet' means any person appointed to undergo training with a view to becoming a constable;

'police fund'—

(a) in relation to a chief officer of police within sub-paragraph (a) of the above definition of that term, has the same meaning as in the Police Act 1996,

(b) in relation to a chief officer of police within sub-paragraph (b) of that definition, means the service fund established under section 16 or (as the case may be) section 61 of the Police Act 1997,

(c) in any other case means money provided by the police authority; and

'specified Act' means the Metropolitan Police Act 1829, the City of London Police Act 1839 or the Police Act 1996.

(8) In relation to a constable of a force who is not under the direction and control of the chief officer of police for that force, references in this regulation to the chief officer of

police are references to the chief officer of the force under whose direction and control he is, and references in this regulation to the police authority are references to the relevant police authority for that force.

12. Barristers

(1) It is unlawful for a barrister or barrister's clerk, in relation to any offer of a pupillage or tenancy, to discriminate against a person—

(a) in the arrangements which are made for the purpose of determining to whom the pupillage or tenancy should be offered;

(b) in respect of any terms on which it is offered; or

(c) by refusing, or deliberately not offering, it to him.

(2) It is unlawful for a barrister or barrister's clerk, in relation to a pupil or tenant in the set of chambers in question, to discriminate against him—

(a) in respect of any terms applicable to him as a pupil or tenant;

(b) in the opportunities for training, or gaining experience, which are afforded or denied to him;

(c) in the benefits which are afforded or denied to him; or

(d) by terminating his pupillage, or by subjecting him to any pressure to leave the chambers or other detriment.

(3) It is unlawful for a barrister or barrister's clerk, in relation to a pupillage or tenancy in the set of chambers in question, to subject to harassment a person who is, or has applied to be, a pupil or tenant.

(4) It is unlawful for any person, in relation to the giving, withholding or acceptance of instructions to a barrister, to discriminate against any person by subjecting him to a detriment, or to subject him to harassment.

(5) In this regulation—

'barrister's clerk' includes any person carrying out any of the functions of a barrister's clerk;

'pupil', 'pupillage' and 'set of chambers' have the meanings commonly associated with their use in the context of barristers practising in independent practice; and

'tenancy' and 'tenant' have the meanings commonly associated with their use in the context of barristers practising in independent practice, but also include reference to any barrister permitted to work in a set of chambers who is not a tenant.

(6) This regulation extends to England and Wales only.

13. Advocates

(1) It is unlawful for an advocate, in relation to taking any person as his pupil, to discriminate against a person—

(a) in the arrangements which he makes for the purpose of determining whom he will take as his pupil;

(b) in respect of any terms on which he offers to take any person as his pupil; or

(c) by refusing to take, or deliberately not taking, a person as his pupil.

(2) It is unlawful for an advocate, in relation to a person who is his pupil, to discriminate against him—

(a) in respect of any terms applicable to him as a pupil;

(b) in the opportunities for training, or gaining experience, which are afforded or denied to him;

(c) in the benefits which are afforded or denied to him; or

(d) by terminating the relationship, or by subjecting him to any pressure to terminate the relationship or other detriment.

(3) It is unlawful for an advocate, in relation to a person who is his pupil or taking any person as his pupil, to subject such a person to harassment.

(4) It is unlawful for any person, in relation to the giving, withholding or acceptance of instructions to an advocate, to discriminate against any person by subjecting him to a detriment, or to subject him to harassment.

(5) In this regulation—

'advocate' means a member of the Faculty of Advocates practising as such; and

'pupil' has the meaning commonly associated with its use in the context of a person training to be an advocate.

(6) This regulation extends to Scotland only.

14. Partnerships

(1) It is unlawful for a firm, in relation to a position as partner in the firm, to discriminate against a person—

(a) in the arrangements they make for the purpose of determining to whom they should offer that position;

(b) in the terms on which they offer him that position;

(c) by refusing to offer, or deliberately not offering, him that position; or

(d) in a case where the person already holds that position—

(i) in the way they afford him access to any benefits or by refusing to afford, or deliberately not affording, him access to them, or

(ii) by expelling him from that position, or subjecting him to any other detriment.

(2) It is unlawful for a firm, in relation to a position as partner in the firm, to subject to harassment a person who holds or has applied for that position.

(3) Paragraphs (1)(a) to (c) and (2) apply in relation to persons proposing to form themselves into a partnership as they apply in relation to a firm.

(4) Paragraph (1) does not apply to any act in relation to a position as partner where, if the position were employment, that act would be lawful by virtue of regulation 7 (exception for genuine occupational requirement).

(5) In the case of a limited partnership references in this regulation to a partner shall be construed as references to a general partner as defined in section 3 of the Limited Partnerships Act 1907.

(6) This regulation applies to a limited liability partnership as it applies to a firm; and, in its application to a limited liability partnership, references to a partner in a firm are references to a member of the limited liability partnership.

(7) In this regulation, 'firm' has the meaning given by section 4 of the Partnership Act 1890.

(8) In paragraph (1)(d) reference to the expulsion of a person from a position as partner includes reference—

(a) to the termination of that person's partnership by the expiration of any period (including a period expiring by reference to an event or circumstance), not being a termination immediately after which the partnership is renewed on the same terms; and

(b) to the termination of that person's partnership by any act of his (including the giving of notice) in circumstances such that he is entitled to terminate it without notice by reason of the conduct of the other partners.

15. Trade organisations

(1) It is unlawful for a trade organisation to discriminate against a person—

(a) in the terms on which it is prepared to admit him to membership of the organisation; or

(b) by refusing to accept, or deliberately not accepting, his application for membership.

(2) It is unlawful for a trade organisation, in relation to a member of the organisation, to discriminate against him—

(a) in the way it affords him access to any benefits or by refusing or deliberately omitting to afford him access to them;

(b) by depriving him of membership, or varying the terms on which he is a member; or

(c) by subjecting him to any other detriment.

(3) It is unlawful for a trade organisation, in relation to a person's membership or application for membership of that organisation, to subject that person to harassment.

(4) In this regulation—

'trade organisation' means an organisation of workers, an organisation of employers, or any other organisation whose members carry on a particular profession or trade for the purposes of which the organisation exists;

'profession' includes any vocation or occupation; and

'trade' includes any business.

16. Qualifications bodies

(1) It is unlawful for a qualifications body to discriminate against a person—

(a) in the terms on which it is prepared to confer a professional or trade qualification on him;

(b) by refusing or deliberately not granting any application by him for such a qualification; or

(c) by withdrawing such a qualification from him or varying the terms on which he holds it.

(2) It is unlawful for a qualifications body, in relation to a professional or trade qualification conferred by it, to subject to harassment a person who holds or applies for such a qualification.

(3) In this regulation—

'qualifications body' means any authority or body which can confer a professional or trade qualification, but it does not include—

(a) an educational establishment to which regulation 20 (institutions of further and higher education) applies, or would apply but for the operation of any other provision of these Regulations, or

(b) a school;

'confer' includes renew or extend;

'professional or trade qualification' means any authorisation, qualification, recognition, registration, enrolment, approval or certification which is needed for, or facilitates engagement in, a particular profession or trade;

'profession' and 'trade' have the same meaning as in regulation 15.

17. Providers of vocational training

(1) It is unlawful, in relation to a person seeking or undergoing training which would help fit him for any employment, for any training provider to discriminate against him—

(a) in the terms on which the training provider affords him access to any training;

(b) by refusing or deliberately not affording him such access;

(c) by terminating his training; or

(d) by subjecting him to any other detriment during his training.

(2) It is unlawful for a training provider, in relation to a person seeking or undergoing training which would help fit him for any employment, to subject him to harassment.

(3) Paragraph (1) does not apply if the discrimination only concerns training for employment which, by virtue of regulation 7 (exception for genuine occupational requirement), the employer could lawfully refuse to offer the person seeking training.

(4) In this regulation—

'training' includes—

(a) facilities for training; and

(b) practical work experience provided by an employer to a person whom he does not employ;

'training provider' means any person who provides, or makes arrangements for the provision of, training which would help fit another person for any employment, but it does not include—

(a) an employer in relation to training for persons employed by him;

(b) an educational establishment to which regulation 20 (institutions of further and higher education) applies, or would apply but for the operation of any other provision of these Regulations; or

(c) a school.

18. Employment agencies, careers guidance etc

(1) It is unlawful for an employment agency to discriminate against a person—

(a) in the terms on which the agency offers to provide any of its services;

(b) by refusing or deliberately not providing any of its services; or

(c) in the way it provides any of its services.

(2) It is unlawful for an employment agency, in relation to a person to whom it provides its services, or who has requested it to provide its services, to subject that person to harassment.

(3) Paragraph (1) does not apply to discrimination if it only concerns employment which, by virtue of regulation 7 (exception for genuine occupational requirement), the employer could lawfully refuse to offer the person in question.

(4) An employment agency shall not be subject to any liability under this regulation if it proves that—

(a) it acted in reliance on a statement made to it by the employer to the effect that, by reason of the operation of paragraph (3), its action would not be unlawful, and

(b) it was reasonable for it to rely on the statement.

(5) A person who knowingly or recklessly makes a statement such as is referred to in paragraph (4)(a) which in a material respect is false or misleading commits an offence, and shall be liable on summary conviction to a fine not exceeding level 5 on the standard scale.

(6) For the purposes of this regulation—

(a) 'employment agency' means a person who, for profit or not, provides services for the purpose of finding employment for workers or supplying employers with workers, but it does not include—

 (i) an educational establishment to which regulation 20 (institutions of further and higher education) applies, or would apply but for the operation of any other provision of these Regulations, or

 (ii) a school; and

(b) references to the services of an employment agency include guidance on careers and any other services related to employment.

19. Assisting persons to obtain employment etc

(1) It is unlawful for the Secretary of State to discriminate against any person by subjecting him to a detriment, or to subject a person to harassment, in the provision of facilities or services under section 2 of the Employment and Training Act 1973 (arrangements for assisting persons to obtain employment).

(2) It is unlawful for Scottish Enterprise or Highlands and Islands Enterprise to discriminate against any person by subjecting him to a detriment, or to subject a person to harassment, in the provision of facilities or services under such arrangements as are mentioned in section 2(3) of the Enterprise and New Towns (Scotland) Act 1990 (arrangements analogous to arrangements in pursuance of the said Act of 1973).

(3) This regulation does not apply in a case where—

(a) regulation 17 (providers of vocational training) applies, or would apply but for the operation of any other provision of these Regulations, or

(b) the Secretary of State is acting as an employment agency within the meaning of regulation 18.

20. Institutions of further and higher education

(1) It is unlawful, in relation to an educational establishment to which this regulation applies, for the governing body of that establishment to discriminate against a person—

(a) in the terms on which it offers to admit him to the establishment as a student;

(b) by refusing or deliberately not accepting an application for his admission to the establishment as a student; or

(c) where he is a student of the establishment—

 (i) in the way it affords him access to any benefits,

 (ii) by refusing or deliberately not affording him access to them, or

 (iii) by excluding him from the establishment or subjecting him to any other detriment.

(2) It is unlawful, in relation to an educational establishment to which this regulation applies, for the governing body of that establishment to subject to harassment a person who is a student at the establishment, or who has applied for admission to the establishment as a student.

(3) Paragraph (1) does not apply if the discrimination only concerns training which would help fit a person for employment which, by virtue of regulation 7 (exception for genuine occupational requirement), the employer could lawfully refuse to offer the person in question.

(4) This regulation applies to the following educational establishments in England and Wales, namely—

(a) an institution within the further education sector (within the meaning of section 91(3) of the Further and Higher Education Act 1992);

(b) a university;

(c) an institution, other than a university, within the higher education sector (within the meaning of section 91(5) of the Further and Higher Education Act 1992).

(5) This regulation applies to the following educational establishments in Scotland, namely—

(a) a college of further education within the meaning of section 36(1) of the Further and Higher Education (Scotland) Act 1992 under the management of a board of management within the meaning of Part I of that Act;

(b) a college of further education maintained by an education authority in the exercise of its further education functions in providing courses of further education within the meaning of section 1(5)(b)(ii) of the Education (Scotland) Act 1980;

(c) any other educational establishment (not being a school) which provides further education within the meaning of section 1 of the Further and Higher Education (Scotland) Act 1992;

(d) an institution within the higher education sector (within the meaning of Part II of the Further and Higher Education (Scotland) Act 1992);

(e) a central institution (within the meaning of section 135 of the Education (Scotland) Act 1980).

(6) In this regulation—

'education authority' has the meaning given by section 135(1) of the Education (Scotland) Act 1980;

'governing body' includes—

(a) the board of management of a college referred to in paragraph (5)(a), and

(b) the managers of a college or institution referred to in paragraph (5)(b) or (e);

'student' means any person who receives education at an educational establishment to which this regulation applies; and

'university' includes a university college and the college, school or hall of a university.

21. Relationships which have come to an end

(1) In this regulation a 'relevant relationship' is a relationship during the course of which an act of discrimination against, or harassment of, one party to the relationship ('B') by the other party to it ('A') is unlawful by virtue of any preceding provision of this Part.

(2) Where a relevant relationship has come to an end, it is unlawful for A—

(a) to discriminate against B by subjecting him to a detriment; or

(b) to subject B to harassment,

where the discrimination or harassment arises out of and is closely connected to that relationship.

(3) In paragraph (1), reference to an act of discrimination or harassment which is unlawful includes, in the case of a relationship which has come to an end before the coming into force of these Regulations, reference to an act of discrimination or harassment which would, after the coming into force of these Regulations, be unlawful.

Part III
Other unlawful acts

22. Liability of employers and principals

(1) Anything done by a person in the course of his employment shall be treated for the purposes of these Regulations as done by his employer as well as by him, whether or not it was done with the employer's knowledge or approval.

(2) Anything done by a person as agent for another person with the authority (whether express or implied, and whether precedent or subsequent) of that other person shall be treated for the purposes of these Regulations as done by that other person as well as by him.

(3) In proceedings brought under these Regulations against any person in respect of an act alleged to have been done by an employee of his it shall be a defence for that person to prove that he took such steps as were reasonably practicable to prevent the employee from doing that act, or from doing in the course of his employment acts of that description.

23. Aiding unlawful acts

(1) A person who knowingly aids another person to do an act made unlawful by these Regulations shall be treated for the purpose of these Regulations as himself doing an unlawful act of the like description.

(2) For the purposes of paragraph (1) an employee or agent for whose act the employer or principal is liable under regulation 22 (or would be so liable but for regulation 22(3)) shall be deemed to aid the doing of the act by the employer or principal.

(3) A person does not under this regulation knowingly aid another to do an unlawful act if—

(a) he acts in reliance on a statement made to him by that other person that, by reason of any provision of these Regulations, the act which he aids would not be unlawful; and

(b) it is reasonable for him to rely on the statement.

(4) A person who knowingly or recklessly makes a statement such as is referred to in paragraph (3)(a) which in a material respect is false or misleading commits an offence, and shall be liable on summary conviction to a fine not exceeding level 5 on the standard scale.

Part IV
General exceptions from parts II and III

24. Exception for national security

Nothing in Part II or III shall render unlawful an act done for the purpose of safeguarding national security, if the doing of the act was justified by that purpose.

25. Exceptions for positive action

(1) Nothing in Part II or III shall render unlawful any act done in or in connection with—

(a) affording persons of a particular religion or belief access to facilities for training which would help fit them for particular work; or

(b) encouraging persons of a particular religion or belief to take advantage of opportunities for doing particular work,

where it reasonably appears to the person doing the act that it prevents or compensates for disadvantages linked to religion or belief suffered by persons of that religion or belief doing that work or likely to take up that work.

(2) Nothing in Part II or III shall render unlawful any act done by a trade organisation within the meaning of regulation 15 in or in connection with—

(a) affording only members of the organisation who are of a particular religion or belief access to facilities for training which would help fit them for holding a post of any kind in the organisation; or

(b) encouraging only members of the organisation who are of a particular religion or belief to take advantage of opportunities for holding such posts in the organisation, where it reasonably appears to the organisation that the act prevents or compensates for disadvantages linked to religion or belief suffered by those of that religion or belief holding such posts or likely to hold such posts.

(3) Nothing in Part II or III shall render unlawful any act done by a trade organisation within the meaning of regulation 15 in or in connection with encouraging only persons of a particular religion or belief to become members of the organisation where it reasonably appears to the organisation that the act prevents or compensates for disadvantages linked to religion or belief suffered by persons of that religion or belief who are, or are eligible to become, members.

26. Protection of Sikhs from discrimination in connection with requirements as to wearing of safety helmets

(1) Where—

(a) any person applies to a Sikh any provision, criterion or practice relating to the wearing by him of a safety helmet while he is on a construction site; and

(b) at the time when he so applies the provision, criterion or practice that person has no reasonable grounds for believing that the Sikh would not wear a turban at all times when on such a site,

then, for the purposes of regulation 3(1)(b)(iii), the provision, criterion or practice shall be taken to be one which cannot be shown to be a proportionate means of achieving a legitimate aim.

(2) Any special treatment afforded to a Sikh in consequence of section 11(1) or (2) of the Employment Act 1989 (exemption of Sikhs from requirements as to wearing of safety helmets on construction sites) shall not be regarded as giving rise, in relation to any other person, to any discrimination falling within regulation 3.

(3) In this regulation—

'construction site' means any place in Great Britain where any building operations or works of engineering construction are being undertaken, but does not include any site within the territorial sea adjacent to Great Britain unless there are being undertaken on that site such operations or works as are activities falling within Article 8(a) of the Health and Safety at Work etc Act 1974 (Application outside Great Britain) Order 2001; and

'safety helmet' means any form of protective headgear.

(4) In this regulation—

(a) any reference to a Sikh is a reference to a follower of the Sikh religion; and

(b) any reference to a Sikh being on a construction site is a reference to his being there whether while at work or otherwise.

Part V

Enforcement

27. Restriction of proceedings for breach of Regulations

(1) Except as provided by these Regulations no proceedings, whether civil or criminal, shall lie against any person in respect of an act by reason that the act is unlawful by virtue of a provision of these Regulations.

(2) Paragraph (1) does not prevent the making of an application for judicial review [or the investigation or determination of any matter in accordance with Part X (investigations: the Pensions Ombudsman) of the Pension Schemes Act 1993 by the Pensions Ombudsman.].

28. Jurisdiction of employment tribunals

(1) A complaint by any person ('the complainant') that another person ('the respondent')—

    (a) has committed against the complainant an act to which this regulation applies; or

    (b) is by virtue of regulation 22 (liability of employers and principals) or 23 (aiding unlawful acts) to be treated as having committed against the complainant such an act,

may be presented to an employment tribunal.

(2) This regulation applies to any act of discrimination or harassment which is unlawful by virtue of any provision of Part II other than—

    (a) where the act is one in respect of which an appeal or proceedings in the nature of an appeal may be brought under any enactment, regulation 16 (qualifications bodies);

    (b) regulation 20 (institutions of further and higher education); or

    (c) where the act arises out of and is closely connected to a relationship between the complainant and the respondent which has come to an end but during the course of which an act of discrimination against, or harassment of, the complainant by the respondent would have been unlawful by virtue of regulation 20, regulation 21 (relationships which have come to an end).

(3) In paragraph (2)(c), reference to an act of discrimination or harassment which would have been unlawful includes, in the case of a relationship which has come to an end before the coming into force of these Regulations, reference to an act of discrimination or harassment which would, after the coming into force of these Regulations, have been unlawful.

(4) In this regulation, 'enactment' includes an enactment comprised in, or in an instrument made under, an Act of the Scottish Parliament.

29. Burden of proof: employment tribunals

(1) This regulation applies to any complaint presented under regulation 28 to an employment tribunal.

(2) Where, on the hearing of the complaint, the complainant proves facts from which the tribunal could, apart from this regulation, conclude in the absence of an adequate explanation that the respondent—

    (a) has committed against the complainant an act to which regulation 28 applies; or

    (b) is by virtue of regulation 22 (liability of employers and principals) or 23 (aiding unlawful acts) to be treated as having committed against the complainant such an act,

the tribunal shall uphold the complaint unless the respondent proves that he did not commit, or as the case may be, is not to be treated as having committed, that act.

30. Remedies on complaints in employment tribunals

(1) Where an employment tribunal finds that a complaint presented to it under regulation 28 is well-founded, the tribunal shall make such of the following as it considers just and equitable—

    (a) an order declaring the rights of the complainant and the respondent in relation to the act to which the complaint relates;

    (b) an order requiring the respondent to pay to the complainant compensation of an amount corresponding to any damages he could have been ordered by a county court or by a sheriff court to pay to the complainant if the complaint had fallen to be dealt with under regulation 31 (jurisdiction of county and sheriff courts);

(c) a recommendation that the respondent take within a specified period action appearing to the tribunal to be practicable for the purpose of obviating or reducing the adverse effect on the complainant of any act of discrimination or harassment to which the complaint relates.

(2) As respects an unlawful act of discrimination falling within regulation 3(1)(b), if the respondent proves that the provision, criterion or practice was not applied with the intention of treating the complainant unfavourably on grounds of religion or belief, an order may be made under paragraph (1)(b) only if the employment tribunal—

(a) makes such order under paragraph (1)(a) (if any) and such recommendation under paragraph (1)(c) (if any) as it would have made if it had no power to make an order under paragraph (1)(b); and

(b) (where it makes an order under paragraph (1)(a) or a recommendation under paragraph (1)(c) or both) considers that it is just and equitable to make an order under paragraph (1)(b) as well.

(3) If without reasonable justification the respondent to a complaint fails to comply with a recommendation made by an employment tribunal under paragraph (1)(c), then, if it thinks it just and equitable to do so—

(a) the tribunal may increase the amount of compensation required to be paid to the complainant in respect of the complaint by an order made under paragraph (1)(b); or

(b) if an order under paragraph (1)(b) was not made, the tribunal may make such an order.

(4) Where an amount of compensation falls to be awarded under paragraph (1)(b), the tribunal may include in the award interest on that amount subject to, and in accordance with, the provisions of the Employment Tribunals (Interest on Awards in Discrimination Cases) Regulations 1996.

(5) This regulation has effect subject to paragraph 7 of Schedule 1A (occupational pension schemes).]

31. Jurisdiction of county and sheriff courts

(1) A claim by any person ('the claimant') that another person ('the respondent')—

(a) has committed against the claimant an act to which this regulation applies; or

(b) is by virtue of regulation 22 (liability of employers and principals) or 23 (aiding unlawful acts) to be treated as having committed against the claimant such an act,

may be made the subject of civil proceedings in like manner as any other claim in tort or (in Scotland) in reparation for breach of statutory duty.

(2) Proceedings brought under paragraph (1) shall—

(a) in England and Wales, be brought only in a county court; and

(b) in Scotland, be brought only in a sheriff court.

(3) For the avoidance of doubt it is hereby declared that damages in respect of an unlawful act to which this regulation applies may include compensation for injury to feelings whether or not they include compensation under any other head.

(4) This regulation applies to any act of discrimination or harassment which is unlawful by virtue of—

(a) regulation 20 (institutions of further and higher education); or

(b) where the act arises out of and is closely connected to a relationship between the claimant and the respondent which has come to an end but during the course of which an act of discrimination against, or harassment of, the claimant by the respondent would have been unlawful by virtue of regulation 20, regulation 21 (relationships which have come to an end).

(5) In paragraph (4)(b), reference to an act of discrimination or harassment which would have been unlawful includes, in the case of a relationship which has come to an end before the coming into force of these Regulations, reference to an act of discrimination or harassment which would, after the coming into force of these Regulations, have been unlawful.

32. Burden of proof: county and sheriff courts

(1) This regulation applies to any claim brought under regulation 31 in a county court in England and Wales or a sheriff court in Scotland.

(2) Where, on the hearing of the claim, the claimant proves facts from which the court could, apart from this regulation, conclude in the absence of an adequate explanation that the respondent—

(a) has committed against the claimant an act to which regulation 31 applies; or

(b) is by virtue of regulation 22 (liability of employers and principals) or 23 (aiding unlawful acts) to be treated as having committed against the claimant such an act,

the court shall uphold the claim unless the respondent proves that he did not commit, or as the case may be, is not to be treated as having committed, that act.

33. Help for persons in obtaining information etc

(1) In accordance with this regulation, a person ('the person aggrieved') who considers he may have been discriminated against, or subjected to harassment, in contravention of these Regulations may serve on the respondent to a complaint presented under regulation 28 (jurisdiction of employment tribunals) or a claim brought under regulation 31 (jurisdiction of county and sheriff courts) questions in the form set out in Schedule 2 or forms to the like effect with such variation as the circumstances require; and the respondent may if he so wishes reply to such questions by way of the form set out in Schedule 3 or forms to the like effect with such variation as the circumstances require.

(2) Where the person aggrieved questions the respondent (whether in accordance with paragraph (1) or not)—

(a) the questions, and any reply by the respondent (whether in accordance with paragraph (1) or not) shall, subject to the following provisions of this regulation, be admissible as evidence in the proceedings;

(b) if it appears to the court or tribunal that the respondent deliberately, and without reasonable excuse, omitted to reply within eight weeks of service of the questions or that his reply is evasive or equivocal, the court or tribunal may draw any inference from that fact that it considers it just and equitable to draw, including an inference that he committed an unlawful act.

(3) In proceedings before a county court in England or Wales or a sheriff court in Scotland, a question shall only be admissible as evidence in pursuance of paragraph (2)(a)—

(a) where it was served before those proceedings had been instituted, if it was so served within the period of six months beginning when the act complained of was done;

(b) where it was served when those proceedings had been instituted, if it was served with the leave of, and within a period specified by, the court in question.

(4) In proceedings before an employment tribunal, a question shall only be admissible as evidence in pursuance of paragraph (2)(a)—

(a) where it was served before a complaint had been presented to the tribunal, if it was so served within the period of three months beginning when the act complained of was done;

(b) where it was served when a complaint had been presented to the tribunal, either—

(i) if it was so served within the period of twenty-one days beginning with the day on which the complaint was presented, or

(ii) if it was so served later with leave given, and within a period specified, by a direction of the tribunal.

(5) A question and any reply thereto may be served on the respondent or, as the case may be, on the person aggrieved—

(a) by delivering it to him;

(b) by sending it by post to him at his usual or last-known residence or place of business;

(c) where the person to be served is a body corporate or is a trade union or employers' association within the meaning of the Trade Union and Labour Relations (Consolidation) Act 1992, by delivering it to the secretary or clerk of the body, union or association at its registered or principal office or by sending it by post to the secretary or clerk at that office;

(d) where the person to be served is acting by a solicitor, by delivering it at, or by sending it by post to, the solicitor's address for service; or

(e) where the person to be served is the person aggrieved, by delivering the reply, or sending it by post, to him at his address for reply as stated by him in the document containing the questions.

(6) This regulation is without prejudice to any other enactment or rule of law regulating interlocutory and preliminary matters in proceedings before a county court, sheriff court or employment tribunal, and has effect subject to any enactment or rule of law regulating the admissibility of evidence in such proceedings.

(7) In this regulation 'respondent' includes a prospective respondent.

34. Period within which proceedings to be brought

(1) An employment tribunal shall not consider a complaint under regulation 28 unless it is presented to the tribunal before the end of—

(a) the period of three months beginning when the act complained of was done; or

(b) in a case to which regulation 36(7) (armed forces) applies, the period of six months so beginning.

(2) A county court or a sheriff court shall not consider a claim brought under regulation 31 unless proceedings in respect of the claim are instituted before the end of the period of six months beginning when the act complained of was done.

(3) A court or tribunal may nevertheless consider any such complaint or claim which is out of time if, in all the circumstances of the case, it considers that it is just and equitable to do so.

(4) For the purposes of this regulation and regulation 33 (help for persons in obtaining information etc)—

(a) when the making of a contract is, by reason of the inclusion of any term, an unlawful act, that act shall be treated as extending throughout the duration of the contract; and

(b) any act extending over a period shall be treated as done at the end of that period; and

(c) a deliberate omission shall be treated as done when the person in question decided upon it,

and in the absence of evidence establishing the contrary a person shall be taken for the purposes of this regulation to decide upon an omission when he does an act inconsistent with doing the omitted act or, if he has done no such inconsistent act, when the period expires within which he might reasonably have been expected to do the omitted act if it was to be done.

Part VI

Supplemental

35. Validity of contracts, collective agreements and rules of undertakings

Schedule 4 (validity of contracts, collective agreements and rules of undertakings) shall have effect.

36. Application to the Crown etc

(1) These Regulations apply—

(a) to an act done by or for purposes of a Minister of the Crown or government department; or

(b) to an act done on behalf of the Crown by a statutory body, or a person holding a statutory office,

as they apply to an act done by a private person.

(2) These Regulations apply to—

(a) service for purposes of a Minister of the Crown or government department, other than service of a person holding a statutory office;

(b) service on behalf of the Crown for purposes of a person holding a statutory office or purposes of a statutory body; or

(c) service in the armed forces,

as they apply to employment by a private person, and shall so apply as if references to a contract of employment included references to the terms of service.

(3) Paragraphs (1) and (2) have effect subject to regulation 11 (police).

(4) Regulation 9(3) (meaning of employment and contract work at establishment in Great Britain) shall have effect in relation to any ship, aircraft or hovercraft belonging to or possessed by Her Majesty in right of the government of the United Kingdom as it has effect in relation to a ship, aircraft or hovercraft specified in regulation 9(3)(a) or (b).

(5) The provisions of Parts II to IV of the Crown Proceedings Act 1947 shall apply to proceedings against the Crown under these Regulations as they apply to proceedings in England and Wales which by virtue of section 23 of that Act are treated for the purposes of Part II of that Act as civil proceedings by or against the Crown, except that in their application to proceedings under these Regulations section 20 of that Act (removal of proceedings from county court to High Court) shall not apply.

(6) The provisions of Part V of the Crown Proceedings Act 1947 shall apply to proceedings against the Crown under these Regulations as they apply to proceedings in Scotland which by virtue of the said Part are treated as civil proceedings by or against the Crown, except that in their application to proceedings under these Regulations the proviso to section 44 of that Act (removal of proceedings from the sheriff court to the Court of Session) shall not apply.

(7) This paragraph applies to any complaint by a person ('the complainant') that another person—

(a) has committed an act of discrimination or harassment against the complainant which is unlawful by virtue of regulation 6 (applicants and employees); or

(b) is by virtue of regulation 22 (liability of employers and principals) or 23 (aiding unlawful acts) to be treated as having committed such an act of discrimination or harassment against the complainant,
if at the time when the act complained of was done the complainant was serving in the armed forces and the discrimination or harassment in question relates to his service in those forces.

(8) A complainant may present a complaint to which paragraph (7) applies to an employment tribunal under regulation 28 only if—

(a) he has made a complaint in respect of the same matter to an officer under the service redress procedures applicable to him; and

(b) that complaint has not been withdrawn.

(9) For the purpose of paragraph (8)(b), a complainant shall be treated as having withdrawn his complaint if, having made a complaint to an officer under the service redress procedures applicable to him, he fails to submit that complaint to the Defence Council under those procedures.

(10) Where a complaint is presented to an employment tribunal under regulation 28 by virtue of paragraph (8), the service redress procedures may continue after the complaint is so presented.

(11) In this regulation—

'armed forces' means any of the naval, military or air forces of the Crown;

'service for purposes of a Minister of the Crown or government department' does not include service in any office mentioned in Schedule 2 (Ministerial offices) to the House of Commons Disqualification Act 1975;

'the service redress procedures' means the procedures, excluding those which relate to the making of a report on a complaint to Her Majesty, referred to in section 180 of the Army Act 1955, section 180 of the Air Force Act 1955 and section 130 of the Naval Discipline Act 1957; and

'statutory body' means a body set up by or in pursuance of an enactment, and 'statutory office' means an office so set up.

37. Application to House of Commons staff

(1) These Regulations apply to an act done by an employer of a relevant member of the House of Commons staff, and to service as such a member, as they apply to an act done by and to service for purposes of a Minister of the Crown or government department, and accordingly apply as if references to a contract of employment included references to the terms of service of such a member.

(2) In this regulation 'relevant member of the House of Commons staff' means any person—

(a) who was appointed by the House of Commons Commission; or

(b) who is a member of the Speaker's personal staff,

and subsections (6) to (12) of section 195 of the Employment Rights Act 1996 (person to be treated as employer of House of Commons staff) apply, with any necessary modifications, for the purposes of these Regulations.

38. Application to House of Lords staff

(1) These Regulations apply in relation to employment as a relevant member of the House of Lords staff as they apply in relation to other employment.

(2) In this regulation 'relevant member of the House of Lords staff' means any person who is employed under a contract of employment with the Corporate Officer of the House of Lords, and section 194(7) of the Employment Rights Act 1996 (continuity of employment) applies for the purposes of this regulation.

39. Savings of, and amendments to, legislation

(1) These Regulations are without prejudice to—

(a) sections 58 to 60 of the School Standards and Framework Act 1998 (appointment and dismissal of teachers in schools with a religious character etc); and

(b) section 21 of the Education (Scotland) Act 1980 (management of denominational schools).

(2) Schedule 5 (amendments to legislation) shall have effect.

SCHEDULES

SCHEDULE 1

Regulation 9(4)
Norwegian part of the Frigg Gas Field

1. The part of the Norwegian sector of the Continental Shelf described in this Schedule is the area defined by—

(a) the sets of lines of latitude and longitude joining the following surface co-ordinates—

Longitude	Latitude
02 degrees 05 minutes 30 seconds E	60 degrees 00 minutes 45 seconds N
02 degrees 05 minutes 30 seconds E	59 degrees 58 minutes 45 seconds N
02 degrees 06 minutes 00 seconds E	59 degrees 58 minutes 45 seconds N
02 degrees 06 minutes 00 seconds E	59 degrees 57 minutes 45 seconds N
02 degrees 07 minutes 00 seconds E	59 degrees 57 minutes 45 seconds N
02 degrees 07 minutes 00 seconds E	59 degrees 57 minutes 30 seconds N
02 degrees 07 minutes 30 seconds E	59 degrees 57 minutes 30 seconds N
02 degrees 07 minutes 30 seconds E	59 degrees 55 minutes 30 seconds N
02 degrees 10 minutes 30 seconds E	59 degrees 55 minutes 30 seconds N
02 degrees 10 minutes 30 seconds E	59 degrees 54 minutes 45 seconds N
02 degrees 11 minutes 00 seconds E	59 degrees 54 minutes 45 seconds N
02 degrees 11 minutes 00 seconds E	59 degrees 54 minutes 15 seconds N
02 degrees 12 minutes 30 seconds E	59 degrees 54 minutes 15 seconds N
02 degrees 12 minutes 30 seconds E	59 degrees 54 minutes 00 seconds N
02 degrees 13 minutes 30 seconds E	59 degrees 54 minutes 00 seconds N
02 degrees 13 minutes 30 seconds E	59 degrees 54 minutes 30 seconds N
02 degrees 15 minutes 30 seconds E	59 degrees 54 minutes 30 seconds N
02 degrees 15 minutes 30 seconds E	59 degrees 53 minutes 15 seconds N
02 degrees 10 minutes 30 seconds E	59 degrees 53 minutes 15 seconds N
02 degrees 10 minutes 30 seconds E	59 degrees 52 minutes 45 seconds N
02 degrees 09 minutes 30 seconds E	59 degrees 52 minutes 45 seconds N
02 degrees 09 minutes 30 seconds E	59 degrees 52 minutes 15 seconds N

Longitude	Latitude
02 degrees 08 minutes 30 seconds E	59 degrees 52 minutes 15 seconds N
02 degrees 08 minutes 30 seconds E	59 degrees 52 minutes 00 seconds N
02 degrees 07 minutes 30 seconds E	59 degrees 52 minutes 00 seconds N
02 degrees 07 minutes 30 seconds E	59 degrees 51 minutes 30 seconds N
02 degrees 05 minutes 30 seconds E	59 degrees 51 minutes 30 seconds N
02 degrees 05 minutes 30 seconds E	59 degrees 51 minutes 00 seconds N
02 degrees 04 minutes 00 seconds E	59 degrees 51 minutes 00 seconds N
02 degrees 04 minutes 00 seconds E	59 degrees 50 minutes 30 seconds N
02 degrees 03 minutes 00 seconds E	59 degrees 50 minutes 30 seconds N
02 degrees 03 minutes 00 seconds E	59 degrees 50 minutes 00 seconds N

(b) a line from the point 02 degrees 03 minutes 00 seconds E 59 degrees 50 minutes 00 seconds N west along the parallel of latitude 59 degrees 50 minutes 00 seconds N until its intersection with the Dividing Line;

(c) a line from the point of intersection specified in sub-paragraph (b) along the Dividing Line until its intersection with the parallel of latitude 60 degrees 00 minutes 45 seconds N;

(d) a line from the point of intersection specified in sub-paragraph (c) east along the parallel of latitude 60 degrees 00 minutes 45 degrees N until its intersection with the meridian 02 degrees 05 minutes 30 seconds E.

2. In this Schedule, the 'Dividing Line' means the dividing line as defined in an Agreement dated 10th March 1965 and made between the government of the United Kingdom of Great Britain and Northern Ireland and the government of the Kingdom of Norway as supplemented by a Protocol dated 22nd December 1978.

SCHEDULE 1A

Regulation 9A(3)
Occupational pension schemes

Interpretation

1.

(1) In this Schedule—

'active member', 'deferred member', 'managers', 'pensioner member' and 'trustees or managers', in relation to an occupational pension scheme, have the meanings given by section 124(1) of the Pensions Act 1995 as at the date of the coming into force of these Regulations;

'member', in relation to an occupational pension scheme, means any active member, deferred member or pensioner member;

'non-discrimination rule' means the rule in paragraph 2;

'occupational pension scheme' has the same meaning as in the Pension Schemes Act 1993 as at the date of the coming into force of these Regulations;

'prospective member', in relation to an occupational pension scheme, means any person who, under the terms of his employment or the rules of the scheme or both—

(a) is able, at his own option, to become a member of the scheme,

(b) shall become so able if he continues in the same employment for a sufficient period of time,

(c) shall be admitted to it automatically unless he makes an election not to become a member, or

(d) may be admitted to it subject to the consent of his employer.

(2) In paragraph 6 (procedure in employment tribunals), 'employer', in relation to an occupational pension scheme, has the meaning given by section 124(1) of the Pensions Act 1995 as at the date of the coming into force of these Regulations.

(3) Any term used in regulation 9A (trustees and managers of occupational pension schemes) and in this Schedule shall have the same meaning in that regulation as it has in this Schedule.

Non-discrimination rule

2. Every occupational pension scheme shall be treated as including a provision ('the non-discrimination rule') containing a requirement that the trustees or managers of the scheme refrain from doing any act which is unlawful by virtue of regulation 9A.

3. The other provisions of the scheme are to have effect subject to the non-discrimination rule.

4. The trustees or managers of an occupational pension scheme may—

(a) if they do not (apart from this paragraph) have power to make such alterations to the scheme as may be required to secure conformity with the non-discrimination rule, or

(b) if they have such power but the procedure for doing so—

(i) is liable to be unduly complex or protracted, or

(ii) involves the obtaining of consents which cannot be obtained, or can only be obtained with undue delay or difficulty,

by resolution make such alterations to the scheme.

5. Alterations made by a resolution such as is referred to in paragraph 4 may have effect in relation to a period before the alterations are made (but may not have effect in relation to any time before the coming into force of these Regulations).

Procedure in employment tribunals

6. Where under regulation 28 (jurisdiction of employment tribunals) a member or prospective member of an occupational pension scheme presents to an employment tribunal a complaint that the trustees or managers of the scheme—

(a) have committed against him an act which is unlawful by virtue of regulation 9A (trustees and managers of occupational pension schemes) or 21 (relationships which have come to an end); or

(b) are by virtue of regulation 22 (liability of employers and principals) or 23 (aiding unlawful acts) to be treated as having committed against him such an act,

the employer in relation to the scheme shall, for the purposes of the rules governing procedure, be treated as a party and be entitled to appear and be heard in accordance with those rules.

Remedies in employment tribunals

7.

(1) This paragraph applies where—

(a) under regulation 28 (jurisdiction of employment tribunals) a member or prospective member of an occupational pension scheme ('the complainant') presents to an employment tribunal a complaint against the trustees or managers of the scheme or an employer;

(b) the complainant is not a pensioner member of the scheme;

(c) the complaint relates to the terms on which persons become members of the scheme, or the terms on which members of the scheme are treated; and

(d) the tribunal finds the complaint to be well-founded.

(2) Where this paragraph applies, the employment tribunal may, without prejudice to the generality of its power under regulation 30(1)(a) (power to make order declaring rights of complainant and respondent), make an order declaring that the complainant has a right—

(a) where the complaint relates to the terms on which persons become members of the scheme, to be admitted to the scheme;

(b) where the complaint relates to the terms on which members of the scheme are treated, to membership of the scheme without discrimination.

(3) An order under sub-paragraph (2)—

(a) may be made in respect of such period as is specified in the order (but may not be made in respect of any time before the coming into force of these Regulations);

(b) may make such provision as the employment tribunal considers appropriate as to the terms on which, or the capacity in which, the complainant is to enjoy such admission or membership.

(4) Where this paragraph applies, the employment tribunal may not make an order for compensation under regulation 30(1)(b), whether in relation to arrears of benefits or otherwise, except—

(a) for injury to feelings;

(b) by virtue of regulation 30(3).'.

SCHEDULE 2

Regulation 33(1)

Questionnaire of person aggrieved

To

. . . .

(*name of person to be questioned*) of

. . . .

(*address*)

    1.—(1) I

. . . .

(*name of questioner*) of

. . . .

. . . .

(*address*)

consider that you may have discriminated against me [subjected me to harassment] contrary to the Employment Equality (Religion or Belief) Regulations 2003.

(2) (*Give date, approximate time and a factual description of the treatment received and of the circumstances leading up to the treatment.*)

(3) I consider that this treatment may have been unlawful [because

. . . .

(*complete if you wish to give reasons, otherwise delete*)].

2. Do you agree that the statement in paragraph 1(2) above is an accurate description of what happened? If not, in what respect do you disagree or what is your version of what happened?

3. Do you accept that your treatment of me was unlawful discrimination [harassment]? If not—

(a) why not,

(b) for what reason did I receive the treatment accorded to me, and (c) how far did considerations of religion or belief affect your treatment of me?

4. (*Any other questions you wish to ask.*)

5. My address for any reply you may wish to give to the questions raised above is [that set out in paragraph 1(1) above] [the following address

. . . .

. . . .].

(*signature of questioner*)

. . . .

(*date*)

N.B.—By virtue of regulation 33 of the Employment Equality (Religion or Belief) Regulations 2003 this questionnaire and any reply are (subject to the provisions of that regulation) admissible in proceedings under the Regulations. A court or tribunal may draw any such inference as is just and equitable from a failure without reasonable excuse to reply within eight weeks of service of this questionnaire, or from an evasive or equivocal reply, including an inference that the person questioned has committed an unlawful act.

SCHEDULE 3

Regulation 33(1)

Reply by respondent
To

. . . .

(*name of questioner*) of

. . . .

(*address*)

1. I

. . . .

(*name of person questioned*) of

....

....

(*address*)
hereby acknowledge receipt of the questionnaire signed by you and dated

....

which was served on me on

....

(*date*).
   2. [I agree that the statement in paragraph 1(2) of the questionnaire is an accurate description of what happened.]
     [I disagree with the statement in paragraph 1(2) of the questionnaire in that

....

....]
   3. I accept/dispute that my treatment of you was unlawful discrimination [harassment]. [My reasons for so disputing are

....

The reason why you received the treatment accorded to you and the answers to the other questions in paragraph 3 of the questionnaire are

....]
   4. (*Replies to questions in paragraph 4 of the questionnaire.*)
   [5. I have deleted (in whole or in part) the paragraph(s) numbered

....

above, since I am unable/unwilling to reply to the relevant questions in the correspondingly numbered paragraph(s) of the questionnaire for the following reasons

....]

(*signature of person questioned*)

....

(*date*)

SCHEDULE 4

Regulation 35

Validity of contracts, collective agreement and rules of undertakings

Part 1
Validity and revision of contracts

1.
   (1) A term of a contract is void where—
     (a) the making of the contract is, by reason of the inclusion of the term, unlawful by virtue of these Regulations;

(b) it is included in furtherance of an act which is unlawful by virtue of these Regulations; or

(c) it provides for the doing of an act which is unlawful by virtue of these Regulations.

(2) Sub-paragraph (1) does not apply to a term the inclusion of which constitutes, or is in furtherance of, or provides for, unlawful discrimination against, or harassment of, a party to the contract, but the term shall be unenforceable against that party.

(3) A term in a contract which purports to exclude or limit any provision of these Regulations is unenforceable by any person in whose favour the term would operate apart from this paragraph.

(4) Sub-paragraphs (1), (2) and (3) shall apply whether the contract was entered into before or after the date on which these Regulations come into force; but in the case of a contract made before that date, those sub-paragraphs do not apply in relation to any period before that date.

2.

(1) Paragraph 1(3) does not apply—

(a) to a contract settling a complaint to which regulation 28(1) (jurisdiction of employment tribunals) applies where the contract is made with the assistance of a conciliation officer within the meaning of section 211 of the Trade Union and Labour Relations (Consolidation) Act 1992;

(b) to a contract settling a complaint to which regulation 28(1) applies if the conditions regulating compromise contracts under this Schedule are satisfied in relation to the contract; or

(c) to a contract settling a claim to which regulation 31 (jurisdiction of county or sheriff courts) applies.

(2) The conditions regulating compromise contracts under this Schedule are that—

(a) the contract must be in writing;

(b) the contract must relate to the particular complaint;

(c) the complainant must have received advice from a relevant independent adviser as to the terms and effect of the proposed contract and in particular its effect on his ability to pursue a complaint before an employment tribunal;

(d) there must be in force, when the adviser gives the advice, a contract of insurance, or an indemnity provided for members of a profession or professional body, covering the risk of a claim by the complainant in respect of loss arising in consequence of the advice;

(e) the contract must identify the adviser; and

(f) the contract must state that the conditions regulating compromise contracts under this Schedule are satisfied.

(3) A person is a relevant independent adviser for the purposes of sub-paragraph (2)(c)—

(a) if he is a qualified lawyer;

(b) if he is an officer, official, employee or member of an independent trade union who has been certified in writing by the trade union as competent to give advice and as authorised to do so on behalf of the trade union; or

(c) if he works at an advice centre (whether as an employee or a volunteer) and has been certified in writing by the centre as competent to give advice and as authorised to do so on behalf of the centre.

(4) But a person is not a relevant independent adviser for the purposes of sub-paragraph (2)(c) in relation to the complainant—

(a) if he is, is employed by or is acting in the matter for the other party or a person who is connected with the other party;

(b) in the case of a person within sub-paragraph (3)(b) or (c), if the trade union or advice centre is the other party or a person who is connected with the other party; or

(c) in the case of a person within sub-paragraph (3)(c), if the complainant makes a payment for the advice received from him.

(5) In sub-paragraph (3)(a) 'qualified lawyer' means—

(a) as respects England and Wales, a barrister (whether in practice as such or employed to give legal advice), a solicitor who holds a practising certificate, or a person other than a barrister or solicitor who is an authorised advocate or authorised litigator (within the meaning of the Courts and Legal Services Act 1990); and

(b) as respects Scotland, an advocate (whether in practice as such or employed to give legal advice), or a solicitor who holds a practising certificate.

(6) In sub-paragraph (3)(b) 'independent trade union' has the same meaning as in the Trade Union and Labour Relations (Consolidation) Act 1992.

(7) For the purposes of sub-paragraph (4)(a) any two persons are to be treated as connected—

(a) if one is a company of which the other (directly or indirectly) has control; or

(b) if both are companies of which a third person (directly or indirectly) has control.

(8) An agreement under which the parties agree to submit a dispute to arbitration—

(a) shall be regarded for the purposes of sub-paragraph (1)(a) and (b) as being a contract settling a complaint if—

(i) the dispute is covered by a scheme having effect by virtue of an order under section 212A of the Trade Union and Labour Relations (Consolidation) Act 1992, and

(ii) the agreement is to submit it to arbitration in accordance with the scheme, but

(b) shall be regarded as neither being nor including such a contract in any other case.

3.

(1) On the application of a person interested in a contract to which paragraph 1(1) or (2) applies, a county court or a sheriff court may make such order as it thinks fit for—

(a) removing or modifying any term rendered void by paragraph 1(1), or

(b) removing or modifying any term made unenforceable by paragraph 1(2);

but such an order shall not be made unless all persons affected have been given notice in writing of the application (except where under rules of court notice may be dispensed with) and have been afforded an opportunity to make representations to the court.

(2) An order under sub-paragraph (1) may include provision as respects any period before the making of the order (but after the coming into force of these Regulations).

Part 2
Collective agreements and rules of undertakings

4.

(1) This Part of this Schedule applies to—

(a) any term of a collective agreement, including an agreement which was not intended, or is presumed not to have been intended, to be a legally enforceable contract;

(b) any rule made by an employer for application to all or any of the persons who are employed by him or who apply to be, or are, considered by him for employment;

(c) any rule made by a trade organisation (within the meaning of regulation 15) or a qualifications body (within the meaning of regulation 16) for application to—

    (i) all or any of its members or prospective members; or

    (ii) all or any of the persons on whom it has conferred professional or trade qualifications (within the meaning of regulation 16) or who are seeking the professional or trade qualifications which it has power to confer.

(2) Any term or rule to which this Part of this Schedule applies is void where—

    (a) the making of the collective agreement is, by reason of the inclusion of the term, unlawful by virtue of these Regulations;

    (b) the term or rule is included or made in furtherance of an act which is unlawful by virtue of these Regulations; or

    (c) the term or rule provides for the doing of an act which is unlawful by virtue of these Regulations.

(3) Sub-paragraph (2) shall apply whether the agreement was entered into, or the rule made, before or after the date on which these Regulations come into force; but in the case of an agreement entered into, or a rule made, before the date on which these Regulations come into force, that sub-paragraph does not apply in relation to any period before that date.

5. A person to whom this paragraph applies may present a complaint to an employment tribunal that a term or rule is void by virtue of paragraph 4 if he has reason to believe—

    (a) that the term or rule may at some future time have effect in relation to him; and

    (b) where he alleges that it is void by virtue of paragraph 4(2)(c), that—

        (i) an act for the doing of which it provides, may at some such time be done in relation to him, and

        (ii) the act would be unlawful by virtue of these Regulations if done in relation to him in present circumstances.

6. In the case of a complaint about—

    (a) a term of a collective agreement made by or on behalf of—

        (i) an employer,

        (ii) an organisation of employers of which an employer is a member, or

        (iii) an association of such organisations of one of which an employer is a member, or

    (b) a rule made by an employer within the meaning of paragraph 4(1)(b),

paragraph 5 applies to any person who is, or is genuinely and actively seeking to become, one of his employees.

7. In the case of a complaint about a rule made by an organisation or body to which paragraph 4(1)(c) applies, paragraph 5 applies to any person—

    (a) who is, or is genuinely and actively seeking to become, a member of the organisation or body;

    (b) on whom the organisation or body has conferred a professional or trade qualification (within the meaning of regulation 16); or

    (c) who is genuinely and actively seeking such a professional or trade qualification which the organisation or body has power to confer.

8.

(1) When an employment tribunal finds that a complaint presented to it under paragraph 5 is well-founded the tribunal shall make an order declaring that the term or rule is void.

(2) An order under sub-paragraph (1) may include provision as respects any period before the making of the order (but after the coming into force of these Regulations).

9. The avoidance by virtue of paragraph 4(2) of any term or rule which provides for any person to be discriminated against shall be without prejudice to the following rights (except in so far as they enable any person to require another person to be treated less favourably than himself), namely—

(a) such of the rights of the person to be discriminated against; and

(b) such of the rights of any person who will be treated more favourably in direct or indirect consequence of the discrimination,

as are conferred by or in respect of a contract made or modified wholly or partly in pursuance of, or by reference to, that term or rule.

10. In this Schedule 'collective agreement' means any agreement relating to one or more of the matters mentioned in section 178(2) of the Trade Union and Labour Relations (Consolidation) Act 1992 (meaning of trade dispute), being an agreement made by or on behalf of one or more employers or one or more organisations of employers or associations of such organisations with one or more organisations of workers or associations of such organisations.

SCHEDULE 5

Regulation 39(2)

Amendments to legislation

1. The Employment Tribunals Act 1996 is amended as follows—

(a) in section 18(1) (cases where conciliation provisions apply)—

(i) at the end of paragraph (j), there is omitted 'or', and

(ii) after paragraph (k) there is inserted—

'or

(1) under regulation 28 of the Employment Equality (Religion or Belief) Regulations 2003';

(b) in section 21 (jurisdiction of the Employment Appeal Tribunal), in subsection (1) (which specifies the proceedings and claims to which the section applies)—

(i) at the end of paragraph (k), there is omitted 'or', and

(ii) after paragraph (l) there is inserted—

'or

(m) the Employment Equality (Religion or Belief) Regulations 2003'.

2. Section 126(1)(b) (compensation for acts which are both unfair dismissal and discrimination) of the Employment Rights Act 1996 is amended as follows—

(a) after 'Disability Discrimination Act 1995' there is omitted 'and'; and

(b) after 'the Employment Equality (Sexual Orientation) Regulations 2003' there is inserted—

'and the Employment Equality (Religion or Belief) Regulations 2003'.

3. Sub-paragraph (b) of the definition of 'an award under the relevant legislation' in regulation 1(2) (interpretation) of the Employment Tribunals (Interest on Awards in Discrimination Cases) Regulations 1996 is amended as follows—

(a) after 'section 8(2)(b) of the 1995 Act' there is omitted 'or'; and

(b) after 'the Employment Equality (Sexual Orientation) Regulations 2003' there is inserted—

'or regulation 30(1)(b) of the Employment Equality (Religion or Belief) Regulations 2003'.

4. In the Employment Act 2002 at the end of each of the following schedules—

(a) Schedule 3 (tribunal jurisdictions to which section 31 applies for adjustment of awards for non-completion of statutory procedure);

(b) Schedule 4 (tribunal jurisdictions to which section 32 applies for complaints where the employee must first submit a statement of grievance to employer); and

(c) Schedule 5 (tribunal jurisdictions to which section 38 applies in relation to proceedings where the employer has failed to give a statement of employment particulars), there is inserted—

'Regulation 28 of the Employment Equality (Religion or Belief) Regulations 2003 (discrimination in the employment field)'.

EXPLANATORY NOTE

(This note is not part of the Regulations)

These Regulations, which are made under section 2(2) of the European Communities Act 1972 (c.68), implement (in Great Britain) Council Directive 2000/78/EC of 27th November 2000 establishing a general framework for equal treatment in employment (OJ L 303, 2.12.2000, p.16) so far as it relates to discrimination on grounds of religion or belief. The Regulations make it unlawful to discriminate on grounds of religion or belief in employment and vocational training. They prohibit direct discrimination, indirect discrimination, victimisation and harassment.

Religion or belief is defined in regulation 2 as meaning any religion, religious belief, or similar philosophical belief.

Direct discrimination, defined in regulation 3(1)(a), occurs where a person is treated less favourably than another on grounds of religion or belief. Indirect discrimination, defined in regulation 3(1)(b), occurs where a provision, criterion or practice, which is applied generally, puts persons of a particular religion or belief at a disadvantage and cannot be shown to be a proportionate means of achieving a legitimate aim. Victimisation, defined in regulation 4, occurs where a person receives less favourable treatment than others by reason of the fact that he has brought (or given evidence in) proceedings, made an allegation or otherwise done anything under or by reference to the Regulations. Harassment, defined in regulation 5, occurs where a person is subjected to unwanted conduct on grounds of religion or belief with the purpose or effect of violating his dignity, or creating an intimidating, hostile, degrading, humiliating or offensive environment for him.

Regulations 6 to 21 prohibit discrimination, victimisation and harassment in the fields of employment and vocational training. In particular, they protect employees (regulation 6), contract workers (regulation 8), office-holders (including constables) (regulations 10 and 11), and partners in firms. They not only prohibit discrimination etc by employers, but also by trade organisations (regulation 15), bodies conferring professional and trade qualifications (regulation 16), training providers (regulation 17), employment agencies (regulation 18), and further and higher education institutions (regulation 20). By virtue of regulation 21, discrimination, victimisation or harassment occurring after the relevant relationship has ended is unlawful if it arises out of, and is closely connected to, the relationship. The Regulations also apply to Crown servants and Parliamentary staff (regulations 36 to 38). Regulation 35 and Schedule 4 address the validity of discriminatory terms in contracts and collective agreements.

Not all differences of treatment on grounds of religion or belief are unlawful. There are exceptions in regulations 24 and 25 for differences of treatment related to national security and positive action, and in regulation 26 for the protection of Sikhs in connection with requirements as to the wearing of safety helmets. Regulation 7 provides an exception where being of a particular religion or belief is a genuine and determining occupational requirement for a post if it is proportionate to apply the requirement in the particular case. Regulation 7 also provides an exception for employers with an ethos based on religion or belief where being of a particular religion or belief is a genuine occupational requirement for a post and it is proportionate to apply the requirement in the particular case.

Regulations 27 to 34 provide remedies for individuals, including compensation, by way of proceedings in employment tribunals and in the county or sheriff courts. There are special provisions about the burden of proof in those cases in regulations 29 and 32, which transfer the burden to a respondent to a case once a complainant has established facts from which a court or tribunal could conclude, in the absence of an adequate explanation, that an act of discrimination or harassment has been committed by the respondent. Regulation 33 and Schedules 2 and 3 also include a questionnaire procedure to assist complainants in obtaining information from respondents.

A full Regulatory Impact Assessment report of the effect that these Regulations would have on the costs to business and a Transposition Note are freely available to the public from the Selected Employment Rights Branch, UG65, Department of Trade and Industry, 1 Victoria Street, London SW1H 0ET. Copies have also been placed in the libraries of both Houses of Parliament.

Appendix 2
The Employment Equality (Sexual Orientation) Regulations 2003

SI 2003 NO. 1661

Made	*26th June 2003*
Coming into force	*1st December 2003*

ARRANGEMENT OF REGULATIONS

Whereas a draft of these Regulations was laid before Parliament in accordance with paragraph 2 of Schedule 2 to the European Communities Act 1972, and was approved by resolution of each House of Parliament;

Now, therefore, the Secretary of State, being a Minister designated for the purposes of section 2(2) of the European Communities Act 1972 in relation to discrimination, in exercise of the powers conferred by that section, hereby makes the following Regulations:—

Part I
General

1. Citation, commencement and extent

(1) These Regulations may be cited as the Employment Equality (Sexual Orientation) Regulations 2003, and shall come into force on 1st December 2003.

(2) These Regulations do not extend to Northern Ireland.

2. Interpretation

(1) In these Regulations, 'sexual orientation' means a sexual orientation towards—

(a) persons of the same sex;

(b) persons of the opposite sex; or

(c) persons of the same sex and of the opposite sex.

(2) In these Regulations, references to discrimination are to any discrimination falling within regulation 3 (discrimination on grounds of sexual orientation) or 4 (discrimination by way of victimisation) and related expressions shall be construed accordingly, and references to harassment shall be construed in accordance with regulation 5 (harassment on grounds of sexual orientation).

(3) In these Regulations—

'act' includes a deliberate omission;

'benefits', except in regulation 9A (trustees and managers of occupational pension schemes), includes facilities and services;

'detriment' does not include harassment within the meaning of regulation 5;

references to 'employer', in their application to a person at any time seeking to employ another, include a person who has no employees at that time;

'employment' means employment under a contract of service or of apprenticeship or a contract personally to do any work, and related expressions shall be construed accordingly;

'Great Britain' includes such of the territorial waters of the United Kingdom as are adjacent to Great Britain;

'Minister of the Crown' includes the Treasury and the Defence Council; and

'school', in England and Wales, has the meaning given by section 4 of the Education Act 1996, and, in Scotland, has the meaning given by section 135(1) of the Education (Scotland) Act 1980, and references to a school are to an institution in so far as it is engaged in the provision of education under those sections.

3. Discrimination on grounds of sexual orientation

(1) For the purposes of these Regulations, a person ('A') discriminates against another person ('B') if—

(a) on grounds of sexual orientation, A treats B less favourably than he treats or would treat other persons; or

(b) A applies to B a provision, criterion or practice which he applies or would apply equally to persons not of the same sexual orientation as B, but—

(i) which puts or would put persons of the same sexual orientation as B at a particular disadvantage when compared with other persons,

(ii) which puts B at that disadvantage, and (iii) which A cannot show to be a proportionate means of achieving a legitimate aim.

(2) A comparison of B's case with that of another person under paragraph (1) must be such that the relevant circumstances in the one case are the same, or not materially different, in the other.

4. Discrimination by way of victimisation

(1) For the purposes of these Regulations, a person ('A') discriminates against another person ('B') if he treats B less favourably than he treats or would treat other persons in the same circumstances, and does so by reason that B has—

(a) brought proceedings against A or any other person under these Regulations;

(b) given evidence or information in connection with proceedings brought by any person against A or any other person under these Regulations;

(c) otherwise done anything under or by reference to these Regulations in relation to A or any other person; or

(d) alleged that A or any other person has committed an act which (whether or not the allegation so states) would amount to a contravention of these Regulations,

or by reason that A knows that B intends to do any of those things, or suspects that B has done or intends to do any of them.

(2) Paragraph (1) does not apply to treatment of B by reason of any allegation made by him, or evidence or information given by him, if the allegation, evidence or information was false and not made (or, as the case may be, given) in good faith.

5. Harassment on grounds of sexual orientation

(1) For the purposes of these Regulations, a person ('A') subjects another person ('B') to harassment where, on grounds of sexual orientation, A engages in unwanted conduct which has the purpose or effect of—

(a) violating B's dignity; or

(b) creating an intimidating, hostile, degrading, humiliating or offensive environment for B.

(2) Conduct shall be regarded as having the effect specified in paragraph (1)(a) or (b) only if, having regard to all the circumstances, including in particular the perception of B, it should reasonably be considered as having that effect.

Part II
Discrimination in employment and vocational training

6. Applicants and employees

(1) It is unlawful for an employer, in relation to employment by him at an establishment in Great Britain, to discriminate against a person—

(a) in the arrangements he makes for the purpose of determining to whom he should offer employment;

(b) in the terms on which he offers that person employment; or

(c) by refusing to offer, or deliberately not offering, him employment.

(2) It is unlawful for an employer, in relation to a person whom he employs at an establishment in Great Britain, to discriminate against that person—

(a) in the terms of employment which he affords him;

(b) in the opportunities which he affords him for promotion, a transfer, training, or receiving any other benefit;

(c) by refusing to afford him, or deliberately not affording him, any such opportunity; or

(d) by dismissing him, or subjecting him to any other detriment.

(3) It is unlawful for an employer, in relation to employment by him at an establishment in Great Britain, to subject to harassment a person whom he employs or who has applied to him for employment.

(4) Paragraph (2) does not apply to benefits of any description if the employer is concerned with the provision (for payment or not) of benefits of that description to the public, or to a section of the public which includes the employee in question, unless—

(a) that provision differs in a material respect from the provision of the benefits by the employer to his employees; or

(b) the provision of the benefits to the employee in question is regulated by his contract of employment; or

(c) the benefits relate to training.

(5) In paragraph (2)(d) reference to the dismissal of a person from employment includes reference—

(a) to the termination of that person's employment by the expiration of any period (including a period expiring by reference to an event or circumstance), not being a termination immediately after which the employment is renewed on the same terms; and

(b) to the termination of that person's employment by any act of his (including the giving of notice) in circumstances such that he is entitled to terminate it without notice by reason of the conduct of the employer.

7. Exception for genuine occupational requirement etc

(1) In relation to discrimination falling within regulation 3 (discrimination on grounds of sexual orientation)—

(a) regulation 6(1)(a) or (c) does not apply to any employment;

(b) regulation 6(2)(b) or (c) does not apply to promotion or transfer to, or training for, any employment; and

(c) regulation 6(2)(d) does not apply to dismissal from any employment,

where paragraph (2) or (3) applies.

(2) This paragraph applies where, having regard to the nature of the employment or the context in which it is carried out—

(a) being of a particular sexual orientation is a genuine and determining occupational requirement;

(b) it is proportionate to apply that requirement in the particular case; and (c) either—

(i) the person to whom that requirement is applied does not meet it, or

(ii) the employer is not satisfied, and in all the circumstances it is reasonable for him not to be satisfied, that that person meets it,

and this paragraph applies whether or not the employment is for purposes of an organised religion.

(3) This paragraph applies where—

(a) the employment is for purposes of an organised religion;

(b) the employer applies a requirement related to sexual orientation—

(i) so as to comply with the doctrines of the religion, or

(ii) because of the nature of the employment and the context in which it is carried out, so as to avoid conflicting with the strongly held religious convictions of a significant number of the religion's followers; and

(c) either—

    (i)   the person to whom that requirement is applied does not meet it, or

    (ii) the employer is not satisfied, and in all the circumstances it is reasonable for him not to be satisfied, that that person meets it.

8. Contract workers

(1) It is unlawful for a principal, in relation to contract work at an establishment in Great Britain, to discriminate against a contract worker—

    (a) in the terms on which he allows him to do that work;

    (b) by not allowing him to do it or continue to do it;

    (c) in the way he affords him access to any benefits or by refusing or deliberately not affording him access to them; or

    (d) by subjecting him to any other detriment.

(2) It is unlawful for a principal, in relation to contract work at an establishment in Great Britain, to subject a contract worker to harassment.

(3) A principal does not contravene paragraph (1)(b) by doing any act in relation to a contract worker where, if the work were to be done by a person taken into the principal's employment, that act would be lawful by virtue of regulation 7 (exception for genuine occupational requirement etc).

(4) Paragraph (1) does not apply to benefits of any description if the principal is concerned with the provision (for payment or not) of benefits of that description to the public, or to a section of the public to which the contract worker in question belongs, unless that provision differs in a material respect from the provision of the benefits by the principal to his contract workers.

(5) In this regulation—

    'principal' means a person ('A') who makes work available for doing by individuals who are employed by another person who supplies them under a contract made with A;

    'contract work' means work so made available; and

    'contract worker' means any individual who is supplied to the principal under such a contract.

9. Meaning of employment and contract work at establishment in Great Britain

(1) For the purposes of this Part ('the relevant purposes'), employment is to be regarded as being at an establishment in Great Britain if the employee—

    (a) does his work wholly or partly in Great Britain; or

    (b) does his work wholly outside Great Britain and paragraph (2) applies.

(2) This paragraph applies if—

    (a) the employer has a place of business at an establishment in Great Britain;

    (b) the work is for the purposes of the business carried on at that establishment; and

    (c) the employee is ordinarily resident in Great Britain—

        (i)   at the time when he applies for or is offered the employment, or

        (ii) at any time during the course of the employment.

(3) The reference to 'employment' in paragraph (1) includes—

    (a) employment on board a ship only if the ship is registered at a port of registry in Great Britain, and

    (b) employment on an aircraft or hovercraft only if the aircraft or hovercraft is registered in the United Kingdom and operated by a person who has his principal place of business, or is ordinarily resident, in Great Britain.

(4) Subject to paragraph (5), for the purposes of determining if employment concerned with the exploration of the sea bed or sub-soil or the exploitation of their natural resources is outside Great Britain, this regulation has effect as if references to Great Britain included—

(a) any area designated under section 1(7) of the Continental Shelf Act 1964 except an area or part of an area in which the law of Northern Ireland applies; and

(b) in relation to employment concerned with the exploration or exploitation of the Frigg Gas Field, the part of the Norwegian sector of the Continental Shelf described in Schedule 1.

(5) Paragraph (4) shall not apply to employment which is concerned with the exploration or exploitation of the Frigg Gas Field unless the employer is—

(a) a company registered under the Companies Act 1985;

(b) an oversea company which has established a place of business within Great Britain from which it directs the exploration or exploitation in question; or

(c) any other person who has a place of business within Great Britain from which he directs the exploration or exploitation in question.

(6) In this regulation—

'the Frigg Gas Field' means the naturally occurring gas-bearing sand formations of the lower Eocene age located in the vicinity of the intersection of the line of latitude 59 degrees 53 minutes North and of the dividing line between the sectors of the Continental Shelf of the United Kingdom and the Kingdom of Norway and includes all other gas-bearing strata from which gas at the start of production is capable of flowing into the above-mentioned gas-bearing sand formations;

'oversea company' has the same meaning as in section 744 of the Companies Act 1985.

(7) This regulation applies in relation to contract work within the meaning of regulation 8 as it applies in relation to employment; and, in its application to contract work, references to 'employee', 'employer' and 'employment' are references to (respectively) 'contract worker', 'principal' and 'contract work' within the meaning of regulation 8.

9A. Trustees and managers of occupational pension schemes

(1) It is unlawful, except in relation to rights accrued or benefits payable in respect of periods of service prior to the coming into force of these Regulations, for the trustees or managers of an occupational pension scheme to discriminate against a member or prospective member of the scheme in carrying out any of their functions in relation to it (including in particular their functions relating to the admission of members to the scheme and the treatment of members of it).

(2) It is unlawful for the trustees or managers of an occupational pension scheme, in relation to the scheme, to subject to harassment a member or prospective member of it.

(3) Schedule 1A (occupational pension schemes) shall have effect for the purposes of—

(a) defining terms used in this regulation and in that Schedule;

(b) treating every occupational pension scheme as including a non-discrimination rule;

(c) giving trustees or managers of an occupational pension scheme power to alter the scheme so as to secure conformity with the non-discrimination rule;

(d) making provision in relation to the procedures, and remedies which may be granted, on certain complaints relating to occupational pension schemes presented to an employment tribunal under regulation 28 (jurisdiction of employment tribunals).

10. Office-holders etc

(1) It is unlawful for a relevant person, in relation to an appointment to an office or post to which this regulation applies, to discriminate against a person—

(a) in the arrangements which he makes for the purpose of determining to whom the appointment should be offered;

(b) in the terms on which he offers him the appointment; or (c) by refusing to offer him the appointment.

(2) It is unlawful, in relation to an appointment to an office or post to which this regulation applies and which is an office or post referred to in paragraph (8)(b), for a relevant person on whose recommendation (or subject to whose approval) appointments to the office or post are made, to discriminate against a person—

(a) in the arrangements which he makes for the purpose of determining who should be recommended or approved in relation to the appointment; or

(b) in making or refusing to make a recommendation, or giving or refusing to give an approval, in relation to the appointment.

(3) It is unlawful for a relevant person, in relation to a person who has been appointed to an office or post to which this regulation applies, to discriminate against him—

(a) in the terms of the appointment;

(b) in the opportunities which he affords him for promotion, a transfer, training or receiving any other benefit, or by refusing to afford him any such opportunity;

(c) by terminating the appointment; or

(d) by subjecting him to any other detriment in relation to the appointment.

(4) It is unlawful for a relevant person, in relation to an office or post to which this regulation applies, to subject to harassment a person—

(a) who has been appointed to the office or post;

(b) who is seeking or being considered for appointment to the office or post; or

(c) who is seeking or being considered for a recommendation or approval in relation to an appointment to an office or post referred to in paragraph (8)(b).

(5) Paragraphs (1) and (3) do not apply to any act in relation to an office or post where, if the office or post constituted employment, that act would be lawful by virtue of regulation 7 (exception for genuine occupational requirement etc); and paragraph (2) does not apply to any act in relation to an office or post where, if the office or post constituted employment, it would be lawful by virtue of regulation 7 to refuse to offer the person such employment.

(6) Paragraph (3) does not apply to benefits of any description if the relevant person is concerned with the provision (for payment or not) of benefits of that description to the public, or a section of the public to which the person appointed belongs, unless—

(a) that provision differs in a material respect from the provision of the benefits by the relevant person to persons appointed to offices or posts which are the same as, or not materially different from, that which the person appointed holds; or

(b) the provision of the benefits to the person appointed is regulated by the terms and conditions of his appointment; or

(c) the benefits relate to training.

(7) In paragraph (3)(c) the reference to the termination of the appointment includes a reference—

(a) to the termination of the appointment by the expiration of any period (including a period expiring by reference to an event or circumstance), not being a termination immediately after which the appointment is renewed on the same terms and conditions; and

(b) to the termination of the appointment by any act of the person appointed (including the giving of notice) in circumstances such that he is entitled to terminate the appointment without notice by reason of the conduct of the relevant person.

(8) This regulation applies to—

(a) any office or post to which persons are appointed to discharge functions personally under the direction of another person, and in respect of which they are entitled to remuneration; and

(b) any office or post to which appointments are made by (or on the recommendation of or subject to the approval of) a Minister of the Crown, a government department, the National Assembly for Wales or any part of the Scottish Administration,

but not to a political office or a case where regulation 6 (applicants and employees), 8 (contract workers), 12 (barristers), 13 (advocates) or 14 (partnerships) applies, or would apply but for the operation of any other provision of these Regulations.

(9) For the purposes of paragraph (8)(a) the holder of an office or post—

(a) is to be regarded as discharging his functions under the direction of another person if that other person is entitled to direct him as to when and where he discharges those functions;

(b) is not to be regarded as entitled to remuneration merely because he is entitled to payments—

(i) in respect of expenses incurred by him in carrying out the functions of the office or post, or

(ii) by way of compensation for the loss of income or benefits he would or might have received from any person had he not been carrying out the functions of the office or post.

(10) In this regulation—

(a) appointment to an office or post does not include election to an office or post;

(b) 'political office' means—

(i) any office of the House of Commons held by a member of it,

(ii) a life peerage within the meaning of the Life Peerages Act 1958, or any office of the House of Lords held by a member of it,

(iii) any office mentioned in Schedule 2 (Ministerial offices) to the House of Commons Disqualification Act 1975,

(iv) the offices of Leader of the Opposition, Chief Opposition Whip or Assistant Opposition Whip within the meaning of the Ministerial and other Salaries Act 1975,

(v) any office of the Scottish Parliament held by a member of it,

(vi) a member of the Scottish Executive within the meaning of section 44 of the Scotland Act 1998, or a junior Scottish Minister within the meaning of section 49 of that Act,

(vii) any office of the National Assembly for Wales held by a member of it,

(viii) in England, any office of a county council, a London borough council, a district council, or a parish council held by a member of it,

(ix) in Wales, any office of a county council, a county borough council, or a community council held by a member of it,

(x) in relation to a council constituted under section 2 of the Local

Government etc (Scotland) Act 1994 or a community council established under section 51 of the Local Government (Scotland) Act 1973, any office of such a council held by a member of it,

    (xi)   any office of the Greater London Authority held by a member of it,

    (xii) any office of the Common Council of the City of London held by a member of it,

    (xiii) any office of the Council of the Isles of Scilly held by a member of it,

    (xiv) any office of a political party;

    (c) 'relevant person', in relation to an office or post, means—

    (i)   any person with power to make or terminate appointments to the office or post, or to determine the terms of appointment,

    (ii) any person with power to determine the working conditions of a person appointed to the office or post in relation to opportunities for promotion, a transfer, training or for receiving any other benefit, and

    (iii) any person or body referred to in paragraph (8)(b) on whose recommendation or subject to whose approval appointments are made to the office or post;

    (d) references to making a recommendation include references to making a negative recommendation; and (e) references to refusal include references to deliberate omission.

11. Police

(1) For the purposes of this Part, the holding of the office of constable shall be treated as employment—

    (a) by the chief officer of police as respects any act done by him in relation to a constable or that office;

    (b) by the police authority as respects any act done by it in relation to a constable or that office.

(2) For the purposes of regulation 22 (liability of employers and principals)—

    (a) the holding of the office of constable shall be treated as employment by the chief officer of police (and as not being employment by any other person); and

    (b) anything done by a person holding such an office in the performance, or purported performance, of his functions shall be treated as done in the course of that employment.

(3) There shall be paid out of the police fund—

    (a) any compensation, costs or expenses awarded against a chief officer of police in any proceedings brought against him under these Regulations, and any costs or expenses incurred by him in any such proceedings so far as not recovered by him in the proceedings; and

    (b) any sum required by a chief officer of police for the settlement of any claim made against him under these Regulations if the settlement is approved by the police authority.

(4) Any proceedings under these Regulations which, by virtue of paragraph (1), would lie against a chief officer of police shall be brought against the chief officer of police for the time being or, in the case of a vacancy in that office, against the person for the time being performing the functions of that office; and references in paragraph (3) to the chief officer of police shall be construed accordingly.

(5) A police authority may, in such cases and to such extent as appear to it to be appropriate, pay out of the police fund—

(a) any compensation, costs or expenses awarded in proceedings under these Regulations against a person under the direction and control of the chief officer of police;

(b) any costs or expenses incurred and not recovered by such a person in such proceedings; and

(c) any sum required in connection with the settlement of a claim that has or might have given rise to such proceedings.

(6) Paragraphs (1) and (2) apply to a police cadet and appointment as a police cadet as they apply to a constable and the office of constable.

(7) Subject to paragraph (8), in this regulation—

'chief officer of police'—

(a) in relation to a person appointed, or an appointment falling to be made, under a specified Act, has the same meaning as in the Police Act 1996,

(b) in relation to a person appointed, or an appointment falling to be made, under section 9(1)(b) or 55(1)(b) of the Police Act 1997 (police members of the National Criminal Intelligence Service and the National Crime Squad) means the Director General of the National Criminal Intelligence Service or, as the case may be, the Director General of the National Crime Squad,

(c) in relation to a person appointed, or an appointment falling to be made, under the Police (Scotland) Act 1967, means the chief constable of the relevant police force,

(d) in relation to any other person or appointment means the officer or other person who has the direction and control of the body of constables or cadets in question;

'police authority'—

(a) in relation to a person appointed, or an appointment falling to be made, under a specified Act, has the same meaning as in the Police Act 1996,

(b) in relation to a person appointed, or an appointment falling to be made, under section 9(1)(b) or 55(1)(b) of the Police Act 1997, means the Service Authority for the National Criminal Intelligence Service or, as the case may be, the Service Authority for the National Crime Squad,

(c) in relation to a person appointed, or an appointment falling to be made, under the Police (Scotland) Act 1967, has the meaning given in that Act,

(d) in relation to any other person or appointment, means the authority by whom the person in question is or on appointment would be paid;

'police cadet' means any person appointed to undergo training with a view to becoming a constable;

'police fund'—

(a) in relation to a chief officer of police within sub-paragraph (a) of the above definition of that term, has the same meaning as in the Police Act 1996,

(b) in relation to a chief officer of police within sub-paragraph (b) of that definition, means the service fund established under section 16 or (as the case may be) section 61 of the Police Act 1997,

(c) in any other case means money provided by the police authority; and

'specified Act' means the Metropolitan Police Act 1829, the City of London Police Act 1839 or the Police Act 1996.

(8) In relation to a constable of a force who is not under the direction and control of the chief officer of police for that force, references in this regulation to the chief officer of police

are references to the chief officer of the force under whose direction and control he is, and references in this regulation to the police authority are references to the relevant police authority for that force.

12. Barristers

(1) It is unlawful for a barrister or barrister's clerk, in relation to any offer of a pupillage or tenancy, to discriminate against a person—

(a) in the arrangements which are made for the purpose of determining to whom the pupillage or tenancy should be offered;

(b) in respect of any terms on which it is offered; or

(c) by refusing, or deliberately not offering, it to him.

(2) It is unlawful for a barrister or barrister's clerk, in relation to a pupil or tenant in the set of chambers in question, to discriminate against him—

(a) in respect of any terms applicable to him as a pupil or tenant;

(b) in the opportunities for training, or gaining experience, which are afforded or denied to him;

(c) in the benefits which are afforded or denied to him; or

(d) by terminating his pupillage, or by subjecting him to any pressure to leave the chambers or other detriment.

(3) It is unlawful for a barrister or barrister's clerk, in relation to a pupillage or tenancy in the set of chambers in question, to subject to harassment a person who is, or has applied to be, a pupil or tenant.

(4) It is unlawful for any person, in relation to the giving, withholding or acceptance of instructions to a barrister, to discriminate against any person by subjecting him to a detriment, or to subject him to harassment.

(5) In this regulation—

'barrister's clerk' includes any person carrying out any of the functions of a barrister's clerk;

'pupil', 'pupillage' and 'set of chambers' have the meanings commonly associated with their use in the context of barristers practising in independent practice; and

'tenancy' and 'tenant' have the meanings commonly associated with their use in the context of barristers practising in independent practice, but also include reference to any barrister permitted to work in a set of chambers who is not a tenant.

(6) This regulation extends to England and Wales only.

13. Advocates

(1) It is unlawful for an advocate, in relation to taking any person as his pupil, to discriminate against a person—

(a) in the arrangements which he makes for the purpose of determining whom he will take as his pupil;

(b) in respect of any terms on which he offers to take any person as his pupil; or

(c) by refusing to take, or deliberately not taking, a person as his pupil.

(2) It is unlawful for an advocate, in relation to a person who is his pupil, to discriminate against him—

(a) in respect of any terms applicable to him as a pupil;

(b) in the opportunities for training, or gaining experience, which are afforded or denied to him;

(c) in the benefits which are afforded or denied to him; or

(d) by terminating the relationship, or by subjecting him to any pressure to terminate the relationship or other detriment.

(3) It is unlawful for an advocate, in relation to a person who is his pupil or taking any person as his pupil, to subject such a person to harassment.

(4) It is unlawful for any person, in relation to the giving, withholding or acceptance of instructions to an advocate, to discriminate against any person by subjecting him to a detriment, or to subject him to harassment.

(5) In this regulation—

'advocate' means a member of the Faculty of Advocates practising as such; and

'pupil' has the meaning commonly associated with its use in the context of a person training to be an advocate.

(6) This regulation extends to Scotland only.

14. Partnerships

(1) It is unlawful for a firm, in relation to a position as partner in the firm, to discriminate against a person—

(a) in the arrangements they make for the purpose of determining to whom they should offer that position;

(b) in the terms on which they offer him that position;

(c) by refusing to offer, or deliberately not offering, him that position; or

(d) in a case where the person already holds that position—

(i)   in the way they afford him access to any benefits or by refusing to afford, or deliberately not affording, him access to them, or

(ii) by expelling him from that position, or subjecting him to any other detriment.

(2) It is unlawful for a firm, in relation to a position as partner in the firm, to subject to harassment a person who holds or has applied for that position.

(3) Paragraphs (1)(a) to (c) and (2) apply in relation to persons proposing to form themselves into a partnership as they apply in relation to a firm.

(4) Paragraph (1) does not apply to any act in relation to a position as partner where, if the position were employment, that act would be lawful by virtue of regulation 7 (exception for genuine occupational requirement etc).

(5) In the case of a limited partnership references in this regulation to a partner shall be construed as references to a general partner as defined in section 3 of the Limited Partnerships Act 1907.

(6) This regulation applies to a limited liability partnership as it applies to a firm; and, in its application to a limited liability partnership, references to a partner in a firm are references to a member of the limited liability partnership.

(7) In this regulation, 'firm' has the meaning given by section 4 of the Partnership Act 1890.

(8) In paragraph (1)(d) reference to the expulsion of a person from a position as partner includes reference—

(a) to the termination of that person's partnership by the expiration of any period (including a period expiring by reference to an event or circumstance), not being a termination immediately after which the partnership is renewed on the same terms; and

(b) to the termination of that person's partnership by any act of his (including the giving of notice) in circumstances such that he is entitled to terminate it without notice by reason of the conduct of the other partners.

15. Trade organisations

(1) It is unlawful for a trade organisation to discriminate against a person—

(a) in the terms on which it is prepared to admit him to membership of the organisation; or

(b) by refusing to accept, or deliberately not accepting, his application for membership.

(2) It is unlawful for a trade organisation, in relation to a member of the organisation, to discriminate against him—

(a) in the way it affords him access to any benefits or by refusing or deliberately omitting to afford him access to them;

(b) by depriving him of membership, or varying the terms on which he is a member; or

(c) by subjecting him to any other detriment.

(3) It is unlawful for a trade organisation, in relation to a person's membership or application for membership of that organisation, to subject that person to harassment.

(4) In this regulation—

'trade organisation' means an organisation of workers, an organisation of employers, or any other organisation whose members carry on a particular profession or trade for the purposes of which the organisation exists;

'profession' includes any vocation or occupation; and

'trade' includes any business.

16. Qualifications bodies

(1) It is unlawful for a qualifications body to discriminate against a person—

(a) in the terms on which it is prepared to confer a professional or trade qualification on him;

(b) by refusing or deliberately not granting any application by him for such a qualification; or

(c) by withdrawing such a qualification from him or varying the terms on which he holds it.

(2) It is unlawful for a qualifications body, in relation to a professional or trade qualification conferred by it, to subject to harassment a person who holds or applies for such a qualification.

(3) Paragraph (1) does not apply to a professional or trade qualification for purposes of an organised religion where a requirement related to sexual orientation is applied to the qualification so as to comply with the doctrines of the religion or avoid conflicting with the strongly held religious convictions of a significant number of the religion's followers.

(4) In this regulation—

'qualifications body' means any authority or body which can confer a professional or trade qualification, but it does not include—

(a) an educational establishment to which regulation 20 (institutions of further and higher education) applies, or would apply but for the operation of any other provision of these Regulations, or

(b) a school;

'confer' includes renew or extend;

'professional or trade qualification' means any authorisation, qualification, recognition, registration, enrolment, approval or certification which is needed for, or facilitates engagement in, a particular profession or trade;

'profession' and 'trade' have the same meaning as in regulation 15.

17. Providers of vocational training

(1) It is unlawful, in relation to a person seeking or undergoing training which would help fit him for any employment, for any training provider to discriminate against him—

    (a) in the terms on which the training provider affords him access to any training;

    (b) by refusing or deliberately not affording him such access;

    (c) by terminating his training; or

    (d) by subjecting him to any other detriment during his training.

(2) It is unlawful for a training provider, in relation to a person seeking or undergoing training which would help fit him for any employment, to subject him to harassment.

(3) Paragraph (1) does not apply if the discrimination only concerns training for employment which, by virtue of regulation 7 (exception for genuine occupational requirement etc), the employer could lawfully refuse to offer the person seeking training.

(4) In this regulation—

    'training' includes—

    (a) facilities for training; and

    (b) practical work experience provided by an employer to a person whom he does not employ;

    'training provider' means any person who provides, or makes arrangements for the provision of, training which would help fit another person for any employment, but it does not include—

    (a) an employer in relation to training for persons employed by him;

    (b) an educational establishment to which regulation 20 (institutions of further and higher education) applies, or would apply but for the operation of any other provision of these Regulations; or

    (c) a school.

18. Employment agencies, careers guidance etc

(1) It is unlawful for an employment agency to discriminate against a person—

    (a) in the terms on which the agency offers to provide any of its services;

    (b) by refusing or deliberately not providing any of its services; or

    (c) in the way it provides any of its services.

(2) It is unlawful for an employment agency, in relation to a person to whom it provides its services, or who has requested it to provide its services, to subject that person to harassment.

(3) Paragraph (1) does not apply to discrimination if it only concerns employment which, by virtue of regulation 7 (exception for genuine occupational requirement etc), the employer could lawfully refuse to offer the person in question.

(4) An employment agency shall not be subject to any liability under this regulation if it proves that—

    (a) it acted in reliance on a statement made to it by the employer to the effect that, by reason of the operation of paragraph (3), its action would not be unlawful, and

    (b) it was reasonable for it to rely on the statement.

(5) A person who knowingly or recklessly makes a statement such as is referred to in paragraph (4)(a) which in a material respect is false or misleading commits an offence, and shall be liable on summary conviction to a fine not exceeding level 5 on the standard scale.

(6) For the purposes of this regulation—

(a) 'employment agency' means a person who, for profit or not, provides services for the purpose of finding employment for workers or supplying employers with workers, but it does not include—

(i) an educational establishment to which regulation 20 (institutions of further and higher education) applies, or would apply but for the operation of any other provision of these Regulations, or

(ii) a school; and

(b) references to the services of an employment agency include guidance on careers and any other services related to employment.

19. Assisting persons to obtain employment etc

(1) It is unlawful for the Secretary of State to discriminate against any person by subjecting him to a detriment, or to subject a person to harassment, in the provision of facilities or services under section 2 of the Employment and Training Act 1973 (arrangements for assisting persons to obtain employment).

(2) It is unlawful for Scottish Enterprise or Highlands and Islands Enterprise to discriminate against any person by subjecting him to a detriment, or to subject a person to harassment, in the provision of facilities or services under such arrangements as are mentioned in section 2(3) of the Enterprise and New Towns (Scotland) Act 1990 (arrangements analogous to arrangements in pursuance of the said Act of 1973).

(3) This regulation does not apply in a case where—

(a) regulation 17 (providers of vocational training) applies, or would apply but for the operation of any other provision of these Regulations, or

(b) the Secretary of State is acting as an employment agency within the meaning of regulation 18.

20. Institutions of further and higher education

(1) It is unlawful, in relation to an educational establishment to which this regulation applies, for the governing body of that establishment to discriminate against a person—

(a) in the terms on which it offers to admit him to the establishment as a student;

(b) by refusing or deliberately not accepting an application for his admission to the establishment as a student; or

(c) where he is a student of the establishment—

(i) in the way it affords him access to any benefits,

(ii) by refusing or deliberately not affording him access to them, or

(iii) by excluding him from the establishment or subjecting him to any other detriment.

(2) It is unlawful, in relation to an educational establishment to which this regulation applies, for the governing body of that establishment to subject to harassment a person who is a student at the establishment, or who has applied for admission to the establishment as a student.

(3) Paragraph (1) does not apply if the discrimination only concerns training which would help fit a person for employment which, by virtue of regulation 7 (exception for genuine occupational requirement etc), the employer could lawfully refuse to offer the person in question.

(4) This regulation applies to the following educational establishments in England and Wales, namely—

(a) an institution within the further education sector (within the meaning of section 91(3) of the Further and Higher Education Act 1992);

(b) a university;

(c) an institution, other than a university, within the higher education sector (within the meaning of section 91(5) of the Further and Higher Education Act 1992).

(5) This regulation applies to the following educational establishments in Scotland, namely—

(a) a college of further education within the meaning of section 36(1) of the Further and Higher Education (Scotland) Act 1992 under the management of a board of management within the meaning of Part I of that Act;

(b) a college of further education maintained by an education authority in the exercise of its further education functions in providing courses of further education within the meaning of section 1(5)(b)(ii) of the Education (Scotland) Act 1980;

(c) any other educational establishment (not being a school) which provides further education within the meaning of section 1 of the Further and Higher Education (Scotland) Act 1992;

(d) an institution within the higher education sector (within the meaning of Part II of the Further and Higher Education (Scotland) Act 1992);

(e) a central institution (within the meaning of section 135 of the Education (Scotland) Act 1980).

(6) In this regulation—

'education authority' has the meaning given by section 135(1) of the Education (Scotland) Act 1980;

'governing body' includes—

(a) the board of management of a college referred to in paragraph (5)(a), and

(b) the managers of a college or institution referred to in paragraph (5)(b) or (e);

'student' means any person who receives education at an educational establishment to which this regulation applies; and

'university' includes a university college and the college, school or hall of a university.

21. Relationships which have come to an end

(1) In this regulation a 'relevant relationship' is a relationship during the course of which an act of discrimination against, or harassment of, one party to the relationship ('B') by the other party to it ('A') is unlawful by virtue of any preceding provision of this Part.

(2) Where a relevant relationship has come to an end, it is unlawful for A—

(a) to discriminate against B by subjecting him to a detriment; or

(b) to subject B to harassment,

where the discrimination or harassment arises out of and is closely connected to that relationship.

(3) In paragraph (1), reference to an act of discrimination or harassment which is unlawful includes, in the case of a relationship which has come to an end before the coming into force of these Regulations, reference to an act of discrimination or harassment which would, after the coming into force of these Regulations, be unlawful.

Part III
Other unlawful acts

22. Liability of employers and principals

(1) Anything done by a person in the course of his employment shall be treated for the purposes of these Regulations as done by his employer as well as by him, whether or not it was done with the employer's knowledge or approval.

(2) Anything done by a person as agent for another person with the authority (whether express or implied, and whether precedent or subsequent) of that other person shall be treated for the purposes of these Regulations as done by that other person as well as by him.

(3) In proceedings brought under these Regulations against any person in respect of an act alleged to have been done by an employee of his it shall be a defence for that person to prove that he took such steps as were reasonably practicable to prevent the employee from doing that act, or from doing in the course of his employment acts of that description.

23. Aiding unlawful acts

(1) A person who knowingly aids another person to do an act made unlawful by these Regulations shall be treated for the purpose of these Regulations as himself doing an unlawful act of the like description.

(2) For the purposes of paragraph (1) an employee or agent for whose act the employer or principal is liable under regulation 22 (or would be so liable but for regulation 22(3)) shall be deemed to aid the doing of the act by the employer or principal.

(3) A person does not under this regulation knowingly aid another to do an unlawful act if—

(a) he acts in reliance on a statement made to him by that other person that, by reason of any provision of these Regulations, the act which he aids would not be unlawful; and

(b) it is reasonable for him to rely on the statement.

(4) A person who knowingly or recklessly makes a statement such as is referred to in paragraph (3)(a) which in a material respect is false or misleading commits an offence, and shall be liable on summary conviction to a fine not exceeding level 5 on the standard scale.

Part IV
General exceptions from parts II and III

24. Exception for national security

Nothing in Part II or III shall render unlawful an act done for the purpose of safeguarding national security, if the doing of the act was justified by that purpose.

25. Exception for benefits dependent on marital status

Nothing in Part II or III shall render unlawful anything which prevents or restricts access to a benefit by reference to marital status.

26. Exceptions for positive action

(1) Nothing in Part II or III shall render unlawful any act done in or in connection with—

(a) affording persons of a particular sexual orientation access to facilities for training which would help fit them for particular work; or

(b) encouraging persons of a particular sexual orientation to take advantage of opportunities for doing particular work, where it reasonably appears to the person doing the act that it prevents or compensates for disadvantages linked to sexual orientation suffered by persons of that sexual orientation doing that work or likely to take up that work.

(2) Nothing in Part II or III shall render unlawful any act done by a trade organisation within the meaning of regulation 15 in or in connection with—

(a) affording only members of the organisation who are of a particular sexual orientation access to facilities for training which would help fit them for holding a post of any kind in the organisation; or

(b) encouraging only members of the organisation who are of a particular sexual orientation to take advantage of opportunities for holding such posts in the organisation,

where it reasonably appears to the organisation that the act prevents or compensates for disadvantages linked to sexual orientation suffered by those of that sexual orientation holding such posts or likely to hold such posts.

(3) Nothing in Part II or III shall render unlawful any act done by a trade organisation within the meaning of regulation 15 in or in connection with encouraging only persons of a particular sexual orientation to become members of the organisation where it reasonably appears to the organisation that the act prevents or compensates for disadvantages linked to sexual orientation suffered by persons of that sexual orientation who are, or are eligible to become, members.

Part V
Enforcement

27. Restriction of proceedings for breach of Regulations

(1) Except as provided by these Regulations no proceedings, whether civil or criminal, shall lie against any person in respect of an act by reason that the act is unlawful by virtue of a provision of these Regulations.

(2) Paragraph (1) does not prevent the making of an application for judicial review [or the investigation or determination of any matter in accordance with Part X (investigations: the Pensions Ombudsman) of the Pension Schemes Act 1993 by the Pensions Ombudsman.].

28. Jurisdiction of employment tribunals

(1) A complaint by any person ('the complainant') that another person ('the respondent')—

(a) has committed against the complainant an act to which this regulation applies; or

(b) is by virtue of regulation 22 (liability of employers and principals) or 23 (aiding unlawful acts) to be treated as having committed against the complainant such an act,

may be presented to an employment tribunal.

(2) This regulation applies to any act of discrimination or harassment which is unlawful by virtue of any provision of Part II other than—

(a) where the act is one in respect of which an appeal or proceedings in the nature of an appeal may be brought under any enactment, regulation 16 (qualifications bodies);

(b) regulation 20 (institutions of further and higher education); or

(c) where the act arises out of and is closely connected to a relationship between the complainant and the respondent which has come to an end but during the course of which an act of discrimination against, or harassment of, the complainant by the respondent would have been unlawful by virtue of regulation 20, regulation 21 (relationships which have come to an end).

(3) In paragraph (2)(c), reference to an act of discrimination or harassment which would have been unlawful includes, in the case of a relationship which has come to an end before the coming into force of these Regulations, reference to an act of discrimination or harassment which would, after the coming into force of these Regulations, have been unlawful.

(4) In this regulation, 'enactment' includes an enactment comprised in, or in an instrument made under, an Act of the Scottish Parliament.

29. Burden of proof: employment tribunals

(1) This regulation applies to any complaint presented under regulation 28 to an employment tribunal.

(2) Where, on the hearing of the complaint, the complainant proves facts from which the tribunal could, apart from this regulation, conclude in the absence of an adequate explanation that the respondent—

(a) has committed against the complainant an act to which regulation 28 applies; or

(b) is by virtue of regulation 22 (liability of employers and principals) or 23 (aiding unlawful acts) to be treated as having committed against the complainant such an act,

the tribunal shall uphold the complaint unless the respondent proves that he did not commit, or as the case may be, is not to be treated as having committed, that act.

30. Remedies on complaints in employment tribunals

(1) Where an employment tribunal finds that a complaint presented to it under regulation 28 is well-founded, the tribunal shall make such of the following as it considers just and equitable—

(a) an order declaring the rights of the complainant and the respondent in relation to the act to which the complaint relates;

(b) an order requiring the respondent to pay to the complainant compensation of an amount corresponding to any damages he could have been ordered by a county court or by a sheriff court to pay to the complainant if the complaint had fallen to be dealt with under regulation 31 (jurisdiction of county and sheriff courts);

(c) a recommendation that the respondent take within a specified period action appearing to the tribunal to be practicable for the purpose of obviating or reducing the adverse effect on the complainant of any act of discrimination or harassment to which the complaint relates.

(2) As respects an unlawful act of discrimination falling within regulation 3(1)(b), if the respondent proves that the provision, criterion or practice was not applied with the intention of treating the complainant unfavourably on grounds of sexual orientation, an order may be made under paragraph (1)(b) only if the employment tribunal—

(a) makes such order under paragraph (1)(a) (if any) and such recommendation under paragraph (1)(c) (if any) as it would have made if it had no power to make an order under paragraph (1)(b); and

(b) (where it makes an order under paragraph (1)(a) or a recommendation under paragraph (1)(c) or both) considers that it is just and equitable to make an order under paragraph (1)(b) as well.

(3) If without reasonable justification the respondent to a complaint fails to comply with a recommendation made by an employment tribunal under paragraph (1)(c), then, if it thinks it just and equitable to do so—

(a) the tribunal may increase the amount of compensation required to be paid to the complainant in respect of the complaint by an order made under paragraph (1)(b); or

(b) if an order under paragraph (1)(b) was not made, the tribunal may make such an order.

(4) Where an amount of compensation falls to be awarded under paragraph (1)(b), the tribunal may include in the award interest on that amount subject to, and in accordance with, the provisions of the Employment Tribunals (Interest on Awards in Discrimination Cases) Regulations 1996.

[(5) This regulation has effect subject to paragraph 7 of Schedule 1A (occupational pension schemes).]

31. Jurisdiction of county and sheriff courts

(1) A claim by any person ('the claimant') that another person ('the respondent')—

(a) has committed against the claimant an act to which this regulation applies; or

(b) is by virtue of regulation 22 (liability of employers and principals) or 23 (aiding unlawful acts) to be treated as having committed against the claimant such an act,

may be made the subject of civil proceedings in like manner as any other claim in tort or (in Scotland) in reparation for breach of statutory duty.

(2) Proceedings brought under paragraph (1) shall—

(a) in England and Wales, be brought only in a county court; and

(b) in Scotland, be brought only in a sheriff court.

(3) For the avoidance of doubt it is hereby declared that damages in respect of an unlawful act to which this regulation applies may include compensation for injury to feelings whether or not they include compensation under any other head.

(4) This regulation applies to any act of discrimination or harassment which is unlawful by virtue of—

(a) regulation 20 (institutions of further and higher education); or

(b) where the act arises out of and is closely connected to a relationship between the claimant and the respondent which has come to an end but during the course of which an act of discrimination against, or harassment of, the claimant by the respondent would have been unlawful by virtue of regulation 20, regulation 21 (relationships which have come to an end).

(5) In paragraph (4)(b), reference to an act of discrimination or harassment which would have been unlawful includes, in the case of a relationship which has come to an end before the coming into force of these Regulations, reference to an act of discrimination or harassment which would, after the coming into force of these Regulations, have been unlawful.

32. Burden of proof: county and sheriff courts

(1) This regulation applies to any claim brought under regulation 31 in a county court in England and Wales or a sheriff court in Scotland.

(2) Where, on the hearing of the claim, the claimant proves facts from which the court could, apart from this regulation, conclude in the absence of an adequate explanation that the respondent—

(a) has committed against the claimant an act to which regulation 31 applies; or

(b) is by virtue of regulation 22 (liability of employers and principals) or 23 (aiding unlawful acts) to be treated as having committed against the claimant such an act,

the court shall uphold the claim unless the respondent proves that he did not commit, or as the case may be, is not to be treated as having committed, that act.

33. Help for persons in obtaining information etc

(1) In accordance with this regulation, a person ('the person aggrieved') who considers he may have been discriminated against, or subjected to harassment, in contravention of these Regulations may serve on the respondent to a complaint presented under regulation 28 (jurisdiction of employment tribunals) or a claim brought under regulation 31 (jurisdiction of county and sheriff courts) questions in the form set out in Schedule 2 or forms to the like effect with such variation as the circumstances require; and the respondent may if he so wishes reply to such questions by way of the form set out in Schedule 3 or forms to the like effect with such variation as the circumstances require.

(2) Where the person aggrieved questions the respondent (whether in accordance with paragraph (1) or not)—

(a) the questions, and any reply by the respondent (whether in accordance with paragraph (1) or not) shall, subject to the following provisions of this regulation, be admissible as evidence in the proceedings;

(b) if it appears to the court or tribunal that the respondent deliberately, and without reasonable excuse, omitted to reply within eight weeks of service of the questions or that his reply is evasive or equivocal, the court or tribunal may draw any inference from that fact that it considers it just and equitable to draw, including an inference that he committed an unlawful act.

(3) In proceedings before a county court in England or Wales or a sheriff court in Scotland, a question shall only be admissible as evidence in pursuance of paragraph (2)(a)—

(a) where it was served before those proceedings had been instituted, if it was so served within the period of six months beginning when the act complained of was done;

(b) where it was served when those proceedings had been instituted, if it was served with the leave of, and within a period specified by, the court in question.

(4) In proceedings before an employment tribunal, a question shall only be admissible as evidence in pursuance of paragraph (2)(a)—

(a) where it was served before a complaint had been presented to the tribunal, if it was so served within the period of three months beginning when the act complained of was done;

(b) where it was served when a complaint had been presented to the tribunal, either—

(i) if it was so served within the period of twenty-one days beginning with the day on which the complaint was presented, or

(ii) if it was so served later with leave given, and within a period specified, by a direction of the tribunal.

(5) A question and any reply thereto may be served on the respondent or, as the case may be, on the person aggrieved—

(a) by delivering it to him;

(b) by sending it by post to him at his usual or last-known residence or place of business;

(c) where the person to be served is a body corporate or is a trade union or employers' association within the meaning of the Trade Union and Labour Relations (Consolidation) Act 1992, by delivering it to the secretary or clerk of the body, union or association at its registered or principal office or by sending it by post to the secretary or clerk at that office;

(d) where the person to be served is acting by a solicitor, by delivering it at, or by sending it by post to, the solicitor's address for service; or

(e) where the person to be served is the person aggrieved, by delivering the reply, or sending it by post, to him at his address for reply as stated by him in the document containing the questions.

(6) This regulation is without prejudice to any other enactment or rule of law regulating interlocutory and preliminary matters in proceedings before a county court, sheriff court or employment tribunal, and has effect subject to any enactment or rule of law regulating the admissibility of evidence in such proceedings.

(7) In this regulation 'respondent' includes a prospective respondent.

34. Period within which proceedings to be brought

(1) An employment tribunal shall not consider a complaint under regulation 28 unless it is presented to the tribunal before the end of—

(a) the period of three months beginning when the act complained of was done; or

(b) in a case to which regulation 36(7) (armed forces) applies, the period of six months so beginning.

(2) A county court or a sheriff court shall not consider a claim brought under regulation 31 unless proceedings in respect of the claim are instituted before the end of the period of six months beginning when the act complained of was done.

(3) A court or tribunal may nevertheless consider any such complaint or claim which is out of time if, in all the circumstances of the case, it considers that it is just and equitable to do so.

(4) For the purposes of this regulation and regulation 33 (help for persons in obtaining information etc)—

(a) when the making of a contract is, by reason of the inclusion of any term, an unlawful act, that act shall be treated as extending throughout the duration of the contract; and

(b) any act extending over a period shall be treated as done at the end of that period; and

(c) a deliberate omission shall be treated as done when the person in question decided upon it,

and in the absence of evidence establishing the contrary a person shall be taken for the purposes of this regulation to decide upon an omission when he does an act inconsistent with doing the omitted act or, if he has done no such inconsistent act, when the period expires within which he might reasonably have been expected to do the omitted act if it was to be done.

Part VI

Supplemental

35. Validity of contracts, collective agreements and rules of undertakings

Schedule 4 (validity of contracts, collective agreements and rules of undertakings) shall have effect.

36. Application to the Crown etc

(1) These Regulations apply—

(a) to an act done by or for purposes of a Minister of the Crown or government department; or

(b) to an act done on behalf of the Crown by a statutory body, or a person holding a statutory office,

as they apply to an act done by a private person.

(2) These Regulations apply to—

(a) service for purposes of a Minister of the Crown or government department, other than service of a person holding a statutory office;

(b) service on behalf of the Crown for purposes of a person holding a statutory office or purposes of a statutory body; or

(c) service in the armed forces,

as they apply to employment by a private person, and shall so apply as if references to a contract of employment included references to the terms of service.

(3) Paragraphs (1) and (2) have effect subject to regulation 11 (police).

(4) Regulation 9(3) (meaning of employment and contract work at establishment in Great Britain) shall have effect in relation to any ship, aircraft or hovercraft belonging to or possessed by Her Majesty in right of the government of the United Kingdom as it has effect in relation to a ship, aircraft or hovercraft specified in regulation 9(3)(a) or (b).

(5) The provisions of Parts II to IV of the Crown Proceedings Act 1947 shall apply to proceedings against the Crown under these Regulations as they apply to proceedings in England and Wales which by virtue of section 23 of that Act are treated for the purposes of Part II of that Act as civil proceedings by or against the Crown, except that in their application to proceedings under these Regulations section 20 of that Act (removal of proceedings from county court to High Court) shall not apply.

(6) The provisions of Part V of the Crown Proceedings Act 1947 shall apply to proceedings against the Crown under these Regulations as they apply to proceedings in Scotland which by virtue of the said Part are treated as civil proceedings by or against the Crown, except that in their application to proceedings under these Regulations the proviso to section 44 of that Act (removal of proceedings from the sheriff court to the Court of Session) shall not apply.

(7) This paragraph applies to any complaint by a person ('the complainant') that another person—

(a) has committed an act of discrimination or harassment against the complainant which is unlawful by virtue of regulation 6 (applicants and employees); or

(b) is by virtue of regulation 22 (liability of employers and principals) or 23 (aiding unlawful acts) to be treated as having committed such an act of discrimination or harassment against the complainant,

if at the time when the act complained of was done the complainant was serving in the armed forces and the discrimination or harassment in question relates to his service in those forces.

(8) A complainant may present a complaint to which paragraph (7) applies to an employment tribunal under regulation 28 only if—

(a) he has made a complaint in respect of the same matter to an officer under the service redress procedures applicable to him; and

(b) that complaint has not been withdrawn.

(9) For the purpose of paragraph (8)(b), a complainant shall be treated as having withdrawn his complaint if, having made a complaint to an officer under the service redress procedures applicable to him, he fails to submit that complaint to the Defence Council under those procedures.

190

(10)   Where a complaint is presented to an employment tribunal under regulation 28 by virtue of paragraph (8), the service redress procedures may continue after the complaint is so presented.

(11)   In this regulation—

'armed forces' means any of the naval, military or air forces of the Crown;

'service for purposes of a Minister of the Crown or government department' does not include service in any office mentioned in Schedule 2 (Ministerial offices) to the House of Commons Disqualification Act 1975;

'the service redress procedures' means the procedures, excluding those which relate to the making of a report on a complaint to Her Majesty, referred to in section 180 of the Army Act 1955, section 180 of the Air Force Act 1955 and section 130 of the Naval Discipline Act 1957; and

'statutory body' means a body set up by or in pursuance of an enactment, and 'statutory office' means an office so set up.

37. Application to House of Commons staff

(1)   These Regulations apply to an act done by an employer of a relevant member of the House of Commons staff, and to service as such a member, as they apply to an act done by and to service for purposes of a Minister of the Crown or government department, and accordingly apply as if references to a contract of employment included references to the terms of service of such a member.

(2)   In this regulation 'relevant member of the House of Commons staff' means any person—

(a)   who was appointed by the House of Commons Commission; or

(b)   who is a member of the Speaker's personal staff,

and subsections (6) to (12) of section 195 of the Employment Rights Act 1996 (person to be treated as employer of House of Commons staff) apply, with any necessary modifications, for the purposes of these Regulations.

38. Application to House of Lords staff

(1)   These Regulations apply in relation to employment as a relevant member of the House of Lords staff as they apply in relation to other employment.

(2)   In this regulation 'relevant member of the House of Lords staff' means any person who is employed under a contract of employment with the Corporate Officer of the House of Lords, and section 194(7) of the Employment Rights Act 1996 (continuity of employment) applies for the purposes of this regulation.

39. Amendments to legislation

Schedule 5 (amendments to legislation) shall have effect.

SCHEDULES
SCHEDULE 1

Regulation 9(4)

Norwegian part of the Frigg Gas Field
1. The part of the Norwegian sector of the Continental Shelf described in this Schedule is the area defined by—
(a) the sets of lines of latitude and longitude joining the following surface co-ordinates—

Longitude	Latitude
02 degrees 05 minutes 30 seconds E	60 degrees 00 minutes 45 seconds N
02 degrees 05 minutes 30 seconds E	59 degrees 58 minutes 45 seconds N
02 degrees 06 minutes 00 seconds E	59 degrees 58 minutes 45 seconds N
02 degrees 06 minutes 00 seconds E	59 degrees 57 minutes 45 seconds N
02 degrees 07 minutes 00 seconds E	59 degrees 57 minutes 45 seconds N
02 degrees 07 minutes 00 seconds E	59 degrees 57 minutes 30 seconds N
02 degrees 07 minutes 30 seconds E	59 degrees 57 minutes 30 seconds N
02 degrees 07 minutes 30 seconds E	59 degrees 55 minutes 30 seconds N
02 degrees 10 minutes 30 seconds E	59 degrees 55 minutes 30 seconds N
02 degrees 10 minutes 30 seconds E	59 degrees 54 minutes 45 seconds N
02 degrees 11 minutes 00 seconds E	59 degrees 54 minutes 45 seconds N
02 degrees 11 minutes 00 seconds E	59 degrees 54 minutes 15 seconds N
02 degrees 12 minutes 30 seconds E	59 degrees 54 minutes 15 seconds N
02 degrees 12 minutes 30 seconds E	59 degrees 54 minutes 00 seconds N
02 degrees 13 minutes 30 seconds E	59 degrees 54 minutes 00 seconds N
02 degrees 13 minutes 30 seconds E	59 degrees 54 minutes 30 seconds N
02 degrees 15 minutes 30 seconds E	59 degrees 54 minutes 30 seconds N
02 degrees 15 minutes 30 seconds E	59 degrees 53 minutes 15 seconds N
02 degrees 10 minutes 30 seconds E	59 degrees 53 minutes 15 seconds N
02 degrees 10 minutes 30 seconds E	59 degrees 52 minutes 45 seconds N
02 degrees 09 minutes 30 seconds E	59 degrees 52 minutes 45 seconds N
02 degrees 09 minutes 30 seconds E	59 degrees 52 minutes 15 seconds N
02 degrees 08 minutes 30 seconds E	59 degrees 52 minutes 15 seconds N
02 degrees 08 minutes 30 seconds E	59 degrees 52 minutes 00 seconds N
02 degrees 07 minutes 30 seconds E	59 degrees 52 minutes 00 seconds N
02 degrees 07 minutes 30 seconds E	59 degrees 51 minutes 30 seconds N
02 degrees 05 minutes 30 seconds E	59 degrees 51 minutes 30 seconds N
02 degrees 05 minutes 30 seconds E	59 degrees 51 minutes 00 seconds N
02 degrees 04 minutes 00 seconds E	59 degrees 51 minutes 00 seconds N
02 degrees 04 minutes 00 seconds E	59 degrees 50 minutes 30 seconds N
02 degrees 03 minutes 00 seconds E	59 degrees 50 minutes 30 seconds N
02 degrees 03 minutes 00 seconds E	59 degrees 50 minutes 00 seconds N

(b) a line from the point 02 degrees 03 minutes 00 seconds E 59 degrees 50 minutes 00 seconds N west along the parallel of latitude 59 degrees 50 minutes 00 seconds N until its intersection with the Dividing Line;

(c) a line from the point of intersection specified in sub-paragraph (b) along the Dividing Line until its intersection with the parallel of latitude 60 degrees 00 minutes 45 seconds N;

(d) a line from the point of intersection specified in sub-paragraph (c) east along the parallel of latitude 60 degrees 00 minutes 45 degrees N until its intersection with the meridian 02 degrees 05 minutes 30 seconds E.

2. In this Schedule, the 'Dividing Line' means the dividing line as defined in an Agreement dated 10th March 1965 and made between the government of the United Kingdom of Great Britain and Northern Ireland and the government of the Kingdom of Norway as supplemented by a Protocol dated 22nd December 1978.

SCHEDULE 1A

Regulation 9A(3)
Occupational pension schemes

Interpretation
1.
(1) In this Schedule—

'active member', 'deferred member', 'managers', 'pensioner member' and 'trustees or managers', in relation to an occupational pension scheme, have the meanings given by section 124(1) of the Pensions Act 1995 as at the date of the coming into force of these Regulations;

'member', in relation to an occupational pension scheme, means any active member, deferred member or pensioner member;

'non-discrimination rule' means the rule in paragraph 2;

'occupational pension scheme' has the same meaning as in the Pension Schemes Act 1993 as at the date of the coming into force of these Regulations;

'prospective member', in relation to an occupational pension scheme, means any person who, under the terms of his employment or the rules of the scheme or both—

(a) is able, at his own option, to become a member of the scheme,

(b) shall become so able if he continues in the same employment for a sufficient period of time,

(c) shall be admitted to it automatically unless he makes an election not to become a member, or

(d) may be admitted to it subject to the consent of his employer.

(2) In paragraph 6 (procedure in employment tribunals), 'employer', in relation to an occupational pension scheme, has the meaning given by section 124(1) of the Pensions Act 1995 as at the date of the coming into force of these Regulations.

(3) Any term used in regulation 9A (trustees and managers of occupational pension schemes) and in this Schedule shall have the same meaning in that regulation as it has in this Schedule.

Non-discrimination rule
2. Every occupational pension scheme shall be treated as including a provision ('the non-discrimination rule') containing a requirement that the trustees or managers of the scheme refrain from doing any act which is unlawful by virtue of regulation 9A.

3. The other provisions of the scheme are to have effect subject to the non-discrimination rule.

4. The trustees or managers of an occupational pension scheme may—

(a) if they do not (apart from this paragraph) have power to make such alterations to the scheme as may be required to secure conformity with the non-discrimination rule, or

(b) if they have such power but the procedure for doing so—

(i) is liable to be unduly complex or protracted, or

(ii) involves the obtaining of consents which cannot be obtained, or can only be obtained with undue delay or difficulty,

by resolution make such alterations to the scheme.

5. Alterations made by a resolution such as is referred to in paragraph 4 may have effect in relation to a period before the alterations are made (but may not have effect in relation to any time before the coming into force of these Regulations).

Procedure in employment tribunals

6. Where under regulation 28 (jurisdiction of employment tribunals) a member or prospective member of an occupational pension scheme presents to an employment tribunal a complaint that the trustees or managers of the scheme—

(a) have committed against him an act which is unlawful by virtue of regulation 9A (trustees and managers of occupational pension schemes) or 21 (relationships which have come to an end); or

(b) are by virtue of regulation 22 (liability of employers and principals) or 23 (aiding unlawful acts) to be treated as having committed against him such an act,

the employer in relation to the scheme shall, for the purposes of the rules governing procedure, be treated as a party and be entitled to appear and be heard in accordance with those rules.

Remedies in employment tribunals

7.

(1) This paragraph applies where—

(a) under regulation 28 (jurisdiction of employment tribunals) a member or prospective member of an occupational pension scheme ('the complainant') presents to an employment tribunal a complaint against the trustees or managers of the scheme or an employer;

(b) the complainant is not a pensioner member of the scheme;

(c) the complaint relates to the terms on which persons become members of the scheme, or the terms on which members of the scheme are treated; and

(d) the tribunal finds the complaint to be well-founded.

(2) Where this paragraph applies, the employment tribunal may, without prejudice to the generality of its power under regulation 30(1)(a) (power to make order declaring rights of complainant and respondent), make an order declaring that the complainant has a right—

(a) where the complaint relates to the terms on which persons become members of the scheme, to be admitted to the scheme;

(b) where the complaint relates to the terms on which members of the scheme are treated, to membership of the scheme without discrimination.

(3) An order under sub-paragraph (2)—

(a) may be made in respect of such period as is specified in the order (but may not be made in respect of any time before the coming into force of these Regulations);

(b) may make such provision as the employment tribunal considers appropriate as to the terms on which, or the capacity in which, the complainant is to enjoy such admission or membership.

(4) Where this paragraph applies, the employment tribunal may not make an order for compensation under regulation 30(1)(b), whether in relation to arrears of benefits or otherwise, except—

(a) for injury to feelings;

(b) by virtue of regulation 30(3).

SCHEDULE 2

Regulation 33(1)
Questionnaire of person aggrieved

To

. . . .

(*name of person to be questioned*) of

. . . .

. . . .

(*address*)

    1.—(1) I

. . . .

(*name of questioner*) of

. . . .

(*address*)

consider that you may have discriminated against me [subjected me to harassment] contrary to the Employment Equality (Sexual Orientation) Regulations 2003.

(2) (*Give date, approximate time and a factual description of the treatment received and of the circumstances leading up to the treatment.*)

(3) I consider that this treatment may have been unlawful [because

. . . .

. . . .

(*complete if you wish to give reasons, otherwise delete*)].

    2. Do you agree that the statement in paragraph 1(2) above is an accurate description of what happened? If not, in what respect do you disagree or what is your version of what happened?

    3. Do you accept that your treatment of me was unlawful discrimination [harassment]? If not—

(a) why not,

(b) for what reason did I receive the treatment accorded to me, and

(c) how far did considerations of sexual orientation affect your treatment of me?

    4. (*Any other questions you wish to ask.*)

5. My address for any reply you may wish to give to the questions raised above is [that set out in paragraph 1(1) above] [the following address

....

....].

(*signature of questioner*)

....

(*date*)

N.B.—By virtue of regulation 33 of the Employment Equality (Sexual Orientation) Regulations 2003 this questionnaire and any reply are (subject to the provisions of that regulation) admissible in proceedings under the Regulations. A court or tribunal may draw any such inference as is just and equitable from a failure without reasonable excuse to reply within eight weeks of service of this questionnaire, or from an evasive or equivocal reply, including an inference that the person questioned has committed an unlawful act.

SCHEDULE 3

Regulation 33(1)
Reply by respondent

To

....

(*name of questioner*) of

....

....

(*address*)
   1. I

....

(*name of person questioned*) of

....

....

(*address*) hereby acknowledge receipt of the questionnaire signed by you and dated

....

which was served on me on

....

(*date*).
   2. [I agree that the statement in paragraph 1(2) of the questionnaire is an accurate description of what happened.]
[I disagree with the statement in paragraph 1(2) of the questionnaire in that

....]

3. I accept/dispute that my treatment of you was unlawful discrimination [harassment]. [My reasons for so disputing are

....

....

The reason why you received the treatment accorded to you and the answers to the other questions in paragraph 3 of the questionnaire are

....

....]

4. *(Replies to questions in paragraph 4 of the questionnaire.)*

[**5.** I have deleted (in whole or in part) the paragraph(s) numbered

....

above, since I am unable/unwilling to reply to the relevant questions in the correspondingly numbered paragraph(s) of the questionnaire for the following reasons

....

....]

(signature of person questioned)

....

(date)

SCHEDULE 4

Regulation 35
Validity of contracts, collective agreements and rules of undertakings

Part 1
Validity and revision of contracts

1.

(1) A term of a contract is void where—

(a) the making of the contract is, by reason of the inclusion of the term, unlawful by virtue of these Regulations;

(b) it is included in furtherance of an act which is unlawful by virtue of these Regulations; or

(c) it provides for the doing of an act which is unlawful by virtue of these Regulations.

(2) Sub-paragraph (1) does not apply to a term the inclusion of which constitutes, or is in furtherance of, or provides for, unlawful discrimination against, or harassment of, a party to the contract, but the term shall be unenforceable against that party.

(3) A term in a contract which purports to exclude or limit any provision of these Regulations is unenforceable by any person in whose favour the term would operate apart from this paragraph.

(4) Sub-paragraphs (1), (2) and (3) shall apply whether the contract was entered into before or after the date on which these Regulations come into force; but in the case of a

contract made before that date, those sub-paragraphs do not apply in relation to any period before that date.

2.

(1) Paragraph 1(3) does not apply—

(a) to a contract settling a complaint to which regulation 28(1) (jurisdiction of employment tribunals) applies where the contract is made with the assistance of a conciliation officer within the meaning of section 211 of the Trade Union and Labour Relations (Consolidation) Act 1992;

(b) to a contract settling a complaint to which regulation 28(1) applies if the conditions regulating compromise contracts under this Schedule are satisfied in relation to the contract; or

(c) to a contract settling a claim to which regulation 31 (jurisdiction of county or sheriff courts) applies.

(2) The conditions regulating compromise contracts under this Schedule are that—

(a) the contract must be in writing;

(b) the contract must relate to the particular complaint;

(c) the complainant must have received advice from a relevant independent adviser as to the terms and effect of the proposed contract and in particular its effect on his ability to pursue a complaint before an employment tribunal;

(d) there must be in force, when the adviser gives the advice, a contract of insurance, or an indemnity provided for members of a profession or professional body, covering the risk of a claim by the complainant in respect of loss arising in consequence of the advice;

(e) the contract must identify the adviser; and

(f) the contract must state that the conditions regulating compromise contracts under this Schedule are satisfied.

(3) A person is a relevant independent adviser for the purposes of sub-paragraph (2)(c)—

(a) if he is a qualified lawyer;

(b) if he is an officer, official, employee or member of an independent trade union who has been certified in writing by the trade union as competent to give advice and as authorised to do so on behalf of the trade union; or

(c) if he works at an advice centre (whether as an employee or a volunteer) and has been certified in writing by the centre as competent to give advice and as authorised to do so on behalf of the centre.

(4) But a person is not a relevant independent adviser for the purposes of sub-paragraph (2)(c) in relation to the complainant—

(a) if he is, is employed by or is acting in the matter for the other party or a person who is connected with the other party;

(b) in the case of a person within sub-paragraph (3)(b) or (c), if the trade union or advice centre is the other party or a person who is connected with the other party; or

(c) in the case of a person within sub-paragraph (3)(c), if the complainant makes a payment for the advice received from him.

(5) In sub-paragraph (3)(a) 'qualified lawyer' means—

(a) as respects England and Wales, a barrister (whether in practice as such or employed to give legal advice), a solicitor who holds a practising certificate, or a person other than a barrister or solicitor who is an authorised advocate or authorised litigator (within the meaning of the Courts and Legal Services Act 1990); and

(b) as respects Scotland, an advocate (whether in practice as such or employed to give legal advice), or a solicitor who holds a practising certificate.

(6) In sub-paragraph (3)(b) 'independent trade union' has the same meaning as in the Trade Union and Labour Relations (Consolidation) Act 1992.

(7) For the purposes of sub-paragraph (4)(a) any two persons are to be treated as connected—

(a) if one is a company of which the other (directly or indirectly) has control; or

(b) if both are companies of which a third person (directly or indirectly) has control.

(8) An agreement under which the parties agree to submit a dispute to arbitration—

(a) shall be regarded for the purposes of sub-paragraph (1)(a) and (b) as being a contract settling a complaint if—

(i) the dispute is covered by a scheme having effect by virtue of an order under section 212A of the Trade Union and Labour Relations (Consolidation) Act 1992, and

(ii) the agreement is to submit it to arbitration in accordance with the scheme, but

(b) shall be regarded as neither being nor including such a contract in any other case.

3.

(1) On the application of a person interested in a contract to which paragraph 1(1) or (2) applies, a county court or a sheriff court may make such order as it thinks fit for—

(a) removing or modifying any term rendered void by paragraph 1(1), or

(b) removing or modifying any term made unenforceable by paragraph 1(2);

but such an order shall not be made unless all persons affected have been given notice in writing of the application (except where under rules of court notice may be dispensed with) and have been afforded an opportunity to make representations to the court.

(2) An order under sub-paragraph (1) may include provision as respects any period before the making of the order (but after the coming into force of these Regulations).

Part 2
Collective agreements and rules of undertakings

4.

(1) This Part of this Schedule applies to—

(a) any term of a collective agreement, including an agreement which was not intended, or is presumed not to have been intended, to be a legally enforceable contract;

(b) any rule made by an employer for application to all or any of the persons who are employed by him or who apply to be, or are, considered by him for employment;

(c) any rule made by a trade organisation (within the meaning of regulation 15) or a qualifications body (within the meaning of regulation 16) for application to—

(i) all or any of its members or prospective members; or

(ii) all or any of the persons on whom it has conferred professional or trade qualifications (within the meaning of regulation 16) or who are seeking the professional or trade qualifications which it has power to confer.

(2) Any term or rule to which this Part of this Schedule applies is void where—

(a) the making of the collective agreement is, by reason of the inclusion of the term, unlawful by virtue of these Regulations;

(b) the term or rule is included or made in furtherance of an act which is unlawful by virtue of these Regulations; or

(c) the term or rule provides for the doing of an act which is unlawful by virtue of these Regulations.

(3) Sub-paragraph (2) shall apply whether the agreement was entered into, or the rule

made, before or after the date on which these Regulations come into force; but in the case of an agreement entered into, or a rule made, before the date on which these Regulations come into force, that sub-paragraph does not apply in relation to any period before that date.

5. A person to whom this paragraph applies may present a complaint to an employment tribunal that a term or rule is void by virtue of paragraph 4 if he has reason to believe—

(a) that the term or rule may at some future time have effect in relation to him; and

(b) where he alleges that it is void by virtue of paragraph 4(2)(c), that—

(i) an act for the doing of which it provides, may at some such time be done in relation to him, and

(ii) the act would be unlawful by virtue of these Regulations if done in relation to him in present circumstances.

6. In the case of a complaint about—

(a) a term of a collective agreement made by or on behalf of—

(i) an employer,

(ii) an organisation of employers of which an employer is a member, or

(iii) an association of such organisations of one of which an employer is a member, or

(b) a rule made by an employer within the meaning of paragraph 4(1)(b),

paragraph 5 applies to any person who is, or is genuinely and actively seeking to become, one of his employees.

7. In the case of a complaint about a rule made by an organisation or body to which paragraph 4(1)(c) applies, paragraph 5 applies to any person—

(a) who is, or is genuinely and actively seeking to become, a member of the organisation or body;

(b) on whom the organisation or body has conferred a professional or trade qualification (within the meaning of regulation 16); or

(c) who is genuinely and actively seeking such a professional or trade qualification which the organisation or body has power to confer.

8.

(1) When an employment tribunal finds that a complaint presented to it under paragraph 5 is well-founded the tribunal shall make an order declaring that the term or rule is void.

(2) An order under sub-paragraph (1) may include provision as respects any period before the making of the order (but after the coming into force of these Regulations).

9. The avoidance by virtue of paragraph 4(2) of any term or rule which provides for any person to be discriminated against shall be without prejudice to the following rights (except in so far as they enable any person to require another person to be treated less favourably than himself), namely—

(a) such of the rights of the person to be discriminated against; and

(b) such of the rights of any person who will be treated more favourably in direct or indirect consequence of the discrimination,

as are conferred by or in respect of a contract made or modified wholly or partly in pursuance of, or by reference to, that term or rule.

10. In this Schedule 'collective agreement' means any agreement relating to one or more of the matters mentioned in section 178(2) of the Trade Union and Labour Relations (Consolidation) Act 1992 (meaning of trade dispute), being an agreement made by or on behalf of one or more employers or one or more organisations of employers or associations of such organisations with one or more organisations of workers or associations of such organisations.

SCHEDULE 5

Regulation 39
Amendments to legislation

1. The Employment Tribunals Act 1996 is amended as follows—
    (a) in section 18(1) (cases where conciliation provisions apply)—
        (i) at the end of paragraph (i), there is omitted 'or', and
        (ii) after paragraph (j), there is inserted—

'or

    (k) under regulation 28 of the Employment Equality (Sexual Orientation) Regulations 2003';

    (b) in section 21 (jurisdiction of the Employment Appeal Tribunal), in subsection (1) (which specifies the proceedings and claims to which the section applies)—
        (i) at the end of paragraph (j), there is omitted 'or', and
        (ii) after paragraph (k) there is inserted—

'or

    (l) the Employment Equality (Sexual Orientation) Regulations 2003'.

2. Section 126 (compensation for acts which are both unfair dismissal and discrimination) of the Employment Rights Act 1996 is amended as follows—
    (a) in subsection (1)(b)—
        (i) after 'Race Relations Act 1976' there is omitted 'and', and
        (ii) after 'Disability Discrimination Act 1995' there is inserted—

'and the Employment Equality (Sexual Orientation) Regulations 2003';
    (b) in subsection (2) after 'those Acts' there is inserted 'or Regulations'.

3. Sub-paragraph (b) of the definition of 'an award under the relevant legislation' in regulation 1(2) (interpretation) of the Employment Tribunals (Interest on Awards in Discrimination Cases) Regulations 1996 is amended as follows—
    (a) after 'section 56(1)(b) of the 1976 Act' there is omitted 'or'; and
    (b) after 'section 8(2)(b) of the 1995 Act' there is inserted—

'or regulation 30(1)(b) of the Employment Equality (Sexual Orientation) Regulations 2003'.

4. In the Employment Act 2002 at the end of each of the following schedules—
    (a) Schedule 3 (tribunal jurisdictions to which section 31 applies for adjustment of awards for non-completion of statutory procedure);
    (b) Schedule 4 (tribunal jurisdictions to which section 32 applies for complaints where the employee must first submit a statement of grievance to employer); and
    (c) Schedule 5 (tribunal jurisdictions to which section 38 applies in relation to

proceedings where the employer has failed to give a statement of employment particulars), there is inserted—

'Regulation 28 of the Employment Equality (Sexual Orientation) Regulations 2003 (discrimination in the employment field)'.

EXPLANATORY NOTE

(This note is not part of the Regulations)

These Regulations, which are made under section 2(2) of the European Communities Act 1972 (c. 68), implement (in Great Britain) Council Directive 2000/78/EC of 27th November 2000 establishing a general framework for equal treatment in employment (OJ L 303, 2.12.2000, p. 16) so far as it relates to discrimination on grounds of sexual orientation. The Regulations make it unlawful to discriminate on grounds of sexual orientation in employment and vocational training. They prohibit direct discrimination, indirect discrimination, victimisation and harassment.

Sexual orientation is defined in regulation 2 as meaning a sexual orientation towards persons of the same sex, persons of the opposite sex, or to both persons of the same sex and of the opposite sex.

Direct discrimination, defined in regulation 3(1)(a), occurs where a person is treated less favourably than another on grounds of sexual orientation. Indirect discrimination, defined in regulation 3(1)(b), occurs where a provision, criterion or practice, which is applied generally, puts persons of a particular sexual orientation at a disadvantage and cannot be shown to be a proportionate means of achieving a legitimate aim. Victimisation, defined in regulation 4, occurs where a person receives less favourable treatment than others by reason of the fact that he has brought (or given evidence in) proceedings, made an allegation or otherwise done anything under or by reference to the Regulations. Harassment, defined in regulation 5, occurs where a person is subjected to unwanted conduct on grounds of sexual orientation with the purpose or effect of violating his dignity, or creating an intimidating, hostile, degrading, humiliating or offensive environment for him.

Regulations 6 to 21 prohibit discrimination, victimisation and harassment in the fields of employment and vocational training. In particular, they protect employees (regulation 6), contract workers (regulation 8), office-holders (including constables) (regulations 10 and 11), and partners in firms. They not only prohibit discrimination etc by employers, but also by trade organisations (regulation 15), bodies conferring professional and trade qualifications (regulation 16), training providers (regulation 17), employment agencies (regulation 18), and further and higher education institutions (regulation 20). By virtue of regulation 21, discrimination, victimisation or harassment occuring after the relevant relationship has ended is unlawful if it arises out of, and is closely connected to, the relationship. The Regulations also apply to Crown servants and Parliamentary staff (regulations 36 to 38). Regulation 35 and Schedule 4 address the validity of discriminatory terms in contracts and collective agreements.

Not all differences of treatment on grounds of sexual orientation are unlawful. There are exceptions in regulations 24 to 26 for differences of treatment related to national security, to benefits which are dependent on marital status, and positive action. Regulation 7 provides an exception where being of a particular sexual orientation is a genuine and determining occupational requirement for a post, if it is proportionate to apply the requirement in the particular case. Regulation 7 also provides an exception for employment for purposes of an organised religion, where a requirement related to sexual orientation is applied so as to comply with the doctrines of the religion or to avoid conflicting with the religious convictions of its followers.

Regulations 27 to 34 provide remedies for individuals, including compensation, by way of proceedings in employment tribunals and in the county or sheriff courts. There are special provisions about the burden of proof in those cases in regulations 29 and 32, which transfer the burden to a respondent to a case once a complainant has established facts from which a court or tribunal could conclude, in the absence of an adequate explanation, that an act of discrimination or harassment has been committed by the respondent. Regulation 33 and Schedules 2 and 3 also include a questionnaire procedure to assist complainants in obtaining information from respondents.

A full Regulatory Impact Assessment report of the effect that these Regulations would have on the costs to business and a Transposition Note are freely available to the public from the Selected Employment Rights Branch, UG65, Department of Trade and Industry, 1 Victoria Street, London SW1H 0ET. Copies have also been placed in the libraries of both Houses of Parliament.

Appendix 3
Council Directive 2000/78/EC
of 27 November 2000
establishing a general framework for equal treatment
in employment and occupation

THE COUNCIL OF THE EUROPEAN UNION,

Having regard to the Treaty establishing the European Community, and in particular Article 13 thereof,

Having regard to the proposal from the Commission[1],

Having regard to the Opinion of the European Parliament[2],

Having regard to the Opinion of the Economic and Social Committee[3],

Having regard to the Opinion of the Committee of the Regions[4],

Whereas:

(1) In accordance with Article 6 of the Treaty on European Union, the European Union is founded on the principles of liberty, democracy, respect for human rights and fundamental freedoms, and the rule of law, principles which are common to all Member States and it respects fundamental rights, as guaranteed by the European Convention for the Protection of Human Rights and Fundamental Freedoms and as they result from the constitutional traditions common to the Member States, as general principles of Community law.

(2) The principle of equal treatment between women and men is well established by an important body of Community law, in particular in Council Directive 76/207/EEC of 9 February 1976 on the implementation of the principle of equal treatment for men and women as regards access to employment, vocational training and promotion, and working conditions[5].

(3) In implementing the principle of equal treatment, the Community should, in accordance with Article 3(2) of the EC Treaty, aim to eliminate inequalities, and to promote equality between men and women, especially since women are often the victims of multiple discrimination.

(4) The right of all persons to equality before the law and protection against discrimination constitutes a universal right recognised by the Universal Declaration of Human Rights, the United Nations Convention on the Elimination of All Forms of Discrimination against Women, United Nations Covenants on Civil and Political Rights and on Economic, Social and Cultural Rights and by the European Convention for the Protection of Human Rights and Fundamental Freedoms, to which all Member States are signatories. Convention No 111 of

---

[1] OJ C 177 E, 27.6.2000, p. 42.
[2] Opinion delivered on 12 October 2000 (not yet published in the Official Journal).
[3] OJ C 204, 18.7.2000, p. 82.
[4] OJ C 226, 8.8.2000, p. 1.
[5] OJ L 39, 14.2.1976, p. 40.

the International Labour Organisation (ILO) prohibits discrimination in the field of employment and occupation.

(5) It is important to respect such fundamental rights and freedoms. This Directive does not prejudice freedom of association, including the right to establish unions with others and to join unions to defend one's interests.

(6) The Community Charter of the Fundamental Social Rights of Workers recognises the importance of combating every form of discrimination, including the need to take appropriate action for the social and economic integration of elderly and disabled people.

(7) The EC Treaty includes among its objectives the promotion of coordination between employment policies of the Member States. To this end, a new employment chapter was incorporated in the EC Treaty as a means of developing a coordinated European strategy for employment to promote a skilled, trained and adaptable workforce.

(8) The Employment Guidelines for 2000 agreed by the European Council at Helsinki on 10 and 11 December 1999 stress the need to foster a labour market favourable to social integration by formulating a coherent set of policies aimed at combating discrimination against groups such as persons with disability. They also emphasise the need to pay particular attention to supporting older workers, in order to increase their participation in the labour force.

(9) Employment and occupation are key elements in guaranteeing equal opportunities for all and contribute strongly to the full participation of citizens in economic, cultural and social life and to realising their potential.

(10) On 29 June 2000 the Council adopted Directive 2000/43/EC[6] implementing the principle of equal treatment between persons irrespective of racial or ethnic origin. That Directive already provides protection against such discrimination in the field of employment and occupation.

(11) Discrimination based on religion or belief, disability, age or sexual orientation may undermine the achievement of the objectives of the EC Treaty, in particular the attainment of a high level of employment and social protection, raising the standard of living and the quality of life, economic and social cohesion and solidarity, and the free movement of persons.

(12) To this end, any direct or indirect discrimination based on religion or belief, disability, age or sexual orientation as regards the areas covered by this Directive should be prohibited throughout the Community. This prohibition of discrimination should also apply to nationals of third countries but does not cover differences of treatment based on nationality and is without prejudice to provisions governing the entry and residence of third-country nationals and their access to employment and occupation.

(13) This Directive does not apply to social security and social protection schemes whose benefits are not treated as income within the meaning given to that term for the purpose of applying Article 141 of the EC Treaty, nor to any kind of payment by the State aimed at providing access to employment or maintaining employment.

(14) This Directive shall be without prejudice to national provisions laying down retirement ages.

(15) The appreciation of the facts from which it may be inferred that there has been direct or indirect discrimination is a matter for national judicial or other competent bodies, in accordance with rules of national law or practice. Such rules may provide, in particular,

---

[6] OJ L 180, 19.7.2000, p. 22.

for indirect discrimination to be established by any means including on the basis of statistical evidence.

(16) The provision of measures to accommodate the needs of disabled people at the workplace plays an important role in combating discrimination on grounds of disability.

(17) This Directive does not require the recruitment, promotion, maintenance in employment or training of an individual who is not competent, capable and available to perform the essential functions of the post concerned or to undergo the relevant training, without prejudice to the obligation to provide reasonable accommodation for people with disabilities.

(18) This Directive does not require, in particular, the armed forces and the police, prison or emergency services to recruit or maintain in employment persons who do not have the required capacity to carry out the range of functions that they may be called upon to perform with regard to the legitimate objective of preserving the operational capacity of those services.

(19) Moreover, in order that the Member States may continue to safeguard the combat effectiveness of their armed forces, they may choose not to apply the provisions of this Directive concerning disability and age to all or part of their armed forces. The Member States which make that choice must define the scope of that derogation.

(20) Appropriate measures should be provided, i.e. effective and practical measures to adapt the workplace to the disability, for example adapting premises and equipment, patterns of working time, the distribution of tasks or the provision of training or integration resources.

(21) To determine whether the measures in question give rise to a disproportionate burden, account should be taken in particular of the financial and other costs entailed, the scale and financial resources of the organisation or undertaking and the possibility of obtaining public funding or any other assistance.

(22) This Directive is without prejudice to national laws on marital status and the benefits dependent thereon.

(23) In very limited circumstances, a difference of treatment may be justified where a characteristic related to religion or belief, disability, age or sexual orientation constitutes a genuine and determining occupational requirement, when the objective is legitimate and the requirement is proportionate. Such circumstances should be included in the information provided by the Member States to the Commission.

(24) The European Union in its Declaration No 11 on the status of churches and non-confessional organisations, annexed to the Final Act of the Amsterdam Treaty, has explicitly recognised that it respects and does not prejudice the status under national law of churches and religious associations or communities in the Member States and that it equally respects the status of philosophical and non-confessional organisations. With this in view, Member States may maintain or lay down specific provisions on genuine, legitimate and justified occupational requirements which might be required for carrying out an occupational activity.

(25) The prohibition of age discrimination is an essential part of meeting the aims set out in the Employment Guidelines and encouraging diversity in the workforce. However, differences in treatment in connection with age may be justified under certain circumstances and therefore require specific provisions which may vary in accordance with the situation in Member States. It is therefore essential to distinguish between differences in treatment which are justified, in particular by legitimate employment policy, labour market and vocational training objectives, and discrimination which must be prohibited.

(26) The prohibition of discrimination should be without prejudice to the maintenance or adoption of measures intended to prevent or compensate for disadvantages suffered by a group of persons of a particular religion or belief, disability, age or sexual orientation, and

such measures may permit organisations of persons of a particular religion or belief, disability, age or sexual orientation where their main object is the promotion of the special needs of those persons.

(27) In its Recommendation 86/379/EEC of 24 July 1986 on the employment of disabled people in the Community[7], the Council established a guideline framework setting out examples of positive action to promote the employment and training of disabled people, and in its Resolution of 17 June 1999 on equal employment opportunities for people with disabilities[8], affirmed the importance of giving specific attention inter alia to recruitment, retention, training and lifelong learning with regard to disabled persons.

(28) This Directive lays down minimum requirements, thus giving the Member States the option of introducing or maintaining more favourable provisions. The implementation of this Directive should not serve to justify any regression in relation to the situation which already prevails in each Member State.

(29) Persons who have been subject to discrimination based on religion or belief, disability, age or sexual orientation should have adequate means of legal protection. To provide a more effective level of protection, associations or legal entities should also be empowered to engage in proceedings, as the Member States so determine, either on behalf or in support of any victim, without prejudice to national rules of procedure concerning representation and defence before the courts.

(30) The effective implementation of the principle of equality requires adequate judicial protection against victimisation.

(31) The rules on the burden of proof must be adapted when there is a prima facie case of discrimination and, for the principle of equal treatment to be applied effectively, the burden of proof must shift back to the respondent when evidence of such discrimination is brought. However, it is not for the respondent to prove that the plaintiff adheres to a particular religion or belief, has a particular disability, is of a particular age or has a particular sexual orientation.

(32) Member States need not apply the rules on the burden of proof to proceedings in which it is for the court or other competent body to investigate the facts of the case. The procedures thus referred to are those in which the plaintiff is not required to prove the facts, which it is for the court or competent body to investigate.

(33) Member States should promote dialogue between the social partners and, within the framework of national practice, with non-governmental organisations to address different forms of discrimination at the workplace and to combat them.

(34) The need to promote peace and reconciliation between the major communities in Northern Ireland necessitates the incorporation of particular provisions into this Directive.

(35) Member States should provide for effective, proportionate and dissuasive sanctions in case of breaches of the obligations under this Directive.

(36) Member States may entrust the social partners, at their joint request, with the implementation of this Directive, as regards the provisions concerning collective agreements, provided they take any necessary steps to ensure that they are at all times able to guarantee the results required by this Directive.

(37) In accordance with the principle of subsidiarity set out in Article 5 of the EC Treaty, the objective of this Directive, namely the creation within the Community of a level

[7] OJ L 225, 12.8.1986, p. 43.
[8] OJ C 186, 2.7.1999, p. 3.

playing-field as regards equality in employment and occupation, cannot be sufficiently achieved by the Member States and can therefore, by reason of the scale and impact of the action, be better achieved at Community level. In accordance with the principle of proportionality, as set out in that Article, this Directive does not go beyond what is necessary in order to achieve that objective,

HAS ADOPTED THIS DIRECTIVE:

CHAPTER I
GENERAL PROVISIONS

Article 1
Purpose

The purpose of this Directive is to lay down a general framework for combating discrimination on the grounds of religion or belief, disability, age or sexual orientation as regards employment and occupation, with a view to putting into effect in the Member States the principle of equal treatment.

Article 2
Concept of discrimination

1. For the purposes of this Directive, the 'principle of equal treatment' shall mean that there shall be no direct or indirect discrimination whatsoever on any of the grounds referred to in Article 1.

2. For the purposes of paragraph 1:

(a) direct discrimination shall be taken to occur where one person is treated less favourably than another is, has been or would be treated in a comparable situation, on any of the grounds referred to in Article 1;

(b) indirect discrimination shall be taken to occur where an apparently neutral provision, criterion or practice would put persons having a particular religion or belief, a particular disability, a particular age, or a particular sexual orientation at a particular disadvantage compared with other persons unless:

(i) that provision, criterion or practice is objectively justified by a legitimate aim and the means of achieving that aim are appropriate and necessary, or

(ii) as regards persons with a particular disability, the employer or any person or organisation to whom this Directive applies, is obliged, under national legislation, to take appropriate measures in line with the principles contained in Article 5 in order to eliminate disadvantages entailed by such provision, criterion or practice.

3. Harassment shall be deemed to be a form of discrimination within the meaning of paragraph 1, when unwanted conduct related to any of the grounds referred to in Article 1 takes place with the purpose or effect of violating the dignity of a person and of creating an intimidating, hostile, degrading, humiliating or offensive environment. In this context, the concept of harassment may be defined in accordance with the national laws and practice of the Member States.

4. An instruction to discriminate against persons on any of the grounds referred to in Article 1 shall be deemed to be discrimination within the meaning of paragraph 1.

5. This Directive shall be without prejudice to measures laid down by national law which, in a democratic society, are necessary for public security, for the maintenance of public order and the prevention of criminal offences, for the protection of health and for the protection of the rights and freedoms of others.

Article 3
Scope

1. Within the limits of the areas of competence conferred on the Community, this Directive shall apply to all persons, as regards both the public and private sectors, including public bodies, in relation to:

(a) conditions for access to employment, to self-employment or to occupation, including selection criteria and recruitment conditions, whatever the branch of activity and at all levels of the professional hierarchy, including promotion;

(b) access to all types and to all levels of vocational guidance, vocational training, advanced vocational training and retraining, including practical work experience;

(c) employment and working conditions, including dismissals and pay;

(d) membership of, and involvement in, an organisation of workers or employers, or any organisation whose members carry on a particular profession, including the benefits provided for by such organisations.

2. This Directive does not cover differences of treatment based on nationality and is without prejudice to provisions and conditions relating to the entry into and residence of third-country nationals and stateless persons in the territory of Member States, and to any treatment which arises from the legal status of the third-country nationals and stateless persons concerned.

3. This Directive does not apply to payments of any kind made by state schemes or similar, including state social security or social protection schemes.

4. Member States may provide that this Directive, in so far as it relates to discrimination on the grounds of disability and age, shall not apply to the armed forces.

Article 4
Occupational requirements

1. Notwithstanding Article 2(1) and (2), Member States may provide that a difference of treatment which is based on a characteristic related to any of the grounds referred to in Article 1 shall not constitute discrimination where, by reason of the nature of the particular occupational activities concerned or of the context in which they are carried out, such a characteristic constitutes a genuine and determining occupational requirement, provided that the objective is legitimate and the requirement is proportionate.

2. Member States may maintain national legislation in force at the date of adoption of this Directive or provide for future legislation incorporating national practices existing at the date of adoption of this Directive pursuant to which, in the case of occupational activities within churches and other public or private organisations the ethos of which is based on religion or belief, a difference of treatment based on a person's religion or belief shall not constitute discrimination where, by reason of the nature of these activities or of the context in which they are carried out, a person's religion or belief constitute a genuine, legitimate and justified occupational requirement, having regard to the organisation's ethos. This difference of treatment shall be implemented taking account of Member States' constitutional provisions and principles, as

210

well as the general principles of Community law, and should not justify discrimination on another ground.

Provided that its provisions are otherwise complied with, this Directive shall thus not prejudice the right of churches and other public or private organisations, the ethos of which is based on religion or belief, acting in conformity with national constitutions and laws, to require individuals working for them to act in good faith and with loyalty to the organisation's ethos.

Article 5
Reasonable accommodation for disabled persons

In order to guarantee compliance with the principle of equal treatment in relation to persons with disabilities, reasonable accommodation shall be provided. This means that employers shall take appropriate measures, where needed in a particular case, to enable a person with a disability to have access to, participate in, or advance in employment, or to undergo training, unless such measures would impose a disproportionate burden on the employer. This burden shall not be disproportionate when it is sufficiently remedied by measures existing within the framework of the disability policy of the Member State concerned.

Article 6
Justification of differences of treatment on grounds of age

1. Notwithstanding Article 2(2), Member States may provide that differences of treatment on grounds of age shall not constitute discrimination, if, within the context of national law, they are objectively and reasonably justified by a legitimate aim, including legitimate employment policy, labour market and vocational training objectives, and if the means of achieving that aim are appropriate and necessary.

Such differences of treatment may include, among others:

(a) the setting of special conditions on access to employment and vocational training, employment and occupation, including dismissal and remuneration conditions, for young people, older workers and persons with caring responsibilities in order to promote their vocational integration or ensure their protection;

(b) the fixing of minimum conditions of age, professional experience or seniority in service for access to employment or to certain advantages linked to employment;

(c) the fixing of a maximum age for recruitment which is based on the training requirements of the post in question or the need for a reasonable period of employment before retirement.

2. Notwithstanding Article 2(2), Member States may provide that the fixing for occupational social security schemes of ages for admission or entitlement to retirement or invalidity benefits, including the fixing under those schemes of different ages for employees or groups or categories of employees, and the use, in the context of such schemes, of age criteria in actuarial calculations, does not constitute discrimination on the grounds of age, provided this does not result in discrimination on the grounds of sex.

Article 7
Positive action

1. With a view to ensuring full equality in practice, the principle of equal treatment shall not prevent any Member State from maintaining or adopting specific measures to prevent or compensate for disadvantages linked to any of the grounds referred to in Article 1.

2. With regard to disabled persons, the principle of equal treatment shall be without prejudice to the right of Member States to maintain or adopt provisions on the protection of health and safety at work or to measures aimed at creating or maintaining provisions or facilities for safeguarding or promoting their integration into the working environment.

Article 8
Minimum requirements

1. Member States may introduce or maintain provisions which are more favourable to the protection of the principle of equal treatment than those laid down in this Directive.

2. The implementation of this Directive shall under no circumstances constitute grounds for a reduction in the level of protection against discrimination already afforded by Member States in the fields covered by this Directive.

CHAPTER II
REMEDIES AND ENFORCEMENT

Article 9
Defence of rights

1. Member States shall ensure that judicial and/or administrative procedures, including where they deem it appropriate conciliation procedures, for the enforcement of obligations under this Directive are available to all persons who consider themselves wronged by failure to apply the principle of equal treatment to them, even after the relationship in which the discrimination is alleged to have occurred has ended.

2. Member States shall ensure that associations, organisations or other legal entities which have, in accordance with the criteria laid down by their national law, a legitimate interest in ensuring that the provisions of this Directive are complied with, may engage, either on behalf or in support of the complainant, with his or her approval, in any judicial and/or administrative procedure provided for the enforcement of obligations under this Directive.

3. Paragraphs 1 and 2 are without prejudice to national rules relating to time limits for bringing actions as regards the principle of equality of treatment.

Article 10
Burden of proof

1. Member States shall take such measures as are necessary, in accordance with their national judicial systems, to ensure that, when persons who consider themselves wronged because the principle of equal treatment has not been applied to them establish, before a court or other competent authority, facts from which it may be presumed that there has been direct or indirect discrimination, it shall be for the respondent to prove that there has been no breach of the principle of equal treatment.

2. Paragraph 1 shall not prevent Member States from introducing rules of evidence which are more favourable to plaintiffs.

3. Paragraph 1 shall not apply to criminal procedures.

4. Paragraphs 1, 2 and 3 shall also apply to any legal proceedings commenced in accordance with Article 9(2).

5. Member States need not apply paragraph 1 to proceedings in which it is for the court or competent body to investigate the facts of the case.

Article 11
Victimisation

Member States shall introduce into their national legal systems such measures as are necessary to protect employees against dismissal or other adverse treatment by the employer as a reaction to a complaint within the undertaking or to any legal proceedings aimed at enforcing compliance with the principle of equal treatment.

Article 12
Dissemination of information

Member States shall take care that the provisions adopted pursuant to this Directive, together with the relevant provisions already in force in this field, are brought to the attention of the persons concerned by all appropriate means, for example at the workplace, throughout their territory.

Article 13
Social dialogue

1. Member States shall, in accordance with their national traditions and practice, take adequate measures to promote dialogue between the social partners with a view to fostering equal treatment, including through the monitoring of workplace practices, collective agreements, codes of conduct and through research or exchange of experiences and good practices.

2. Where consistent with their national traditions and practice, Member States shall encourage the social partners, without prejudice to their autonomy, to conclude at the appropriate level agreements laying down anti-discrimination rules in the fields referred to in Article 3 which fall within the scope of collective bargaining. These agreements shall respect the minimum requirements laid down by this Directive and by the relevant national implementing measures.

Article 14
Dialogue with non-governmental organisations

Member States shall encourage dialogue with appropriate non-governmental organisations which have, in accordance with their national law and practice, a legitimate interest in contributing to the fight against discrimination on any of the grounds referred to in Article 1 with a view to promoting the principle of equal treatment.

CHAPTER III
PARTICULAR PROVISIONS

Article 15
Northern Ireland

1. In order to tackle the under-representation of one of the major religious communities in the police service of Northern Ireland, differences in treatment regarding recruitment into that

service, including its support staff, shall not constitute discrimination insofar as those differences in treatment are expressly authorised by national legislation.

2. In order to maintain a balance of opportunity in employment for teachers in Northern Ireland while furthering the reconciliation of historical divisions between the major religious communities there, the provisions on religion or belief in this Directive shall not apply to the recruitment of teachers in schools in Northern Ireland in so far as this is expressly authorised by national legislation.

CHAPTER IV
FINAL PROVISIONS

Article 16
Compliance

Member States shall take the necessary measures to ensure that:

(a) any laws, regulations and administrative provisions contrary to the principle of equal treatment are abolished;

(b) any provisions contrary to the principle of equal treatment which are included in contracts or collective agreements, internal rules of undertakings or rules governing the independent occupations and professions and workers' and employers' organisations are, or may be, declared null and void or are amended.

Article 17
Sanctions

Member States shall lay down the rules on sanctions applicable to infringements of the national provisions adopted pursuant to this Directive and shall take all measures necessary to ensure that they are applied. The sanctions, which may comprise the payment of compensation to the victim, must be effective, proportionate and dissuasive. Member States shall notify those provisions to the Commission by 2 December 2003 at the latest and shall notify it without delay of any subsequent amendment affecting them.

Article 18
Implementation

Member States shall adopt the laws, regulations and administrative provisions necessary to comply with this Directive by 2 December 2003 at the latest or may entrust the social partners, at their joint request, with the implementation of this Directive as regards provisions concerning collective agreements. In such cases, Member States shall ensure that, no later than 2 December 2003, the social partners introduce the necessary measures by agreement, the Member States concerned being required to take any necessary measures to enable them at any time to be in a position to guarantee the results imposed by this Directive. They shall forthwith inform the Commission thereof.

In order to take account of particular conditions, Member States may, if necessary, have an additional period of 3 years from 2 December 2003, that is to say a total of 6 years, to implement the provisions of this Directive on age and disability discrimination. In that event they shall inform the Commission forthwith. Any Member State which chooses to use this additional period shall report annually to the Commission on the steps it is taking to tackle age and disability discrimination and on the progress it is making towards implementation. The Commission shall report annually to the Council.

When Member States adopt these measures, they shall contain a reference to this Directive or be accompanied by such reference on the occasion of their official publication. The methods of making such reference shall be laid down by Member States.

Article 19
Report

1. Member States shall communicate to the Commission, by 2 December 2005 at the latest and every five years thereafter, all the information necessary for the Commission to draw up a report to the European Parliament and the Council on the application of this Directive.

2. The Commission's report shall take into account, as appropriate, the viewpoints of the social partners and relevant non-governmental organisations. In accordance with the principle of gender mainstreaming, this report shall, inter alia, provide an assessment of the impact of the measures taken on women and men. In the light of the information received, this report shall include, if necessary, proposals to revise and update this Directive.

Article 20
Entry into force

This Directive shall enter into force on the day of its publication in the Official Journal of the European Communities.

Article 21
Addressees

This Directive is addressed to the Member States.
Done at Brussels, 27 November 2000.
For the Council
The President
E. Guigou

Appendix 4

ACAS GUIDANCE
RELIGION OR BELIEF AND THE WORKPLACE

Putting the
Employment Equality (Religion or Belief) Regulations
2003 into practice

For Employers and Their Staff

INDEX

INTRODUCTION

From 2nd December, 2003, when the Employment Equality (Religion or Belief) Regulations come into force, it will be unlawful to discriminate against workers because of religion or similar belief. The regulations also cover providers of vocational training. This booklet describes the regulations and gives guidance on associated good employment practice.

Fairness at work and good job performance go hand in hand. Tackling discrimination helps to attract, motivate and retain staff and enhances an organisation's reputation as an employer. Eliminating discrimination helps everyone to have an equal opportunity to work and to develop their skills.

There is already legislation to protect people against discrimination on the grounds of sex, race, disability and gender reassignment. From December 1st 2003 separate regulations to protect people from discrimination on the grounds of sexual orientation also come into force.

A lot of the good practice in this booklet will be familiar from existing advice on avoiding sex, race and disability discrimination. The new regulations should pose few difficulties in organisations where people are treated fairly and with consideration.

WHAT THE REGULATIONS SAY—IN SUMMARY

These Regulations apply to vocational training and all facets of employment—including recruitment, terms and conditions, promotions, transfers, dismissals and training. They make it unlawful on the grounds of religion or belief to

➢ discriminate directly against anyone. That is, to treat them less favourably than others because of their religion or belief;

➢ discriminate indirectly against anyone. That is, to apply a criterion, provision or practice which disadvantages people of a particular religion or belief unless it can be objectively justified

➢ subject someone to harassment. Harassment is unwanted conduct that violates a person's dignity or creates an intimidating, hostile, degrading, humiliating or offensive environment having regard to all the circumstances and the perception of the victim.

➢ victimise someone because they have made or intend to make a complaint or allegation or have given or intend to give evidence in relation to a complaint of discrimination on the grounds of religion or belief;

➢ discriminate or harass someone in certain circumstances after the working relationship has ended.

Exceptions may be made in very limited circumstances if there is a genuine occupational requirement for the worker to be of a particular religion or belief in order to do the job or to comply with the religious or belief ethos of the organisation.

Religion or belief is defined as being any religion, religious belief or similar philosophical belief. This does not include any philosophical or political belief unless it is similar to religious belief. It will be for the Employment Tribunals and other Courts to decide whether particular circumstances are covered by the regulations.

---

1. WHAT DO THE REGULATIONS MEAN?
A BRIEF EXPLANATION OF THE REGULATIONS

1.1 **Religion or belief** is not explicitly defined in the Regulations. In most applications to a tribunal it will be clear what is or is not a religion or a similar belief. It will be for the tribunals and higher courts to decide where the issue is disputed. They may consider a number of factors when deciding what is a religion or similar belief. It is likely that they will consider things such as collective worship, a clear belief system, a profound belief affecting the way of life or view of the world. Employers should be aware that these

Regulations extend beyond the more well known religions and faiths to include beliefs such as Paganism and Humanism. The Regulations also cover those without religious or similar beliefs.

1.2 **Direct discrimination** means that workers or job applicants must not be treated less favourably than others because they follow, are perceived to follow, or do not follow a particular (or any) religion or belief. For example it is unlawful to

- decide not to employ someone
- dismiss them
- refuse to provide them with training
- deny them promotion
- give them adverse terms and conditions

because they follow, or do not follow, a particular religion or belief.

> *Example: At interview it becomes apparent that a job applicant is Hindu. Although the applicant has all the skills and competences required of the job, the organisation decides not to offer him the job because he is a Hindu. This is direct discrimination.*
>
> *NB A job applicant can make a claim to an Employment Tribunal. It is not necessary for them to have been employed by the organisation to make a claim of discrimination.*

Direct discrimination may only be justified in the very limited circumstances where a genuine occupational requirement can be shown to apply.

1.3 **Indirect discrimination** means that an organisation must not have selection criteria, policies, employment rules or any other practices which although they are applied to all employees, have the effect of disadvantaging people of a particular religion or belief unless the practice can be justified. Indirect discrimination is unlawful whether it is intentional or not.

> *Example: Disliking the baseball caps his delivery drivers like to wear, a Chief Executive applies a 'no headwear' policy to all his staff. The policy, although applied to all employees, disadvantages his Sikh staff who wear turbans for religious reasons. This policy is indirect discrimination.*

The example above is already well recognised. However, there are less well documented examples which are equally important to the followers of particular religions.

> *Example: An organisation has a dress code which states that men may not wear ponytails. This may indirectly disadvantage Hindu men some of whom wear a Shika, (a small knotted tuft of hair worn at the back of the head, as a symbol of their belief). Such a policy could be discriminatory if it cannot be justified.*

In contrast to direct discrimination, indirect discrimination will not be unlawful if it can be justified. To justify it, an employer must show that there is a legitimate aim, (ie a real business need) and that the practice is proportionate to that aim (ie necessary and there is no alternative means available).

Example: A small finance company needs its staff to work late on a Friday afternoon to analyse stock prices in the American finance market. The figures arrive late on Friday because of the global time differences. During the winter months some staff would like to be released early on Friday afternoon in order to be home before nightfall—a requirement of their religion. They propose to make the time up later during the remainder of the week.

The company is not able to agree to this request because the American figures are necessary to the business, they need to be worked on immediately and the company is too small to have anyone else able to do the work.

The requirement to work on Friday afternoon is not unlawful discrimination as it meets a legitimate business aim and there is no alternative means available.

1.4 **Harassment** includes behaviour that is offensive, frightening or in any way distressing. It may be intentional bullying which is obvious or violent, but it can also be unintentional or subtle and insidious. It may involve nicknames, teasing, name calling or other behaviour which may not be intended to be malicious but nevertheless is upsetting. It may be about the individual's religion or belief or it may be about the religion or belief of those with whom the individual associates. It may not be targeted at an individual(s) but consist of a general culture which, for instance, appears to tolerate the telling of religious jokes.

Organisations may be held responsible for the actions of their staff as well as the staff being individually responsible for their own actions. If harassment takes place in the workplace or at a time and/or place associated with the workplace, for example a work related social gathering, the organisation may be liable and may be ordered to pay compensation unless it can show that it took reasonable steps to prevent harassment. Individuals who harass may also be ordered to pay compensation.

Employers should, where possible, also protect their workers from harassment by third parties such as service users and customers.

Employers investigating claims of harassment should consider all the circumstances before reaching a conclusion, and particularly the views of the person making the complaint; harassment is often subjective. Having gathered all the evidence, employers should ask themselves 'could what has taken place be reasonably considered to have caused offence?'

Example: A member of staff is devout in her belief. She continually refers to her colleagues as 'heathens' and warns them of the consequences they may suffer as a result of their lack of belief. Distressed by her intimidating behaviour, her colleagues complain to their manager that they are being harassed.

NB The harassment is unlawful because it is directed at work colleagues because they have different beliefs or no beliefs.

220

> *Example: Mr. 'A' is continually teased about his partner's religious convictions. He finds being subjected to such teasing offensive and distressing and complains to his manager His manager tells him not to be silly, that the teasing is only harmless workplace banter and is nothing to do with the organisation.*
>
> *This is harassment on the grounds of religion or belief even though it is not the victim's own religion or belief that is the subject of the teasing. Mr 'A' is able to complain through an Employment Tribunal. His colleagues may have to pay compensation. The organisation may have to pay compensation because it has liability for the actions of its staff.*

1.5 **Victimisation** is when an individual is treated detrimentally because they have made a complaint or intend to make a complaint about discrimination or harassment or have given evidence or intend to give evidence relating to a complaint about discrimination or harassment. They may become labelled 'troublemaker', denied promotion or training, or be 'sent to Coventry' by their colleagues. If this happens or if organisations fail to take reasonable steps to prevent it from happening, they will be liable and may be ordered to pay compensation. Individuals who victimise may also be ordered to pay compensation.

> *Example: After giving evidence for a colleague who had brought an Employment Tribunal claim against the organisation on the grounds of religion or belief, a worker applies for promotion. Her application is rejected even though she shows that she has all the necessary skills and experience. Her manager says she is a 'troublemaker' because she has given evidence at the Tribunal and as a result should not be promoted. This would be victimisation.*

Discrimination, harassment or victimisation following the end of a working relationship covers issues such as references either written or verbal.

> *Example: A manager is approached by someone from another organisation saying that Mr. Z' has applied for a job and asks for a reference. The manager says that he cannot recommend the worker on the grounds that he did not 'fit in' because he refused to socialise in the pub with his colleagues (his religion forbade alcohol). This worker may have been discriminated against on the grounds of his religion after his working relationship with the organisation has ended.*

> *Example: Some time after resigning from employment with an organisation, a Muslim man meets his ex-colleagues at a football match. They are hostile towards him, alluding to current world events. He is distressed by their attitude but has no claim against the organisation as the harassment is not connected with nor arises out of his previous working relationship with the company.*
>
> *NB The individual in this example has no recourse through employment law but may be able to make a complaint through other legal avenues.*

1.6   A genuine occupational requirement. In very limited circumstances it will be lawful for an employer to treat people differently if it is a genuine occupational requirement that the job holder must be of a particular religion or belief. When deciding if this applies it is necessary to consider the nature of the work and the context in which it is carried out. Jobs may change over time and organisations should periodically consider whether the requirement continues to apply, particularly when recruiting. Further guidance is given in Appendix 1.

> *Example: A hospital which is not a religious foundation wishes to appoint a chaplain to minister to the spiritual needs of patients and staff who are mainly Christian. The hospital may be able to show that in the context in which the job is carried out it is a genuine occupational requirement that the appointee be a minister of the Christian faith.*

An occupational requirement on the grounds of religion or belief, as in the example above, must not be used as a basis for discrimination on other grounds such as race or disability.

Some organisations have an ethos based on a religion or belief, for instance a care home managed by a religious charity. Where organisations can show that they are founded on such an ethos they may be able to apply a genuine occupational requirement to jobs where in other circumstances such a requirement would not apply. In these cases the need for a particular religion or belief may not be a 'decisive' factor for the job but organisations must still be able to show that it is a requirement of the job in order to adhere to the ethos of the organisation and that it is proportionate to apply the requirement. Such an organisation should not assume that it is able to apply a 'blanket' GOR to all posts as they may be required to show that each GOR is reasonable when considering the nature of the job and the context within which it is carried out.

> *Example: A faith based care home may be able to show that being of a particular faith is a genuine requirement of its carers because they are required to carry out their duties in a manner that fulfils both the physical and spiritual needs of its patients.*
>
> *However, they may not be able to justify a similar requirement for their maintenance or reception staff whose jobs do not require them to provide spiritual leadership or support to the patients.*

1.7   Positive Action. Selection for recruitment or promotion must be on merit, irrespective of religion or belief. However, it is possible to take certain steps to redress the effects of previous inequality of opportunity. This is called positive action. Employers may give special encouragement to, or provide specific training for people from religions or beliefs who are in a minority in the workplace. Employers may wish to consider positive measures such as:

—training their existing employees for work which has historically been the preserve of individuals from a particular religion or belief:

—advertisements which encourage applications from a minority religion but making it clear that selection will be on merit without reference to religion or belief.

* * *

There is a sound business case for eliminating discrimination in the workplace. Staff who are subjected to discrimination, harassment or victimisation may

♦ be unhappy, less productive and demotivated
♦ resign
♦ make a complaint to an Employment Tribunal.

If staff are subjected to discrimination, harassment or victimisation this may affect an organisation in terms of

♦ damage to reputation both as a business and as an employer
♦ increased costs of staff leaving and consequent recruitment and training
♦ cost of compensation if they take a claim to an Employment Tribunal—there is no upper limit to the amount of compensation you may be ordered to pay.

2. RECRUITMENT

2.1 It makes sound business sense for an organisation to attract a wide field of job applicants—it is not a good idea to rely on the friends or family of current staff as this may limit the diversity of the organisation.

2.2 Advertising is best undertaken in a form accessible to a diverse audience. For instance, use of a wide interest publication or agency rather than one focussed on a niche or specialist culture or interest area which will limit the diversity of applicants and may constitute indirect discrimination.

> *Example: An advertisement placed only in a particular religious magazine may constitute indirect discrimination as it is unlikely to be seen by people of other religions or beliefs. Although the magazine may be available to all potential applicants, it effectively disadvantages groups of people who for religious or belief reasons may not subscribe to that particular publication.*

2.3 Organisations should be clear about what skills they actually need for the post, differentiating them from those which are merely desirable or reflect the personal preferences of the selector. They should recruit and/or promote for those skills and aptitudes—there is nothing to prevent an employer from deciding not to recruit or promote someone if they do not have the necessary skills or abilities.

2.4 Organisations should ensure they do not set unnecessary selection criteria or standards which might prevent people from applying because of their religion or belief.

2.5 Organisations should make sure that job applicants are clear about what the post actually entails. This should give applicants the opportunity to consider fully whether there is any chance the job might conflict with their religious or belief convictions enabling them to make an informed decision about whether to apply.

2.6 Where it is reasonable to do so, organisations should adapt their methods of recruitment so that anyone who is suitably qualified can apply and attend for selection. Some flexibility around interview/selection times allowing avoidance of significant religious times (for example Friday afternoons) is good practice.

> *Example: Where the recruitment process includes a social gathering care should be taken to avoid disadvantaging anyone for whom alcohol is prohibited on the grounds of religion or belief. For instance, holding the gathering in a hotel bar may pose particular difficulties for those whose religion forbids association with alcohol.*
>
> *Invitations should make it clear that applicants with specific dietary requirements (which may be associated with their religion or belief) will not be disadvantaged by the process or the venue. Employers do not have to provide specific food such as Halal or Kosher if it is not proportionate for them to do so but they should ensure that there is some appropriate food available (eg vegetarian).*

2.7 Where employers believe a genuine religious occupational requirement applies to a post, this should be made clear in the advertisement. The reasoning should also be explained in any application pack and during the selection process. More guidance is given in Appendix 1.

2.8 Whilst organisations should be sensitive to the religious or belief needs of job applicants, individuals invited to attend a selection process should ensure that they make their needs known to the organisation in good time so that employers have an opportunity to take them into account when arranging the selection process. It is a good idea for organisations to specifically invite applicants to make any special needs known.

2.9 At the interview or selection process questions should be asked, or tests set, to check for the skills and competences needed for the post. Interviewers should not be tempted to ask personal questions which may be perceived to be intrusive and imply potential discrimination. Where applicants volunteer personal information, those selecting should take particular care not to be influenced by such information. An organisation only needs to know if the person can do the job and if they are willing to do the job. Assumptions should not be made about who will and who will not fit in.

Where personal information is required for purposes such as security clearance, it should be sought in confidence and retained separately. It should not be available to those conducting the selection process.

> *Good Practice: The perception of the interviewee is important. Questions not obviously related to the post may be perceived as providing a basis for discrimination. It is accepted good practice to avoid irrelevant questions relating to marital status, or child care arrangements from which the applicant could infer an intention to discriminate on grounds of sex. To the category of questions best avoided should be added unnecessary questions about religion or belief such as ones about place or frequency of worship, communal involvement, or the religious ethos of educational establishments attended.*

2.10 At recruitment and beyond, staff welcome an organisation having a robust Equality Policy which includes religion or belief as well as other forms of discrimination and which takes the matter seriously if the policy is contravened. Although not a legal necessity, such a policy makes applicants feel confident and serves to discourage those whose attitudes and behaviours do not embrace equality of opportunity. Acas can help organisations to draw up and implement such a policy and with their training needs.

2.11 Sunday Working: The Employment Rights Act 1996 provides for those working in the retail or betting trades to opt out of Sunday working by giving their employer three months notice of their intention to stop working on Sundays. This does not apply to those working only on Sundays. This provision remains unchanged. This provision is currently applicable only in England and Wales although the law in Scotland is likely to change to make similar provision in the latter part of 2003.

Where other employees request cessation of Sunday working on the grounds of their religion or belief, employers should consider whether Sunday working can be justified as a legitimate business need and whether it is proportionate to apply that justification to the individual. Refusal to adjust the individual's working patterns may be indirect discrimination if adequate justification cannot be shown.

3. RETAINING GOOD STAFF

3.1 Opportunities for promotion and training should be made known to all staff and be available to everyone on a fair and equal basis.

3.2 Where staff apply for internal transfers it should be remembered that informal references, including verbal references, between departmental heads, supervisors etc. should be fair and non-discriminatory. Such informal references are covered by the Regulations

3.3 If it is reasonable to do so, organisations should consider adapting their methods of delivering training if current arrangements have the effect of disadvantaging someone because of religion or belief. This may be particularly relevant if training takes place outside normal working hours, work place or in a residential environment.

Some things to consider:

—times within work schedules for religious observance
—special dietary requirements, for example kosher, halal and vegetarian food
—avoid ice breakers and training activities that use language or physical contact that might be inappropriate for some beliefs.
—avoid exercises which require the exchange of personal information
—ensure related social activities do not exclude people by choice of venue
—avoid significant religious festivals such as Ramadan

3.4 Whilst organisations should be sensitive to the needs of their staff, staff have a responsibility to ensure that their managers and training departments are aware of their individual needs in good time so that there is an opportunity for them to be met.

3.5 Everyone should understand what harassment is and that it is hurtful, unlawful and totally unacceptable. However large or small an organisation, it is good practice for them to have an Equality Policy, to train all staff on its application and to update everyone on a regular basis. This will help to reduce the likelihood of discrimination, harassment and victimisation taking place and may help to limit liability if a complaint is made.

3.6 Organisations should ensure that their staff understand that if they harass their colleagues, they could be personally liable and may have to pay compensation in addition to anything that the organisation may have to pay. Handouts to workers visiting your premises could include a summary of your Equality Policy as well as he more usual Health & Safety instructions.

> *An Employment Tribunal Case brought under the Sex Discrimination Act . A male public service worker wrote down sexual comments about a woman colleague which, together with the general behaviour of the men towards women in her section, caused her distress. When she complained the management sought to minimise the matter. An employment tribunal found that her complaints were justified. She was awarded £15,000 injury to feelings against the employer and £1,000 against the individual concerned. Tribunals may be expected to adopt a similar approach in religion or belief cases as they do in existing discrimination legislation.*

3.7 Staff should be aware of what steps they could take if they feel they have been discriminated against, harassed or victimised. They should feel confident that their complaint will be treated seriously, that management will deal with the cause of the problem and that the process will be undertaken in confidence. If it is practical, it is a good idea to have a named individual who is trained and specifically responsible for dealing with employment equality issues and complaints.

> *Example: A particular religion featured largely in the media due to an international crisis. Stereotypical, pejorative and hurtful comments in the workplace were routinely made about all followers of that religion. A group of distressed workers complained to, managers who promptly arranged a training session during which it was explained that not all followers of that religion agreed with what was happening elsewhere and that they were hurt and worried by their colleagues' comments. Better understanding helped to resolve the situation.*

4. RELIGIOUS OBSERVANCE IN THE WORKPLACE

4.1 The Regulations do not say that employers must provide time and facilities for religious or belief observance in the workplace. However, employers should consider whether their policies, rules and procedures indirectly discriminate against staff of particular religions or beliefs and if so whether reasonable changes might be made.

4.2 Many religions or beliefs have special festival or spiritual observance days. A worker may request holiday in order to celebrate festivals or attend ceremonies. An employer should sympathetically consider such a request where it is reasonable and practical for the employee to be away from work, and they have sufficient holiday entitlement in hand.

　　While it may be practical for one or a small number to be absent it might be difficult if numerous such requests are made. In these circumstances the employer should discuss the matter with the employees affected, and with any recognised trade union, with the aim of balancing the needs of the business and those of other employees. Employers should carefully consider whether their criteria for deciding who should and who should not be granted leave may indirectly discriminate.

> *Some things to consider:*
>
> *Successful equality policies may mean that your longest serving staff are less likely to be from, minority groups than your more recently recruited staff. Could seniority of service therefore indirectly discriminate?*
>
> *Women from some cultural backgrounds may be less assertive than men from the same backgrounds. Would a 'first come/first served' policy disadvantage them?*

> *Example: A small toy shop employing 4 staff may be unable to release an individual for a religious festival in the busy pre-Christmas period. It may be justifiable to refuse a request for such absence.*
>
> *A large department store employing 250 staff would probably be unable to justify refusing the same absence for one person because it would not substantially impact on the business as other staff would be able to cover for the absence.*

4.3 Employers who operate a holiday system whereby the organisation closes for specific periods when all staff must take their annual leave should consider whether such closures are justified as they may prevent individuals taking annual leave at times of specific religious significance to them. Such closures may be justified by the business need to undertake machinery maintenance for instance. However, it would be good practice for such employers to consider how they might balance the needs of the business and those of their staff.

4.4 Organisations should have clear, reasonable procedures for handling requests for leave and ensure that all staff are aware of and adhere to the procedures. Staff should give as much notice as possible when requesting leave and in doing so should also consider that there may be a number of their colleagues who would like leave at the same time. Employers should be aware that some religious or belief festivals are aligned with lunar phases and therefore dates change from year to year; the dates for some festivals do not become clear until quite close to the actual day. Discussion and flexibility between staff and managers will usually result in a mutually acceptable compromise. Organisations should take care not to disadvantage those workers who do not hold any specific religion or belief.

4.5 Some religions or beliefs have specific dietary requirements. If staff bring food into the workplace they may need to store and heat food separately from other food, for example Muslims will wish to ensure their food is not in contact with pork (or anything that may have been in contact with pork, such as cloths or sponges). It is good practice to consult your employees on such issues and find a mutually acceptable solution to any dietary problems.

> *Example: A worker who for religious reasons is vegetarian felt unable to store her lunch in a refrigerator next to the meat sandwiches belonging to a co-worker. Following consultation with the staff and their representatives, the organisation introduced a policy by which all food must be stored in sealed containers and shelves were separately designated 'meat' and 'vegetarian'. This arrangement met the needs of all staff and at no cost to the employer.*

4.6 Some religions require their followers to pray at specific times during the day. Staff may therefore request access to an appropriate quiet place (or prayer room) to undertake their religious observance. Employers are not required to provide a prayer room. However, if a quiet place is available and allowing its use for prayer does not cause problems for other workers or the business, organisations should agree to the request.

Where possible, it is good employee relations practice for organisations to set aside a quiet room or area for prayer or private contemplation. In consultation with staff, it may be possible to designate an area for all staff for the specific purpose of prayer or contemplation rather than just a general rest room. Such a room might also be welcomed by those for whom prayer is a religious obligation and also by those who, for example, have suffered a recent bereavement. Organisations should consider providing separate storage facilities for ceremonial objects.

4.7 Employers are not required to enter into significant expenditure and/or building alterations to meet religious needs. In any event many needs will involve little or no change. For instance some religions or beliefs require a person to wash before prayer. This is often done symbolically or by using the existing facilities. However, it is good practice to consult with staff and to consider whether there is anything reasonable and practical which can be done to help staff meet the ritual requirements of their religion. It may help, for example, if all workers understand the religious observances of their colleagues thus avoiding embarrassment or difficulties for those practicing their religious obligations.

4.8 Some religions or beliefs do not allow individuals to undress or shower in the company of others. If an organisation requires its staff, for reasons of health and safety, to change their clothing and/or shower, it is good employee relations practice to explore how such needs can be met. Insistence upon same-sex communal shower and changing facilities could constitute indirect discrimination (or harassment) as it may disadvantage or offend staff of a particular religion or belief whose requirement for modesty extend to changing their clothing in the presence of others, even of the same sex.

4.9 Some religions require extended periods of fasting. Employers may wish to consider how they can support staff through such a period. However, employers should take care to ensure that they do not place unreasonable extra burdens on other workers which may cause conflict between workers or claims of discrimination.

4.10 If it is practical and safe to do so, staff may welcome the opportunity to wear clothing consistent with their religion. Where organisations adopt a specific dress code careful consideration should be given to the proposed code to ensure it does not conflict with the dress requirements of some religions. General dress codes which have the effect of conflicting with religious requirements may constitute indirect discrimination unless they can be justified for example, on the grounds of health & safety.

> *Example: Some religions require their female followers to dress particularly modestly. A dress code which requires a blouse to be tucked inside a skirt may conflict with that requirement as it accentuates body shape. However, if the individual is allowed to wear the blouse over the outside of the skirt it may be quite acceptable.*

4.11 If organisations have a policy on the wearing of jewellery, having tattoos or other markings, they should try and be flexible and reasonable concerning items of jewellery and markings which are traditional within some religions or beliefs. Unjustifiable policies and rules may constitute indirect discrimination.

> *Example: In addition to a wedding ring, many Hindu women wear a necklace (Mangal Sutra) which is placed around their neck during the wedding ceremony and is therefore highly symbolic. Some may find it distressing if they are not allowed to wear it in their place of work, unless the rule was for health & safety or other justifiable reasons.*

5. KNOW YOUR STAFF

5.1 There is no legal requirement to keep information on how staff groups are made up (gender, ethnic groups, and age, those with disabilities) other than in the public sector where racial monitoring is a statutory requirement. However, such monitoring is considered good practice. Information helps organisations to make sure their equality policy is working to the benefit of all concerned and to test whether recruitment or training policies are reaching a wide audience reflecting the local community. It can also help organisations understand their employees' needs (eg when they may want to request leave for festivals),and monitor recourse to grievance procedures and ensure that staff turnover does not reflect a disproportionate number of people from specific religions or beliefs.

5.2 If organisations decide to include religion or belief in their equality monitoring processes, staff should be told why such information is being collected and how it will be used. Staff should be assured of confidentiality and anonymity. It should be explained that they are under no obligation to give such information. Employers are reminded that such information is sensitive under the Data Protection Act.

5.3 If organisation decide not to include religion or belief in their equality monitoring processes, they may consider including a question on their staff attitude surveys to ascertain whether workers have ever felt harassed on a range of issues which should include religion or belief. Employers should take these issues seriously and make it known that discrimination is a disciplinary issue and give support to the victims.

5.4 Managers/supervisors should be as flexible and open minded as the operating environment allows. This will encourage staff to be equally flexible and open minded, and is the best way of making sure that both the needs of the organisation and those of individuals can be met.

6. WHAT TO DO IF YOU THINK YOU HAVE SUFFERED DISCRIMINATION OR HARASSMENT

6.1 If you think you are being harassed or discriminated against it is a good idea to make it clear to the person who is harassing you that their behaviour is unwelcome and that you want it to stop. However, you do not have to do this, particularly if you are feeling bullied or intimidated. If you do choose to address your concerns to the person be clear and assertive but take care that you are not perceived to be bullying the individual. Individuals may find it helpful to ask a friend, colleague, welfare officer or trade union representative to be with them in a support role.

6.2 If speaking to the person in question has failed to stop the problem, you should talk to your manager or your trade union representative. If it is your manager or supervisor who is harassing you, speak to someone higher up. Employers should deal with such complaints quickly, thoroughly and sympathetically.

6.3 It is usually best to try and sort things out quickly and as close to the problem as possible. If your organisation has a personnel or human resources department or an equality adviser you might find it helpful to talk to them. Discrimination can happen accidentally or through thoughtlessness. Harassment can be unintentional. Often, once a manager understands the problem, he or she will be willing to try and put things right.

6.4 If your manager is unable to help you, or refuses to help you, you should use your organisation's grievance procedure. Organisations with 20 or more employees should have a grievance procedure and this requirement will be extended to all employers once Section 36 of the Employment Act 2002 is commenced (probably in late 2004). You have a legal right to be accompanied by a trade union representative or a work colleague at any hearing into your grievance.

6.5 If you are not satisfied with the result of a grievance procedure, you have a right of appeal which should be heard, if the organisation's size allows it, by someone different from the person who conducted the original grievance hearing. You have a right to be accompanied by a trade union representative or a work colleague during the appeal hearing.

6.6 If you have tried all these things, or if your employer does not have a grievance procedure, you may be able to bring a complaint to an employment tribunal under the Employment Equality (Religion or Belief) Regulations 2003. You do not have to hand in your notice to bring such a complaint.

6.7 You and any witnesses have a right not to be victimised for following up a grievance or complaining to an employment tribunal under these Regulations provided the complaint was made in good faith.

6.8 If you have been dismissed because you objected to conduct towards you, you may be able to bring a complaint of unfair dismissal to an employment tribunal.

6.9 Complaints to an employment tribunal must normally be brought within three months of the act you are complaining about. Care should be taken to ensure that the three month point is not exceeded during any internal grievance/appeals process.

7. SOME FREQUENTLY ASKED QUESTIONS

Q Do organisations have to do anything new or different when the legislation comes in?

A They should ensure that religion and belief are included in their Equality Policy. It is a good idea to revisit the Equality Policy from time to time to ensure it has not become outdated, to test any new employment policies and procedures for discrimination and to ensure the policy itself meets current legislation requirements.

Staff need to be made aware (through training, notice boards, circulars, contracts of employment etc.) that it is not only unacceptable to discriminate, harass or victimise someone on the grounds of religion or belief, it is also unlawful. Organisations should also make it clear that they will not tolerate such behaviour. Staff should know what to do if they believe they have been discriminated against or harassed, or if they believe someone else is being discriminated against or harassed, and this should be included in the grievance procedure. Organisations should also consider adding all forms of discrimination and harassment (religion or belief, sex, race, disability, gender reassignment and sexual orientation) to their disciplinary rules which should also include bullying. It is good practice to include age in your policies ahead of age discrimination becoming unlawful in October 2006.

> *Reminder: The Employment Act 2002 requires all employers, however large or small, to have both a disciplinary procedure and a grievance procedure The requirement is expected to take effect in late 2004.*

Q Must Organisations have an Equality Policy?

A Whilst organisations do not have to have an Equality Policy, implementing and observing such a policy is a commonplace means of demonstrating that an employer has taken reasonably practicable steps to prevent employees discriminating against or harassing other employees. The policy should set out minimum standards of behaviour expected of all staff through recruitment and onwards and what staff can expect of the organisation. It acts as a reminder, gives staff confidence that they will be treated with dignity and respect, and may be used as an integral part of a grievance or disciplinary process if necessary.

If organisations do not have an Equality Policy and would like help in putting in place an effective policy Acas can help.

Q Do the Regulations cover all religions and beliefs?

A It is unlawful to discriminate against a person on the grounds of religion, religious belief, perceived religion or religious belief, or similar philosophical belief. Political beliefs are specifically excluded from these Regulations.(see 1.7)

It is as unlawful to discriminate against a person for not holding a specific religion or belief as it is to discriminate against someone for actually holding to or subscribing to a particular religion or belief.

Q Do these Regulations cover all workers?

A The Regulations apply to all workers, including office holders, police, barristers, partners in a business and members of the armed forces. They also cover related areas such as

231

membership of trade organisations, the award of qualifications, the serices of careers guidance organisations, employment agencies and vocational training providers, including further and higher education institutions.

The Regulations cover anyone who applies to an organisation for work, or who already works for an organisation whether they are directly employed or work under some other kind of contract or are an agency worker. Organisations are also responsible for the behaviour of their staff towards an individual working for someone else but on their premises, for example someone from another organisation repairing a piece of equipment.

Workers are sometimes harassed by third parties, such as customers or clients. Where possible organisations should protect their staff from such harassment and should take steps to deal with actual or potential situations of this kind. This will enhance the organisation's reputation as a good employer and make the organisation a welcoming and safe place to work.

Many organisations provide visitors and visiting workers with guidance on Health & Safety matters. It may be appropriate to include some comments in any policy your organisation has on harassment.

Q Do organisations have to ask about someone's religion or belief at interview?

A No. Interviews are about finding out whether someone has the right skills for the job. Personal questions about an individual's beliefs should not be asked unless they are relevant to the duties of the job in question. It is good practice not to ask any personal questions at interview unless it is to make sure that appropriate adjustments are made for anyone with a disability.

Organisations do not have to employ people whose beliefs mean they are unable to undertake essential parts of the job. It should be made clear to candidates what type of work the organisation does and what duties the job involves so they can consider whether there is any chance it might conflict with their religion or beliefs.

> *Example: An individual applying for a job in a large supermarket stacking shelves may not be willing to handle pork products for religious reasons. Such products probably represent only a small proportion of the goods displayed on the shelves. It may not be reasonable to reject such job applicants if it is practicable to allocate work in a way that does not involve handling pork products.*
>
> *However, it may not be practical for the store to adjust the work of a check-out operative in order that they are not required to handle pork products.*

> *Example: A waiter who is a Humanist or Sikh may not be prepared to serve meat which has not been slaughtered in a manner he or she considers to be humane. In this case redistribution of the work may not be possible if the restaurant serves such meat and it may be reasonable to reject the job application on the grounds of religion or belief.*

If an organisation changes the type of work it does they should give careful consideration to the effect it may have on their staff for reasons of religion or belief. Early consultation with staff and/or their trade union will usually result in a mutually acceptable arrangement.

Q Do organisations have to collect data on religion or belief?

A The Regulations do not require the collection of such data but it may help organisations to provide appropriate facilities for their staff and to understand employees' needs (eg when they might seek annual leave). It is important that managers talk to people and/or their trades unions to ensure an understanding of individual needs and to avoid making assumptions about them. Not all followers of each religion or belief will necessarily have the same practices or follow their religion in exactly the same way.

If an organisation decides to collect data, it may give staff added confidence if it is made clear why they want the information, how it is going to be used and that giving such information is entirely voluntary. All such information should be confidential and anonymous. It is designated 'sensitive' under the Data Protection Act 1998. Staff permission should be obtained before using such information.

Q How will organisations know if they are discriminating inadvertently?

A Individual staff, or their trade union, will generally tell managers, particularly if managers are able to create a culture whereby staff feel comfortable in sharing such information. It can be helpful for organisations to have a designated individual to whom people can go in confidence. It is a good idea for management teams, staff representatives or a specially convened group of employees to think through and test whether any organisational policies and procedures impact on people's religion or belief, or discriminate on any other grounds such as disability, sexual orientation, sex or race. It is good practice to include age in your equality policies ahead of age discrimination becoming unlawful in October 2006.

Organisations should consider carefully whether they are inadvertently discriminating indirectly. For example, if team meetings always take place on a Friday afternoon this may discriminate against Jewish and Muslim staff for whom Friday afternoon has a particular religious significance, although not everyone follows their faith in the same way. Employers will not escape liability in an Employment Tribunal by showing that discrimination was inadvertent or accidental.

Q No one in my organisation has ever complained of discrimination or harassment so we don't need to do anything new, do we?

A People do not always feel able or confident enough to complain, particularly if the harasser is a manager or senior executive. Sometimes they will simply resign. One way to find out is to undertake exit interviews when people leave your organisation and as part of that process to ask if they have ever felt harassed, bullied or discriminated against at work. If it is possible, exit interviews should be undertaken by someone out of the individual's line of management, for instance a personnel officer.

Discrimination includes harassment which can take place without management being aware of it. Organisations should make sure all their staff understand that harassment means any unwanted behaviour that makes someone feel either intimidated, humiliated or offended and that includes teasing, tormenting, name calling etc. and applies whoever the perpetrator may be. The victim's perception of the effect of the behaviour is also important. Managers should take all practical steps to make sure staff understand that organisations and their management teams will not tolerate such behaviour and that they will deal with whoever is causing the problem through the disciplinary process.

Q Should we ban discussions about religion and belief in the workplace? We are concerned that someone might complain about harassment.

A If harassment has been explained to staff they should be able to distinguish between reasonable discussion and offensive behaviour. Staff should be aware that if their discussions cause offence then this may be considered to be harassment and therefore unlawful. A ban on discussions about religion or belief may create more bad feeling amongst staff and cause more problems than it solves.

Q Do organisations have to provide a prayer room?

A The Regulations do not say that organisations have to provide a prayer room (see 4.4). However, if employees request access to a quiet place in which to meet their religious obligations and such a place is available without it having any adverse impact on the business or other staff, then employers may be acting in a discriminatory way if they refuse such a request.

> *Example: It may not be reasonable or practical to provide a prayer room for staff in a small motor garage employing 12 staff, where the only space available is a communal kitchen/rest room.*
>
> *However, a larger organisation with meeting/conference rooms that are often unused may be considered unreasonable if it is not willing to organise its operations in such a way as to make such a room available for prayer at specific and known times each day.*

If employers are able to do so, it is good practice to consider providing a suitable area for religious observance or private contemplation by anyone wishing to use it for that purpose.

Be careful when providing such a room not to put staff that do not have need of a prayer room at an unjustifiable disadvantage. For example, if an organisation were to convert their only rest room into a prayer room then staff who do not have need of a prayer room would be disadvantaged and may have a grievance on the grounds of religion or belief.

It is a good idea to consult with staff representatives or individuals about policies for the use of such a room. Amicable agreement can be reached on issues such as the storage and display of religious symbols and the wearing or otherwise of shoes within the room.

Q Do organisations have to release staff for prayer outside normal rest/break periods or religious festivals?

A Organisations do not have to release staff for prayer outside normal rest breaks or holiday periods. Under the Working Time Regulations 1998, (further details available at Appendix 2) staff are, in general, entitled to a rest break of not less than 20 minutes where working time is more than 6 hours. Staff may request that their rest break coincide with their religious obligations to pray at certain times of the day. Employers may be justified in refusing such a request if, for example, it conflicts with legitimate business needs which they are unable to meet in any other way. If they are unable to justify such a refusal this may be discrimination.

The Working Time Regulations also provide that staff are entitled to not less than 4 weeks annual leave each year (see introduction to Appendix 2). Staff may request annual leave to coincide with religious festivals (see 4.1 and 4.2). Refusal to grant such leave may be discriminatory if it cannot be justified by a legitimate business need which cannot be met by any other reasonable means.

Managers should try to be flexible about when rest breaks or annual holidays are taken. It is good practice to ensure that staff know how to request such flexibility and how much reasonable notice is required to meet their needs. There may be a few jobs where it is not possible to be flexible but explanation and discussion may enable a compromise to be achieved. No organisation is expected to accept unreasonable disruption to its activities. Managers may wish to consider that the time taken for prayer is rarely longer than that of a tea or coffee break. Staff need to understand that they have a responsibility to be reasonable to both their employer and their colleagues when asking for time off.

Q My organisation has rules on personal appearance and dress. Are we in breach of the legislation?

A If your company rules are in place for health and safety reasons or to protect your image with customers they may be lawful. It is important to explain the company's policy on dress and appearance, but organisations should try to be flexible where they can to enable staff to dress in accordance with their beliefs but still meet the organisation's requirements.

Some religions require their women to dress modestly and organisations should consider whether this requirement is contravened by their dress code. For example Jewish women may wish to wear a shirt or blouse outside their skirt in order to avoid accentuating their body shape. This may also apply to women from other religions.

There are items of jewellery which are culturally specific to some religions, for instance Hindu men wear neck beads (known as Kanthi Mala) which are an indication of their faith. Additionally, some religions are designated by body markings such as a red spot on the forehead (Bindi Sindur) and organisations should consider allowing for these within their policies.

Q I am concerned that, on the grounds of religion, some of my staff may refuse to work with their gay or lesbian colleagues.

A Some religions do have strong views concerning sexual orientation but most do not advocate persecution of people because of their sexual orientation. Everyone has the right to be treated with dignity and respect in the workplace whatever their sex, race, colour, disability, age, religion or sexual orientation. You should include this over-riding premise in your Equality Policy and show that you take a robust view when this principal is not adhered to. Your workers do not have to be friends but you can insist that they treat each other professionally.

Q Our organisation has a religious ethos. How do we determine if a person's religion or belief can be justified as a genuine occupational requirement for a post?

A Staff can be recruited on the basis of their religion or belief where this is a genuine occupational requirement for the job. The Regulations require you to consider the nature of the job and the context within which it is carried out when considering whether the job holder needs to practice a specific religion in order to undertake the role within the ethos of the organisation. Appendix 1 provides some further guidance on this subject.

When considering applying such a requirement look at each post individually both in terms of the duties of the job and the context within which it is carried out. Organisations should not expect to apply a blanket requirement to all its posts even if it has a religious ethos.

Organisations should consider whether there are alternatives to applying an occupational requirement. For instance, if only a small part of the job needs someone from that religion then it may be possible to redistribute work or reorganise roles in such a way as to avoid applying a religious requirement to a particular post. Organisations can reasonably expect their staff to keep to their organisational values and culture and should bear in mind that people may be able to maintain those values and culture, and therefore the ethos of the organisation, without actually belonging to the particular religion or belief.

Organisations should be clear about the link between the requirements of the job and the requirement to be of a particular religion or belief. as, in the event of an Employment Tribunal claim on the grounds of religious or belief discrimination, the burden of proof will be on the employer to show a genuine occupational requirement. Tribunals tend to interpret such requirements very narrowly since they effectively go against the principle of equal treatment.

A genuine occupational requirement on the grounds of religion or belief should not be used to discriminate on any other grounds such as sex, race or disability; although in some very limited circumstances a religious organisation may lawfully be able to discriminate on the grounds of sexual orientation or sex.

APPENDIX 1
GENUINE OCCUPATIONAL REQUIREMENTS—GUIDANCE

Employers wishing to claim a genuine occupational requirement (GOR) should bear in mind the following points.

1. GORs should be identified at the beginning of the recruitment, training or promotion process, before the vacancy is advertised. Advertisements and material sent to potential applicants should clearly show that the employer considers that a GOR applies and the point should be reiterated during the selection process.

   Reminder: Applicants who do not agree that there is a GOR for the post holder are at liberty to make a claim to an Employment Tribunal because they believe they have been prevented from applying for the post on the grounds of religion or belief. It would be for the employer to show that such a GOR is justified.

2. If an employer wishes to claim a GOR s/he must consider what the duties are,for which an exemption is to be claimed; a GOR cannot be claimed unless some or all of those duties, or the totality of the role, are covered by a specific exemption and an assessment has been made showing that it would be unreasonable to require other employees of the appropriate religion or belief to undertake those duties. Also it must be shown that those duties must be carried out to achieve the objectives of the job.

3. In an organisation a GOR exemption cannot be claimed in relation to particular duties if the employer already has sufficient employees who are capable of carrying out the required duties and whom it would be reasonable to employ on those duties without undue inconvenience.

   Where the organisation has a religious ethos, a GOR exemption cannot be claimed if the nature of the role and the context within which it is carried out is not of sufficient profile or impact within the organisation to affect the overall ethos of the organisation.

4. Each job for which a GOR may apply must be considered individually; it should not be assumed that because a GOR exists for one job it also exists for jobs of a similar nature or in a similar location. The nature or extent of the relevant duties may be different or, for instance, there may be other employees who could undertake those duties.

5. A GOR can be claimed where it is necessary for the relevant duties to be carried out by someone of a specific religion or belief because being of that religion or belief is a 'determining' factor, for example in the Islamic faith a halal butcher must be Muslim.

6. A GOR must be reassessed on each occasion a post becomes vacant to ensure that it can still be validly claimed. Circumstances may have changed, rendering the GOR inapplicable.

7. A GOR cannot be used to establish or maintain a balance or quota of employees of a particular religion or belief.

8. GORs are always open to challenge by an individual. The burden of proof lies with the employer to establish the validity of a GOR by providing evidence to substantiate a claim.

9. Only an Employment Tribunal or a higher court can give an authoritative ruling as to whether or not a GOR is valid.

10. The following legislation remains extant
    The School Standards and Framework Act 1998
    The Amendments to the School Standards and Framework Act 2003
    The Education (Scotland) Act 1980

APPENDIX 2

The Regulations cover religion, religious belief and similar philosophical beliefs. Until the Courts and Tribunals have had an opportunity to consider which religions or beliefs are covered by these Regulations it is not possible to provide definitive guidance. However, those listed below are some of the most commonly practised religions and beliefs in Britain. They are listed in alphabetical order for ease of reference only. However, there are many more and this list should not be considered to be exhaustive.

The information is intended for guidance only. It may assist employers to plan and implement policies and systems which meet the needs of both the employer and employee. Calendars indicating festivals in world religions are available from a number of sources.

Not all members of each religion follow all the practices and observances. Neither will every member of each religion request time off for each and every festival. In some instances an adjustment to the working day to allow time to attend a prayer meeting before or after work may be all that is requested. In many instances nothing will be requested. Whilst employers are encouraged to be flexible where reasonable and appropriate, employees should recognise that they also have a responsibility to be reasonable and to consider the needs of the business in which they are employed.

Reminder: The Working Time Regulations 1998 provide most workers with an entitlement to 4 weeks annual leave per year ; that is 4 weeks x normal working week. If a worker normally works a 6 day week his/her leave annual entitlement is 24 days per year. If a worker works a 2 day week his/her annual leave entitlement is 8 days. The Working Time Regulations do not apply to workers on board sea-going fishing vessels, to certain sea-farers nor to workers on board most ships which operate on inland waterways. In addition, the annual leave entitlement does not apply to the armed forces, police nor to certain specific activities in the civil protection services; to mobile staff in vicil aviation; nor, until 1 August 2004, to doctors in training. Under the Regulations this leave entitlement is not additional to bank holidays, unless otherwise stated in the workers Terms & Conditions.

Employers can set the times that staff take their leave, for example, for a Christmas shutdown. However, employers should consider whether setting times for annual leave may be discriminatory because of religion or belief.

Under the Working Time Regulations an employer can require an employee to give twice as many days notice of annual leave as the number of days to be taken as annual leave. Therefore 2 days annual leave may require 4 days notice.

Further information on the Working Time Regulations is available from Acas or the DTI

Baha'i

Baha'is should say one of three obligatory prayers during the day. Prayers need to be recited in a quiet place where the Baha'i will wish to face the Qiblih (the Shrine of Baha'u'llah, near Akka, Israel), which is in a south-easterly direction from the UK. Two of the prayers require movement and prostrations.

Baha'is are required to wash their hands and face before prayers but can use a normal washroom facility for this purpose.

Festivals

Baha'i festivals take place from sunset to sunset and followers may wish to leave work early in order to be home for sunset on the day prior to the festival date. Baha'is will wish to refrain from working on the key festival dates.

The Baha'i Fast	2 March–20 March

Baha'is refrain from eating or drinking from sunrise to sunset during this period. Baha'is working evening or night shifts will appreciate the opportunity to prepare food at sundown. There are exemptions from fasting for sickness, pregnancy, travelling and strenuous physical work.

Naw-Ruz (Baha'i New Year)	21 March
Ridvan	21 April–2 May

Ridvan is the most important of the Baha'i festivals and includes 3 holy days on which Baha'is would wish to refrain from working. They are:

1st	Day of Ridvan	21 April
9th	Day of Ridvan	29 April
12th	Day of Ridvan	2 May
Declaration of the Bab		23 May
Ascension of the Baha'u'llah		29 May
Martyrdom of the Bab		9 July
Birth of the Bab		20 October
Birth of Baha'u'llah		12 November

Food As a matter of principal most Baha'is do not take alcohol. Otherwise there are no dietary restrictions.

Bereavement Burial should take place as soon as possible after legal formalities and funeral arrangements can be put in hand. The body should be transported no more than one hour's journey from the place where the person died, so funerals take place relatively close to the place of death. The usual arrangements for compassionate leave should generally suffice. Baha'is have no specific period of mourning.

238

Buddhism

Festivals There are a number of different traditions in Buddhism arising from different cultural and ethnic backgrounds. Different traditions will celebrate different festivals. Some Buddhist traditions do not celebrate any festivals. Buddhist members of staff should be asked which festivals are important to them.

Festivals follow the lunar calendar and will therefore not take place on the same day each year.

Saindran Memorial Day	January
Parinirvana	February
Magha Puja Day	February/March
Honen Memorial Day	March
Buddha Day (Vesak or Visakah Puja)	May
The Ploughing Festival	May
Buddhist New Year	Varies according to tradition
Asalha Puja Day (Dhamma Day)	July
Ulambana (Ancestor Day)	July
Abhidhamma Day	October
Kathina Day	October
The Elephant Festival	November
Loy Krathorg	December
Bodhi Day	December
Uposatha	weekly on the lunar quarter day
Avalokitesvara's Birthday	

Food Most Buddhists are vegetarian reflecting their adherence to the precept of non-harm to self and others. Many would not want to prepare or serve meat for others. Buddhists upholding the precept to avoid intoxication may not wish to drink alcohol, or serve it.

Clothing Many Buddhists would prefer to wear clothing which reflects their adherence to non-harm eg not wearing leather clothing and leather shoes.

Christianity There are a wide variety of Christian Churches and organisations all of which have their own specific needs, rituals and observations.

Festivals

Christmas Day	December 25th
Ash Wednesday	Feb/March (date set by lunar calendar)

This is a day of fasting/abstinence for many Christians.

Maunday Thursday	March/April (date set by lunar calendar)
Good Friday	March/April (date set by lunar calendar)
Easter Sunday	March/April (date set by lunar calendar)
All Saints Day	1 November
Christmas Eve	24 December

In addition there are a number of 'holy days of obligation' when Christians may wish to attend a church service and request a late start to the working day, or early finish in order that they can attend their local church. Many practicing Christians will wish to attend their Church on Sundays throughout the year.

Food Some Christians avoid alcohol.

Clothing Some Christian churches forbid the use of cosmetics and require their female members to dress particularly modestly.

Bereavement No special requirements beyond normal compassionate leave.

Hinduism
Festival Days
Hinduism is a diverse religion and not all Hindus will celebrate the same festivals.

Makar Sakranti	January 14th
Maha Shiva Ratri	February
Holi	March
Ramnavami	April
Rakshabandham	August
Janmashtami	August
Ganesh Chaturthi	August/September
Navaratri	September/October
Dushera (aka Vijayadashmi)	September/October
Karava Chauth	October
Diwali	Late October/Early November
New Year	Late October/Early November

There are a number of occasions through the year when some Hindus fast .

Clothing Hindu women will often wear a *bindi* which is a red spot worn on the forehead and denotes that she is of the Hindu faith. In addition, many married Hindu women wear a necklace (*mangal sutra*) which is placed around their necks during the marriage ceremony and is in addition to a wedding ring.

A few Orthodox Hindu men wear a small tuft of hair (*shikha*) similar to a ponytail but this is often hidden beneath the remaining hair. Some Orthodox Hindu men also wear a clay marking on their foreheads known as a *tilak.*

Food Most Hindus are vegetarian and will not eat meat, fish or eggs. None eat beef.

Bereavement Following cremation, close relatives of the deceased will observe a 13 day mourning period during which they will wish to remain at home. The closest male relatives may take the ashes of the deceased to the Ganges, in India. They may therefore request extended leave. Close male relatives of the deceased may shave their heads as a mark of respect.

Islam (Muslims)
Observant Muslims are required to pray five times a day. Each prayer time takes about 15 minutes and can take place anywhere clean and quiet. Prayer times are:—

At dawn (Fajr)
At mid-day (Zuhr) in Winter sometime between 1200–1300hrs and in Summer between 1300–1600hrs.
Late Afternoon (Asr) in Winter 1430–1530
After Sunset (Maghrib)
Late Evening (Isha)

240

Friday mid-day prayers are particularly important to Muslims and may take a little longer than other prayer times. Friday prayers must be said in congregation and may require Muslims to travel to the nearest mosque or prayer gathering.

Before prayers, observant Muslims undertake a ritual act of purification. This involves the use of running water to wash hands, face, mouth, nose, arms up to the elbows and feet up to the ankles, although often the washing of the feet will be performed symbolically.

Festivals

The dates of festivals are reliant on a sighting of the new moon and will therefore vary from year to year. Whilst approximate dates will be know well in advance, it is not always possible to give a definitive date until much nearer to the time.

Ramadan, which takes place in the 9th month of the Muslim lunar calendar, is a particularly significant time for Muslims. Fasting is required between dawn and sunset. Most Muslims will attend work in the normal way but in the winter they may wish to break fast with other Muslims at sunset. This could be seen as a delayed lunch break. For those working evening or night shifts, the opportunity to heat food at sunset and/or sunrise will be appreciated.

Eid Al-Fitr—3 days to mark the end of Ramadan—most Muslims will only seek annual leave for the first of the three days.

Eid al-Adha takes place 2 months and 10 days after Eid Al-Fitr and is a 3 day festival. Again, most Muslims will usually only seek leave for the first of the three days.

All Muslims are required to make a pilgrimage to Mecca once in their lifetime. Muslims may therefore seek one extended leave period in which to make such a pilgrimage.

Clothing Muslims are required to cover the body. Men may therefore be unwilling to wear shorts. Women may wish to cover their whole body, except their face, hands and feet.

Food Muslims are forbidden to eat any food which is derived from the pig, this includes lard which may be present in bread or even ice cream. In addition they are forbidden to eat any food which is derived from a carnivorous animal. Meat that may be consumed must be slaughtered by the Halal method. Islam also forbids the consumption of alcohol which includes its presence in dishes such as risotto or fruit salad.

Bereavement Burial must take place as soon as possible following death and may therefore occur at short notice.

Other

1. Any form of gambling is forbidden under Islam.
2. Observant Muslims are required to wash following use of the toilet and will therefore appreciate access to water in the toilet cubicle, often Muslims will carry a small container of water into the cubicle for this purpose. By agreement with other staff and cleaners, these containers could be kept in the cubicle.
3. Physical contact between the sexes is discouraged and some Muslims may politely refuse to shake hands with the opposite sex. This should not be viewed negatively.

Jainism

Jains are required to worship three times daily, before dawn, at sunset and at night. Jains working evening or night shifts may wish to take time out to worship or take their meals before sunset.

Festivals

Jain festivals are spiritual in nature.

Oli	April and October

8 days semi-fasting twice a year when some take one bland, tasteless meal during day time.

Mahavira Jayanti	April—birth anniversary of Lord Mahavira
Paryusan	August/September

During this sacred period of fasting and forgiveness for 8 days Jains fast, observe spiritual rituals, meditate and live a pious life taking only boiled water during day time.

Samvatsari	September

The last day of Paryushan when Jains ask for forgiveness and forgive on another.

Diwali	October/November

Death anniversary of Lord Mahavira, includes a 2 day fast and listening to the last message of Mahavira.

Food Jains practice avoidance of harm to all life—self and others. They are, therefore, strict vegetarians including the avoidance of eggs; some may take milk products. Many also avoid root vegetables. Jains do not eat between sunset and sunrise. Jains do not drink alcohol.

Bereavement Cremation will take place as soon as practical after death (usually 3–5 days). There is no specified mourning period and normal compassionate leave arrangements will suffice.

Judaism (Jews)

Observant Jews are required to refrain from work on the Sabbath and Festivals, except where life is at risk. This includes travelling (except on foot), writing, carrying, switching on and off electricity, using a telephone and transactions of a commercial nature (that is buying and sell-ing) The Sabbath and all other Festivals begin one hour before dusk and so practising Jews need to be home by then. Sabbath begins one hour before dusk on Friday.

Festival Days

Passover	March/April	2 sets of 2 days
Pentecost (Shavuoth)	May/June	2 days
New Year	Sept.Oct	2 days
Day of Atonement	Sept/Oct	1 day fasting
Tabernacles (Sukkot)	Sept/Oct	2 sets of 2 days

Clothing Orthodox Jewish men keep their head covered at all times. Orthodox Jewish women will wish to dress modestly and may not want to wear trousers, short skirts or short sleeves; some may wish to keep their heads covered by a scarf or beret.

Food Jews are required to eat only kosher food (which has been treated and prepared in a particular manner).

Bereavement Funerals must take place as soon as possible following the death—the same day where possible—and therefore take place at short notice. Following a death, the immedi-ate family must stay at home and mourn for 7 days (Shiva). Following the death of a Father or Mother, an observant Jewish man will be required to go to a Synagogue to pray morning, afternoon and evening for 11 months of the Jewish calendar.

Muslim (see Islam)

Other Ancient Religions
These include religions covered by the Council of British Druid Orders and examples are Druidry, Paganism and Wicca.

Some examples of Festivals

Candlemas	2 February
Spring Equinox*	21/22 March
Beltaine	30 April
Summer Solstice*	21/22 June
Lughnasadh	2 August
Autumn Equinox*	21/22 September
Samhain 3	1 October
Winter Solstice*	21/22 December

* Dates moveable due to astronomical times set in accordance with GMT.

Food Generally vegetarian or vegan, although not always.

Clothing Some items of jewellery as associated with Pagan faiths such as ankh, pentagram, hammer and crystal.

Bereavement No specific requirements beyond that of normal compassionate leave.

There are also other ancient religions such as Astaru, Odinism and Shamanism.

Parsi (see Zorastrianism)

Rastafarianism
Festivals

Birthday of Haile Selassie 1	July 23rd
Ethiopian New Year	Sept 11th
Anniversary of the Crowning of Haile Selassie 1	Nov 2nd
Christmas	Dec 25th

Food Vegetarian including the avoidance of eggs. Many Rastafarians eat only organic food as close to its raw state as possible.

Clothing Hair is worn uncut and plaited into 'dreadlocks'. It is often covered by a hat which is usually red, green and gold.

Other Whilst the faith supports the smoking of ganga (marijuana) this practice remains unlawful in the UK. and is unaffected by the Employment Equality (Religion or Belief) Regulations 2003.

Bereavement No specific requirements beyond that of normal compassionate leave.

Sikhism
Festival Days

Birthday of Guru Gobind Singh	5 January
Vaisakhi	14 April

Martyrdom of Guru Arjan Dev	16 June
Sri Guru Granth Sahib Day	1 September
Divali (Diwali)	October/November (date set by lunar calender
Martyrdom of Guru Tegh Bahadur	24 November
Birthday of Guru Nanak	November

Food Sikhs do not eat Halal meat. Some do not eat beef and many are vegetarian.

Clothes Practicing male Sikhs observe the 5 Ks of the faith. These are

Kesh	Uncut hair. Observant Sikhs do not remove or cut any hair from their body. Sikh men and some women will wear a turban.
Kangha	Wooden comb usually worn in the hair.
Kara	Metal bracelet worn on the wrist
Kachhahera	Knee length underpants
Kirpan	Short sword worn under the clothing so that it is not visible.

Bereavement Sikhs are cremated and have a preference for this to take place as soon after the death as possible. There is no specified mourning period and normal compassionate leave arrangements will suffice.

Zoroastrians (Parsi)

Zoroastrians are required to pray 5 times during the day, saying a special prayer for each part of the day.

Hawab	(sunrise to midday)
Rapithwin	(midday to mid-afternoon)
Uzerin	(mid-afternoon to sunset)
Aiwisruthrem	(sunset to midnight)
Ushahin	(midnight to dawn)

Prayers should be said in front of a fire—or a symbolic replica of fire.

In addition, a ritual is performed each time a Zorostrain washes his/her hands although the ritual is not always strictly performed in all its detail. When it is performed, the individual will stand on the same spot and must speak to no one during the ritual. No special facilities are required. A prayer will also be said before eating.

Festivals

Dates follow the lunar calendar and will therefore vary from year to year.

Khordad Sal—The Prophet's Birthday
Fravardigan—Remembrance of departed souls.
Tiragan—Water Festival
Mehergan—Harvest Festival
Ave roj nu Parab—Water Festival
Adar roj nu Parab—Fire Festival
Jashn-e-Sadeh—Mid Winter Festival
Zardosht no Disco—Death of the Prophet
Maktad—Festival of All Souls
NoRuz—New Year

In addition there are 6 seasonal festivals

Maidyoizaremaya	Mid Spring
Maidyoishema	Mid Summer
Paitishahya	Early Autumn
Ayathrima	Mid Autumn
Maidhyairya	Mid Winter
Hamaspathmaedaya	Pre-Spring

Clothes Zoroastrians, both male and female, wear two pieces of sacred clothing. The Sudreh (shirt) and the Kusti (cord) which is a string which passes loosely around the waist three times and is tied in a double knot at the back. It is the Kusti which is ritualistically retied each time the hands are washed.

Bereavement Following the death of a close family member there is a mourning period of 10 days followed by a ceremony to mark the 1st month, the 6th month and the 12th month of bereavement.

Appendix 5

ACAS GUIDANCE
SEXUAL ORIENTATION AND THE WORKPLACE

Putting the
Employment Equality (Sexual Orientation) Regulations
2003 into practice

For Employers and their Staff

INDEX

INTRODUCTION

From 1 December, 2003, when the Employment Equality (Sexual Orientation) Regulations come into force, it will be unlawful to discriminate against workers because of sexual orientation. The regulations also cover providers of vocational training. This booklet describes the regulations and gives guidance on associated good employment practice

Fairness at work and good job performance go hand in hand. Tackling discrimination helps to attract, motivate and retain staff and enhances an organisation's reputation as an employer. Eliminating discrimination helps everyone to have an equal opportunity to work and to develop their skills.

There is already legislation to protect people against discrimination on the grounds of sex, race, disability and gender reassignment. From December 2 separate regulations to protect people from discrimination on the grounds of religion or belief also come into force.

A lot of the good practice in this booklet will be familiar from existing advice on avoiding sex, race and disability discrimination. The new regulations should pose few difficulties in organisations where people are treated fairly and with consideration.

Employers are encouraged to consider whether their policies and procedures respect the sensitivity of individuals' sexual orientation and the importance of maintaining a high level of confidentiality. Workers of all sexual orientations should feel welcome and safe in their workplace and the dignity of all should be respected.

WHAT THE REGULATIONS SAY—IN SUMMARY

These Regulations apply to all employment and vocational training and include recruitment, terms and conditions, promotions, transfers, dismissals and vocational training. They make it unlawful on the grounds sexual orientation to

➤ discriminate directly against anyone—that is, to treat them less favourably than others because of their actual or perceived sexual orientation;

➤ discriminate indirectly against anyone—that is, to apply a criterion, provision or practice which disadvantages people of a particular sexual orientation unless it can be objectively justified.

➤ subject someone to harassment. Harassment is unwanted conduct that violates a person's dignity or creates an intimidating, hostile, degrading, humiliating or offensive environment for them having regard to all the circumstances including the perception of the victim

➤ victimise someone because they have made or intend to make a complaint or allegation or have given or intend to give evidence in relation to a complaint of discrimination on grounds of sexual orientation;

➤ discriminate against someone, in certain circumstances, after the working relationship has ended.

Within the Regulations, sexual orientation is defined as—

➤ Orientation towards persons of the same sex (lesbians and gay men)
➤ Orientation towards persons of the opposite sex (heterosexual)
➤ Orientation towards persons of the same sex and the opposite sex (bisexual)

---

1. A BRIEF EXPLANATION OF THE REGULATIONS

1.1 Direct discrimination means that workers or job applicants must not be treated less favourably because of their sexual orientation or their perceived sexual orientation. For example it is unlawful to

- decide not to employ someone,
- dismiss them
- refuse to provide them with training
- deny them promotion

- give them adverse terms and conditions
- deny them access to benefits available to individuals of a different sexual orientation (unless the benefits are dependent on marital status) because they are, or are thought to be, lesbian, gay, bisexual or heterosexual.

> *Example: Whilst being interviewed, a job applicant says that she has a same sex partner. Although she has all the skills and competences required of the job holder, the organisation decides not to offer her the job because she is lesbian. This is direct discrimination.*
>
> *NB A job applicant can make a claim to an Employment Tribunal, it is not necessary for them to have been employed by the organisation to make a claim of discrimination.*

Direct discrimination may only be justified in the very limited circumstances where a genuine occupational requirement can be shown to apply.

1.2 Indirect discrimination means that an organisation must not have selection criteria, policies, benefits, employment rules or any other practices which, although they are applied to all employees, have the effect of disadvantaging people of a particular sexual orientation unless the practice can be justified. Indirect discrimination is unlawful whether it is intentional or not.

In contrast to direct discrimination, indirect discrimination will not be unlawful if it can be justified. To justify it, an employer must show that there is a legitimate aim (e.g. a real business need) and that the practice is proportionate to that aim (i.e. necessary, and there is no alternative means available).

1.3 Harassment includes behaviour that is offensive, frightening or in any way distressing. It may be intentional bullying which is obvious or violent, but it can also be unintentional, subtle and insidious. It may involve nicknames, teasing, name calling or other behaviour which is not with malicious intent but which is upsetting. It may be about the individual's sexual orientation (real or perceived) or it may be about the sexual orientation (real or perceived) of those with whom the individual associates. It may not be targeted at an individual(s) but consist of a general culture which, for instance, appears to tolerate the telling of homophobic jokes.

The Regulations apply as equally to the harassment of heterosexual people as they do to the harassment of lesbians, gay men, and bisexual people.

Organisations may be held responsible for the actions of their staff as well as the staff being individually responsible. If harassment takes place in the workplace or at a time and place associated with the workplace, for example a work related social gathering, the organisation may be liable and may be ordered to pay compensation unless it can be shown that it took reasonable steps to prevent harassment. Individuals who harass may also be ordered to pay compensation.

It is good practice for employers to protect their workers from harassment by third parties, such as service users and customers.

Employers investigating claims of harassment should consider all the circumstances before reaching a conclusion, and particularly the perception of the complainant as harassment is often subjective. Having gathered all the evidence employers should ask themselves 'could what has taken place be reasonably considered to have caused offence?'

> *Example: A male worker who has a same sex partner is continually referred to by female nicknames which he finds humiliating and distressing. This is harassment.*

> *Example: A worker has a son who is gay. People in the workplace often tell jokes about gay people and tease the worker about his son's sexual orientation. This may be harassment on grounds of sexual orientation, despite it not being the victim's own sexuality that is the subject of the teasing.*

1.4 **Victimisation** is when an individual is treated detrimentally because they have made a complaint or intend to make a complaint about discrimination or harassment or have given evidence or intend to give evidence relating to a complaint about discrimination or harassment. They may become labelled 'troublemaker', denied promotion or training, or be 'sent to Coventry' by their colleagues. If this happens or if organisations fail to take reasonable steps to prevent it from happening, they will be liable and may be ordered to pay compensation. Individuals who victimise may also be ordered to pay compensation.

> *Example: A worker gives evidence for a colleague who has brought an Employment Tribunal claim against the organisation of discrimination on grounds of sexual orientation. When that worker applies for promotion her application is rejected even though she is able to show she has all the necessary skills and experience. Her manager maintains she is a 'troublemaker' because she had given evidence at the Tribunal and therefore should not be promoted. This would be victimisation.*

1.5 Discrimination, harassment or victimisation following the end of a working relationship covers issues such as references either written or verbal.

> *Example: A manager is approached by someone from another organisation. He says that Ms 'A' has applied for a job and asks for a reference. The manager says that he cannot recommend the worker as she was not accepted by other staff because she was bisexual. This is direct discrimination because of sexual orientation.*

1.6 **A genuine occupational requirement** In very limited circumstances it will be lawful for an employer to treat people differently if it is a genuine occupational requirement that the job holder must be of a particular sexual orientation. When deciding if this applies it is necessary to consider the nature of the work and the context in which it is carried out. Jobs may change over time and organisations should, from time to time, consider whether the requirement continues to apply, particularly when recruiting. Further guidance is given in Appendix 1.

> *Example An organisation advising on and promoting gay rights may be able to show that it is essential to the credibility of its chief executive who will be the public face of the organisation that s/he should be gay. The sexual orientation of the holder of that post may therefore be a genuine occupational requirement.*

The Regulations also permit differences of treatment on grounds of sexual orientation where the employment is for the purposes of an organised religion—such as the leader of a faith or of an establishment such as a mosque or temple. Any organisation wishing to rely on this provision will also need to establish that the requirement is necessary to comply with religious doctrine; or—because of the nature of the work and the context in which it is carried out—to avoid conflicting with the strongly held religious convictions of a significant number of the religion's followers.

1.7 **The Regulations only relate to sexual orientation**, that is lesbians and gay men, heterosexual people and bisexual people.

1.8 Any laws relating to sexual practices, whether gender or nongender specific, consensual or otherwise remain unchanged.

* * *

There is a sound business case for eliminating discrimination in the workplace. Staff who are subjected to discrimination, harassment or victimisation may

♦ be unhappy, less productive and demotivated
♦ resign
♦ make a complaint to an Employment Tribunal

If staff are subjected to discrimination, harassment or victimisation this may affect an organisation in terms of

♦ damage to reputation both as a business and as an employer
♦ cost of staff leaving and consequent recruitment and training
♦ cost of compensation if they take a claim to an Employment Tribunal—there is no upper limit to the amount of compensation an organisation may be ordered to pay.

2. RECRUITMENT

2.1 It makes sound business sense for an organisation to attract a wide field of applicants—it is not a good idea to rely on the friends or family of current staff as this may limit the diversity of the organisation.

2.2 Advertising is best undertaken in a form accessible to a diverse audience. For instance, use of a wide interest publication or agency rather than one focussed on a niche or specialist culture or interest area which will limit the diversity of applicants and may constitute indirect discrimination.

> *Example: An advertisement placed only in a magazine aimed at gay men and lesbians may indirectly discriminate against people who are heterosexual because they are less likely to subscribe to the magazine and therefore less likely to find out about the vacancy and apply.*

2.3 Organisations should be clear about what skills they actually need for the post, differentiating them from those which are merely desirable or reflect the personal preferences of the selector. They should recruit and/or promote for those skills and aptitudes—there is nothing to prevent an employer from deciding not to recruit or promote someone if the applicant does not have the necessary skills or abilities.

2.4 Organisations should ensure they do not set unnecessary selection criteria or standards which might prevent people from applying because of their sexual orientation.

> *Example: A sports club requires two individuals to manage the bar and other facilities. They advertise for a husband and wife team. This may discriminate against same sex partners.*

2.5 At the interview or selection process questions should be asked or tests set to check for the skills and competences needed for the post. Interviewers should not be tempted to ask personal questions, which may be perceived to be intrusive and imply potential discrimination. Where such information is volunteered, selectors should take particular care not to allow themselves to be influenced by that information. An organisation only needs to know if the person can do the job and if they are willing to do the job. Assumptions should not be made about who will and who will not fit in.

> *Good practice: The perception of the interviewee is important. Questions not obviously related to the post may be perceived as providing a basis for discrimination and, in addition, the interviewer may subconsciously take personal matters into consideration. It is good practice to avoid enquiring about marital status, number of children and arrangements for their care, sexual orientation, and social life.*

2.6 Care should be taken with the wording on application forms. It is most unlikely, for instance, that an organisation needs to know the marital status of the applicant. If such information is required for purposes such as security clearance, it can be sought in confidence when the selection process has been completed.

2.7 Employers may wish to consider that the laws relating to gay men have changed significantly over time. It is possible that applicants may have acquired a criminal conviction many years before for a matter no longer unlawful, (such as consensual adult gay sex). This is unlikely to have any bearing on the individual's skills and suitability for the job or training advertised. Generally a subsequent change in the criminal law does not affect whether an existing sentence becomes spent, the sentence still stands.

2.8 At recruitment and beyond, staff welcome an organisation having a robust Equality Policy which includes sexual orientation as well as other forms of discrimination, and which takes the matter seriously if the policy is contravened. Although not a legal necessity, such a policy makes applicants feel confident and serves to discourage those whose attitudes and behaviours do not embrace equality of opportunity.

Applicants who are not heterosexual may be discouraged from applying for posts in organisations that do not specifically include sexual orientation in their Equality Policy.

Acas can help organisations to draw up and implement such a policy and with their training needs.

2.9 Selection for recruitment or promotion must be on merit, irrespective of sexual orientation. Where employers have reason to believe that persons of a particular sexual orientation are under-represented in the workforce, it is possible to take certain steps to redress the effects of any previous inequality of opportunity. This is called 'positive action'. Employers may wish to consider positive measures such as:

—training their existing employees for work which has historically been the preserve of individuals of a particular sexual orientation.

—Advertisements which encourage applications from people of a particular sexual orientation but making it clear that selection will be on merit without reference to sexual orientation.

3. RETAINING GOOD STAFF

3.1 Opportunities for promotion and training should be made known to all staff and be available to everyone on a fair and equal basis.

3.2 Where staff apply for internal transfers it should be remembered that informal and verbal references between departmental heads, supervisors etc. should be fair and non-discriminatory and are covered by the Regulations.

3.3 Organisations and their staff should not assume that everyone is heterosexual. If organisations offer the opportunity for social gatherings which extend to the partners of staff, care should be taken with the wording of invitations, posters etc. to ensure inclusivity for those with same sex partners. Where opposite sex partners are invited, the exclusion of same sex partners is hurtful and may constitute discrimination.

3.4 Everyone should understand what discrimination and harassment is and that it is hurtful, unlawful and totally unacceptable. However large or small an organisation, it is good practice for them to have an Equality Policy and to train all staff and update them on a regular basis. This will help to reduce the likelihood of discrimination, harassment and victimisation taking place and may help to limit liability if a complaint is made.

3.5 When delivering equality training an organisation should cover issues such as homophobic comments and jokes and the use of inappropriate language which may simply have been intended as 'banter' but which have the effect of being degrading or distressing. Some words can be seen as offensive, and may be viewed as harassment When talking about sexual orientation, words such as heterosexual, bisexual, lesbian and gay are generally acceptable.

3.6 Organisations should ensure that their staff understand that if they harass colleagues, they could be personally liable and may have to pay compensation themselves. Such liability is separate from, and in addition to, any compensation that the organisation is ordered to pay. Workers should understand that saying 'no offence was intended' may not constitute a defence. In addition, an absence of complaint from the individual being harassed does not mean that harassment has not taken place.

Handouts to workers visiting your premises could include a summary of your Equality Policy as well as the more usual Health & Safety instructions.

> *An Employment Tribunal case brought under the Sex Discrimination Act A male public service worker wrote down sexual comments about a woman colleague which together with the general behaviour of the men towards women in her section caused her distress. When she complained managers sought to minimise the matter. An employment tribunal found that her complaints were justified. She was awarded £15,000 injury to feelings against the employer and £1000 against the individual concerned. Tribunals may be expected to adopt a similar approach in sexual orientation cases as they do in existing discrimination legislation.*

3.7 Staff should be made aware of what steps they could take if they feel they have been discriminated against, harassed or victimised. They should feel confident that their complaint will be treated seriously, that managers will deal with the cause of the problem and that the process will be undertaken in confidence. If it is practical, it is a good idea for organisations to have a named individual who is trained and specifically responsible for dealing with employment equality issues and complaints.

> *Example: As part of their equality training, an organisation produces an article in a newsletter to reinforce the message that homophobia and inappropriate jokes will not be tolerated. Copies of the newsletters are subsequently defaced with offensive words and drawings. Managers do nothing about it, simply saying 'it is only to be expected'. Confidence amongst their gay and lesbian staff might be badly affected and they may have a claim of harassment. The organisation may be liable if they had failed to act on the complaint.*

3.8 By their very nature, sexual matters are private and confidential. Although some people are comfortable talking about their partner, many people do not share such information with their managers and colleagues. They may find it very difficult to make a complaint or be fearful that by making a complaint they will be *'outed' in the workplace. Organisations should make strenuous efforts to ensure confidentiality of procedures and information management systems and reassure their staff that policies to ensure confidentiality are in place.

*'outing' is when, against their wishes, a person's sexual orientation is revealed by another person. 'Outing' someone without their clear permission is inappropriate and a breach of that person's privacy. It may constitute harassment and/or a breach of the Data Protection Act.

3.9 Lesbians, gay men and bisexual people are sometimes 'outed' for malicious reasons and consequently suffer harassment by colleagues or service users/customers. Employers should treat such a matter seriously.

3.10 Personal information should be maintained in the strictest confidence. Managers should not forget that even basic information such as a partner's name is confidential, nor should they assume that it is common knowledge.

> *Example: On a residential training course, delegates are required to give the tutor the name, telephone number and relationship of an emergency contact. The completed forms are left on the tutor's desk where they can be seen by other delegates. As a result it becomes common knowledge that one of the delegates has a same sex partner. The delegate is distressed and as a result resigns from the company.*

3.11 Take care to avoid stereotyping. For instance, gay men are sometimes assumed to be HIV positive and consequently suffer exclusion by their managers and colleagues and can be subjected to offensive comments. It can be a good idea to include HIV/Aids awareness training in your equality programme but care should be taken not to reinforce stereotyping whether adverse or otherwise.

4. KNOW YOUR STAFF

4.1 There is no legal requirement to keep information on how staff groups are made up (gender, ethnic groups, and age, those with disabilities) other than in the public sector where racial monitoring is a statutory requirement. Monitoring generally is good practice, underpinning the success of equality policies. However, monitoring for sexual orientation raises some issues where there is a variety of opinion amongst employers, employees and within the lesbian and gay communities.

4.2 Organisations may consider asking a question about sexual orientation on their equal opportunities questionnaire. It is perhaps unlikely that this will give an accurate picture as many people will see the question as an invasion of privacy and staff are under no obligation to give such information. Additionally without accurate statistics on sexual orientation in the community as a whole it is difficult to determine whether employees of any particular sexual orientation are under represented.

It is good practice to monitor disciplinary and grievance procedures as a means of alerting management to homophobic attitudes within the organisation. Employers should take these issues seriously and make it known that discrimination is a disciplinary issue and give support to the victims.

4.3 Initially, organisations may wish to consider including a question on their anonymous staff attitude surveys to ascertain whether workers have ever felt harassed on a range of issues which should include sexual orientation.

4.4 Organisations wishing to implement monitoring may wish to consider seeking specialist assistance concerning the methods and format of monitoring in this sensitive area. Raising awareness of sexual orientation issues amongst their workforce is considered to provide a sound foundation before moving to monitoring at a later date.

There are a number of organisations providing assistance in this field, (Stonewall, Lager and others) and most trade unions have Lesbian, Gay, Bisexual Committees all of whom would be happy to assist. The Acas Equality Direct helpline can also provide assistance.

4.5 If organisations decide to include sexual orientation in their equality monitoring processes, staff should be told why the information is being collected and how it is intended it will be used. Such information is governed by the Data Protection Act 1998 and staff should be assured of both confidentiality and genuine anonymity They should be informed that they are under no obligation to give such information. Employers must ensure confidentiality and anonymity.

5. WHAT TO DO IF YOU THINK YOU HAVE SUFFERED DISCRIMINATION OR HARASSMENT

5.1 If you think you are being harassed or discriminated against it is a good idea to make it clear to the person who is harassing you that their behaviour is unwelcome and that you want it to stop. However, you do not have to do this, particularly if you are feeling bullied or intimidated.

If you do choose to address your concerns to the person, be clear and assertive but take care that you are not perceived to be bullying the individual. Some people may find it helpful to ask a friend, colleague, welfare officer or trade union representative to be with them in a support role.

5.2 If speaking to the person in question has failed to stop the problem, you should talk to your manager or your trade union representative. If it is your manager or supervisor who is harassing you, speak to someone higher up. Employers should deal with such complaints quickly, thoroughly and sympathetically.

5.3 It is usually best to try and sort things out quickly and as close to the problem as possible. If your organisation has a personnel or human resources department or an equality adviser you might find it helpful to talk to them. Discrimination can happen accidentally or through thoughtlessness. Harassment can be unintentional. Often, once a manager understands the problem, he or she will be willing to try and put things right.

5.4 If your manager is unable to help you, or refuses to help you, you should use your organisation's grievance procedure. Organisations with 20 or more employees should have a grievance procedure and this requirement will be extended to all employers once Section 36 of the Employment Act 2002 is commenced (probably in late 2004). You have a legal right to be accompanied by a trade union representative or a work colleague at any hearing into your grievance.

5.5 If you are not satisfied with the result of a grievance procedure, you have a right of appeal which should be heard, if the organisation's size allows it, by someone different from the person who conducted the original grievance hearing. You have a right to be accompanied by a trade union representative or a work colleague during the appeal hearing.

5.6 If you have tried all these things, or if your employer does not have a grievance procedure, or if you feel too intimidated to use the internal procedures, you may be able to bring a complaint to an employment tribunal under the Employment Equality (Sexual Orientation) Regulations 2003. You do not have to hand in your notice to bring such a complaint.

5.7 You and any witnesses have a right not to be victimised for following up a grievance or complaining to an employment tribunal under these Regulations provided the complaint was made in good faith.

5.8 If you have been dismissed because you objected to conduct towards you, you may be able to bring a complaint of unfair dismissal to an employment tribunal.

5.9 Complaints to an employment tribunal must normally be brought within three months of the act you are complaining about. Care should be taken to ensure that the three month point is not exceeded during any internal grievance/appeals process.

6. SOME FREQUENTLY ASKED QUESTIONS

Q Do organisations have to do anything new or different when the legislation comes in?

A They should ensure that sexual orientation is included in their Equality Policy. It is a good idea for them to revisit the Equality Policy from time to time to ensure it has not become outdated, to test any new employment policies and procedures for discrimination and to ensure the policy itself meets current legislation requirements.

Staff need to be made aware (through training, notice boards, circulars, contracts of employment etc.) that it is not only unacceptable to discriminate, harass or victimise someone on the grounds of sexual orientation, it is also unlawful. Organisations should also make it clear that they will not tolerate such behaviour. Staff should know what to do if they believe they have been discriminated against or harassed, or if they believe someone else is being discriminated against or harassed, and this should be included in the grievance procedure. Organisations should also consider adding all forms of discrimination and harassment (sex, race, disability, gender reassignment, sexual orientation and religion or belief) to their disciplinary rules which should also include bullying. It is good practice to include age discrimination within your policies ahead of the legislation due in October 2006.

> *Reminder: The Employment Act 2002 requires all employers, however large or small, to have both a disciplinary procedure and a grievance procedure The requirement is expected to take effect in late 2004.*

Q Must organisations have an Equality Policy?

A Whilst organisations do not have to have an Equality Policy, implementing and observing such a policy is a commonplace means of demonstrating that an employer has taken reasonably practicable steps to prevent employees discriminating against or harassing other employees. The policy should set the minimum standard of behaviour expected of all staff through recruitment and onwards and what staff can expect of the organisation. It acts as a reminder, gives staff confidence that they will be treated with dignity and respect, and may be used as an integral part of a grievance or disciplinary process if necessary. If organisations do not have an Equality Policy and would like help in putting in place an effective policy Acas can help.

Q Do these Regulations cover all workers?

A The Regulations apply to all workers, including office holders, police, barristers, partners in a business and members of the armed forces. They also cover related areas such as membership of trade organisations, the award of qualifications, the services of careers guidance organisations, employment agencies and vocational training providers, including further and higher education institutions.

The Regulations cover anyone who applies to an organisation for work, or who already works for an organisation—whether they are directly employed, work under some other kind of contract, or are an agency worker. Organisations will also be responsible for the behaviour of their staff towards an individual working for someone else but on their premises, for example someone from another organisation repairing a piece of your equipment.

Staff are sometimes harassed by third parties, such as customers or clients. Where possible organisations should protect their staff from such harassment and should take steps to deal with actual or potential situations of this kind. This will enhance the organisation's reputation as a good employer and make the organisation a welcoming and safe place to work.

Many organisations provide visitors and visiting workers with guidance on Health & Safety matters. It may be appropriate to include some comments in any policy your organisation has on harassment.

Q Do organisations have to collect data on sexual orientation?

A The Regulations do not require organisations to collect such data. If they decide to include sexual orientation in their equality monitoring process they should first consider taking expert advice as it is a particularly sensitive issue.

Staff should be told why the organisation wishes to collect the data, how the organisation intends to use such information, and should be assured of confidentiality and anonymity They should be informed that they are under no obligation to give such information. Under the Data Protection Act, organisations require the consent of individuals to collect and use such information.

The best way for an organisation to make sure it does not discriminate is to have a robust, regularly reviewed Equality Policy and a good supportive training programme to make sure everyone understands and implements the policy.

Q How will an organisation know if it is discriminating inadvertently?

A Individuals, or their trade union, will usually tell the employer, particularly if they are in a culture whereby staff feel comfortable in sharing such information. It can be helpful for organisations to have a designated individual to whom people can go in confidence. However, staff may be worried about raising issues which relate to their sexual orientation or their personal life. It is a good idea for organisations to get their management team, staff representatives or a specially convened group of employees to think through and test whether any policies and procedures impact on sexual orientation or discriminate on any other grounds such as disability, religion or belief, sex, gender reassignment, age or race. Discrimination on the grounds of age will become unlawful in October 2006.

Q Are staff entitled to claim time off to deal with emergencies involving same sex partners?

A Under the terms of the Employment Rights Act 1996 (as amended by the Employment Relations Act 1999) employees are entitled to unpaid leave to deal with unexpected or sudden problems concerning a dependent or close family member including a same sex partner. This particular Regulation does not apply to those who are self employed, members of the police service or armed forces.

Organisations should consider whether their policies and procedures for granting time off for dependents or bereavement leave, discriminate on the grounds of sexual orientation either intentionally or implicitly by the use of language.

> *Reminder: Parental leave is available to anyone who has, or expects to have, parental responsibility for a child under the age of 5 years or under the age of 18 years if the child is disabled*

If the individual meets the relevant conditions, Adoption Leave is available to an individual who adopts a child and two weeks paternity leave is available to their partner, whether opposite sex partners or same sex partners. Paternity leave is perhaps more easily understood if considered to be 'maternity (or adoption) support leave'.

Q No one in my organisation has ever complained of discrimination or harassment so I don't need to do anything new, do I?

A People do not always feel able or confident enough to complain, particularly if the harasser is a manager or senior executive. Sometimes they will simply resign. One way to find out is to undertake exit interviews when people leave and to include the question of whether they have ever felt harassed, bullied or discriminated against in the workplace. If it is possible, exit interviews should be undertaken by someone out of the individual's line of management, for instance a personnel officer.

Discrimination includes harassment which can take place without management being aware of it. Organisations should make sure all their staff understand that harassment means any unwanted behaviour that makes someone feel either intimidated, degraded, humiliated or offended and that includes teasing, tormenting, name calling and gossip and it applies whoever the perpetrator may be. The victim's perception of the effect of the behaviour is also important. Organisations should take all possible steps to make sure staff understand that they and their management teams will not tolerate such behaviour and that they will deal with whoever is causing the problem.

Q What about benefits for same sex partners?

A If organisations give benefits such as insurance or private healthcare to opposite sex unmarried partners then refusing to give the same benefits to same sex partners would be discrimination. If benefits specify 'married' partners or 'spouse' then they do not have to be extended to cover unmarried partners.

Organisations should take care not to unjustifiably change their existing policies in order to exclude same sex partners in the light of the new legislation. This may be viewed as discrimination and be unlawful.

Q What about transgender people?

A Gender reassignment is a separate issue and unrelated to sexual orientation despite a common misunderstanding that the two issues are part of the same picture.

It is unlawful to discriminate against or harass anyone on the grounds that the person intends to undergo treatment to change their sex, or is undergoing treatment to change their sex, or has undergone such treatment. These issues are already covered by the Sex Discrimination (Gender Reassignment) Regulations 1999.

If the person has completed gender reassignment treatment, organisations may never know. If the person is undergoing treatment (or raises questions about it) it is good practice to agree with the individual how they would prefer it to be dealt with and to follow a process agreed with them.

Q Should organisations introduce positive action programmes on sexual orientation?

A The law allows organisations to introduce positive action measures where they can demonstrate that staff of a particular sexual orientation are at a career disadvantage or are under represented in the organisation.

Q A member of staff has made a complaint of harassment which involves an inaccurate perception of their sexual orientation. Is this covered by the law?

A Yes, any harassment based on sexual orientation is covered by the Regulations. A worker harassed by their colleagues or manager on an inaccurate suspicion of or speculation about their sexual orientation has grounds for complaint and may take their case to Employment Tribunal if their employer fails to deal with the matter in a timely and proper manner.

Q I am being harassed by my colleagues. Must I use the internal grievance procedure before making an Employment Tribunal claim?

A It is usually quicker and easier to deal with issues as close to the problem as possible. It is also fairer to your employer, who may not know there is a problem. Talk to your manager or supervisor, or to someone else that you trust such as your trade union representative. If it is your manager or supervisor who is causing the problem, then seek help from someone in a more senior position.

If you are dissatisfied with the measures taken by your organisation or have reason not to feel able to access the internal procedures, you can make a claim to an Employment Tribunal. Tribunals will usually expect you to have tried to sort things out before making a claim. However, sometimes there are special circumstances (such as your feeling bullied or intimidated) which make it particularly difficult for you to deal with the situation in the workplace and Tribunals will take this into account.

Q We are an organisation providing employment rights advice to lesbian, gay and bisexual people and would therefore like job holders to be of a particular sexual orientation. Are we allowed to do this?

A Staff can be recruited on the basis of their sexual orientation where this is a genuine occupational requirement (GOR) for the job. You must be able to show that being of a specific sexual orientation is a requirement of the job. Appendix 1 provides some further guidance on this subject.

It is important that each post be considered individually both in terms of the duties of the job and the context within which it is carried out. For instance, an organisation should ask 'Is a particular sexual orientation a *requirement* of the job?' 'Would someone not of that sexual orientation be unable to do the job?' Organisations should not expect to apply a blanket GOR to all its posts.

Organisations should consider whether it is proportionate to apply a GOR to the job. For instance, if only a small part of the job qualifies for a GOR then it may be possible to redistribute work or reorganise roles in such a way as to avoid the necessity to apply a GOR to a particular post.

Organisations should be clear about the link between the requirements of the job and sexual orientation as, in the event of an employment tribunal claim on the grounds of sexual orientation, the burden of proof will be on the employer to show a GOR. Tribunals tend to interpret GORs very narrowly since they effectively go against the principal of equal treatment.

A GOR on the grounds of sexual orientation is specific and cannot be lawfully used to discriminate on any other grounds such as religion or belief, sex, disability or race.

Q **I am concerned that on the grounds of religion, some of my staff may refuse to work with their gay or lesbian colleagues.**

A Some religions do have strong views concerning sexual orientation but most do not advocate persecution of people because of their sexual orientation. Everyone has the right to be treated with dignity and respect in the workplace whatever their sex, race, colour, disability, age, religion or sexual orientation. You should include this over-riding premise in your Equality Policy and show that you take a robust view when this principal is not adhered to. Your workers do not have to be friends but you can insist that they treat each other professionally.

APPENDIX 1
GENUINE OCCUPATIONAL REQUIREMENTS—GUIDANCE

Employers wishing to claim a GOR should bear in mind the following points.

1. GORs should be identified at the beginning of the recruitment, training or promotion process, before the vacancy is advertised. Advertisements and material sent to potential applicants should clearly show that the employer considers that a GOR applies and the point should be reiterated during the selection process.

   Reminder: Applicants who do not agree that there is a GOR for the post are at liberty to make a claim to an Employment Tribunal because they believe they have been prevented from applying for the post on the grounds of sexual orientation. It would be for the employer to show that such a GOR is justified.

2. If an employer wishes to claim a GOR s/he must consider what the duties are for which an exemption is to be claimed; a GOR cannot be claimed unless some or all of those duties require a person of that sexual orientation to undertake those duties.

3. A GOR exemption cannot be claimed in relation to particular duties if the employer already has sufficient employees who are capable of carrying out the required duties and whom it would be reasonable to employ on those duties without undue inconvenience.

4. Each job for which a GOR may apply must be considered individually; it should not be assumed that because a GOR exists for one job it also exists for jobs of a similar nature or in a similar location. The nature or extent of the relevant duties may be different or there may be other employees who could undertake those duties.

5. A GOR can only be claimed where it is necessary for the relevant duties to be carried out by someone of a particular sexual orientation, not merely because it is preferable. The regulations allow organised religions to claim a GOR in very narrow circumstances to

comply with the doctrines of the religion or to avoid conflicting with a significant number of followers' strongly held religious convictions.

6. A GOR must be reassessed on each occasion a post becomes vacant to ensure that it can still be validly claimed. Circumstances may have changed, rendering the GOR inapplicable.

7. A GOR cannot be used to establish or maintain a balance or quota of employees of a particular sexual orientation.

8. GORs are always open to challenge by an individual. The burden of proof lies with the employer to establish the validity of a GOR by providing evidence to substantiate a claim.

9. Only an Employment Tribunal or a higher court can give an authoritative ruling as to whether or not a GOR is valid.

Appendix 6
Useful Contact Details

ADVISORY, CONCILIATION AND ARBITRATION SERVICE (ACAS)
Independent providers of help and advice, conflict resolution and assistance in settling complaints to employment tribunals.
Telephone: 0121 456 5856 (England); 0141 204 2677 (Scotland); 029 2076 1126 (Wales)
Website: www.acas.org.uk

BUSINESS LINK
Providers of advice to business owners and managers on all aspects of setting up and running a business.
Telephone: 0845 600 9006
Website: www.businesslink.gov.uk

CITIZENS ADVICE BUREAU
Free, confidential, impartial, and independent advice on citizen's problems including employment and discrimination. Advisers can help fill out forms, write letters, negotiate and represent clients at Court or Tribunals.
Telephone: Listed in local directories
Website: www.nacab.org.uk

COMMISSION FOR RACIAL EQUALITY (CRE)
Non-governmental body set up under the Race Relations Act 1976 to tackle racial discrimination, promote racial equality, and assist in some employment tribunal complaints.
Telephone: 020 7939 0000 (England); 0131 524 2000 (Scotland); 029 2038 8977 (Wales)
Website: www.cre.gov.uk

DEPARTMENT OF TRADE AND INDUSTRY (DTI)
Government department offering employers information on legislative provisions.
Telephone: 020 7215 5000
Website: www.dti.gov.uk

THE DISABILITY RIGHTS COMMISSION (DRC)
Independent statutory body set to help secure civil rights for disabled people.
Telephone: 08457 622 633
Website: www.drc-gb.org

DIVERSITY ACTION IN LOCAL GOVERNMENT UNIT (DIALOG)
Information for local authority managers on legislative developments and good practice on equality matters.
Website: www.lg-employers.gov.uk

THE EQUAL OPPORTUNITIES COMMISSION (EOC)
Agency working to eliminate sex discrimination.
Telephone: 08456 015901 (England); 0141 245 1800 (Scotland) 029 2034 3552 (Wales)
Website: www.eoc.org.uk

EQUALITY DIRECT
Easy access advice service for business managers on a wide range of equality issues.
Telephone: 0845 600 3444
Website: www.equalitydirect.org.uk

THE EMPLOYMENT TRIBUNAL SERVICE
Website includes details of local tribunals, how to make a complaint to an employment tribunal, and the relevant forms for making a complaint in downloadable form.
Telephone: See local directories
Website: http://www.employmenttribunals.gov.uk

THE EUROPEAN UNION
Institution responsible for large body of employment and discrimination law
Website: http://europa.eu.int/index_en.htm

TRADES UNION CONGRESS (TUC)
Umbrella organization of national trade unions, offers employees and their representatives advice on employment and equality issues.
Telephone: 020 7636 4030
Website: http://www.tuc.org.uk

Index

Please note that references in italics are references to the appendices

United States
  positive action 76
  segregation of black people 20–1

vicarious liability 59–62
  course of employment, acts done in 59–60
  defence where reasonable steps taken 60–1
  small businesses 61
victimization 27–30
  allegations of acts contrary to regulations 30
  bad faith 28
  bringing proceedings under regulations ,
    victimized for 29
  comparators 28
  conduct falling within Regulation 4(1) 29–30
  definition 11
  discrimination prohibited 14
  establishing 27–30
  evidence in connection with proceedings under
    regulations 29

genuine occupational requirement (GOR) 66
good faith, allegations in 30–1
less favourable treatment 27–8
  reason is protected act 28–9
mixed motives 29
motive 28–9
protected acts 27
reason for less favourable treatment is
  protected act 28–9
religion or belief, discrimination on grounds of
  14, *132*
sexual orientation discrimination 14, *170*
vocational training providers
  employment discrimination 47, 52, *143*

washing and showering facilities
  religion or belief, discrimination on grounds of
  110–11

Zoroastrians 103